Buddhism
and Women

The Middle Way Journal of The Buddhist Society, covers by Hassuko (Aileen Humphreys)

Edited by Darcy Flynn

Buddhism
and Women

IN THE MIDDLE WAY

THE BUDDHIST SOCIETY TRUST

The Buddhist Society Trust is a distinguished press in the United Kingdom which enriches lives around the world by advancing the study and practice of Buddhism. Its activities are supported by charitable contributions from individuals and institutions.

For more information visit www.thebuddhistsociety.org
E: middlewayandpublishing@gmail.com

© The Buddhist Society Trust

ISBN: 978-0-90103261-4 (The Buddhist Society Trust)

A catalogue record for this book is available from the British Library

Frontispiece: Louise Janin, *Gravure Composition Musicalisme*, 1940. © ADAGP, Paris and DACS, London, 2021.

Editor: Darcy Flynn
Designer: Avni Patel

Printed in Cornwall, TJ Books Limited

CONTENTS

Foreword, **HH Dalai Lama** v
Preface, **Dr Desmond Biddulph CBE** vii
Introduction, **Darcy Flynn** ix
Editor's Note xi

Otagaki Rengetsu, biography. 1

Caroline Augusta Foley Rhys Davids, biography 7
Caroline Augusta Foley Rhys Davids, *Mind in Buddhism*, 1934 9

Alexandra David-Néel, biography 21
Alexandra David-Néel,
Does Buddhism Respond to the Needs of Today?, 1932 26
Alexandra David-Néel and The Lama Yongden,
Mahayanist Theories of Tibet, 1938 32

Carmen Blacker, biography 41
Mihoko Okamura, biography 43
Carmen Blacker and Mihoko Okamura,
The Early Memories of Daisetz Teitaro Suzuki, 1964 44

Beatrice Erskine Lane Suzuki, biography 55
Beatrice Lane Suzuki, *Zen at Engakuji*, 1936 59
Beatrice Lane Suzuki, *Characteristics of Mahayana*, 1938 63

Miriam Salanave, biography 86
Miriam Salanave, *Learning to Die*, 1934 88

CONTENTS

POEMS

Introduction to **Kaga no Chiyo-jo** 95
Kaga no Chiyo-jo, *The Morning Glory Haiku* 96

Introduction to **Yamada Fusako** 98
Yamada Fusako, *The Love Song of Akegarasu Fusako* 99

Introduction to **Kujo Takeko** 101
Kujo Takeko, *Whispers* 102

Introduction to **Okamoto Kanoko** 104
Okamoto Kanoko, *The Universe of Motherly Love* 105

Aileen Humphreys, biography 107
Aileen Humphreys, *Why Not Now?*, 1932 109

Ruth Fuller Everett Sasaki, biography 116
Ruth Fuller Everett Sasaki,
A Zen Student's Experience and Advice, 1933 120

Louise Janin, biography 129

Isaline Blew Horner, biography 137
Isaline Blew Horner, *The Foundations of Theravada*, 1949 139

Princess Poon Pismal Diskul, biography 144
Princess Poon Pismal Diskul,
The Three Worlds of Existence, 1947 146

CONTENTS

Dharma-Mother Ekai, biography 148
Dharma-Mother Ekai,
On the Way to the Land of Happiness, 2020..149

Li Gotami, biography..155

Norma Levine, *Freda Bedi: A Spiritual Odyssey*, 2018............................159

Joan and Anne Watts,
The Collected Letters of Alan Watts, 2019 169

Freda Wint, biography 179
Freda Wint, *The Luminous Mind*, 1988..181

Venerable Myokyo-ni, biography 188
Venerable Myokyo-ni,
Reflections on the Direct Teaching of the Buddha, 2006 190

Ayya Khema, biography,..193
Ayya Khema, *Unhappiness is a Defilement*, 1992 195

Nina Coltart, biography 200
Nina Coltart,
The Practice of Buddhism and Psychoanalysis, a Freudian View, 1991 201

Gelongma Tsultrim Zangmo, biography..208
Gelongma Tsultrim Zangmo, *Pilgrimages to India and Nepal*, 1999 209

Francesca Fremantle, biography 212
Francesca Fremantle, *What is Tantra?*, 2018..213

CONTENTS

Roshi Joan Halifax, biography 225
Roshi Joan Halifax, *Mindfulness Practice,* 2020 226

Robina Courtin, biography 232
Robina Courtin, *Love or Attachment?,* 2020 233

Ajahn Sundara, biography 240
Ajahn Sundara, *The Wisdom of Emotions,* 2014 241

Ajahn Candasiri, biography 245
Ajahn Candasiri, *My Life as a Nun,* 2018 246

Lama Zangmo, biography 249
Lama Zangmo,
The Four Thoughts that Turn the Mind to the Dharma, 2016 251

Maura Soshin O'Halloran, biography 261

Darcy Flynn, *The Buddhist Perspective on Evil,* 2023 267

Interview with **Jetsun Pema,**
The Compassionate Work of Ama-la, 2023 272

Bibliography and books written by contributors 291
Acknowledgments 298
Glossary 299

THE DALAI LAMA

FOREWORD

When I talk to Buddhist communities around the world, I always emphasize on the need to become 21st century Buddhists. In a scientifically highly advanced world, faith alone is insufficient to sustain our religious practice. Scientific progress has allowed us to use our human intelligence to investigate and experiment with reality. Buddhism places strong importance on strictly ascertaining reality, even if it conflicts with traditional beliefs. Along with that the main purpose of Buddha Shakyamuni's vast and profound teachings is to cultivate wisdom and compassion. An intelligent mind in the absence of compassion could become very destructive. However, if intelligence is supported by a compassionate motivation and vice versa, joy and satisfaction will naturally follow.

Generally, we are all endowed with some level of compassionate feelings. However, scientific researches point out that women have more natural empathy for other's suffering than men. This natural gift of kindness must be treasured and encouraged. I have maintained that if we have more women in the leadership around the world, our world would become more peaceful and happier. In any case, the inherent compassion that we all have should be nurtured through further study, contemplation and habituation. One innovation that we have accomplished in recent years is to have encouraged nuns to do in-depth study and also become Geshemas, which is equivalent to attaining Doctorate in Buddhist Philosophy.

There are many women around the world who have contributed in their own ways towards the wellbeing of others and left legacies that many find inspirational. Therefore, I welcome this book that includes biographies and works of some well-known women in the Buddhist world. I commend the Buddhist Society Trust (U.K.) for bringing out this book and hope it will be of benefit to many people.

H H The Dalai Lama
10 May 2023

PREFACE

This anthology celebrates the one hundreth anniversary of the charity The Buddhist Society, established in 1924. Women have been for the most part overlooked in the history of the transmission of the Dharma, with but few exceptions. This volume hopes to correct that imbalance in a small way, showing the contribution that women have and continue to make in bringing the dharma west.

The texts in the following anthology have been chosen by Darcy Flynn and were all originally published in *The Middle Way* and its predecessor *Buddhism in England* the quarterly journal of The Buddhist Society. Shared language, common culture and religious heritage, meant the United Kingdom and the United States have benefited equally from many of the same contributors. Material and social conditions brought about by the industrial revolution and two world wars, the availability of higher education for women, women's suffrage led towards both economic and political equality. The biographical details of the lives of the contributors included show that many were ahead of their time, compared to most of their contemporaries, many knew each other, and helped each other, and their lives were often quite closely intertwined. Times were changing and women could find new ways to express themselves, that a hundred years before would have been much more difficult, although the spiritual life has never discriminated on the basis of sex.

In the early days of the Society, The Theosophical Society played a very important part in this – it had an international membership and its network of centres, located all over the world, facilitated communication between like-minded but diverse minds. It drew together scholars, philosophers, artists and scientists, and seekers from all walks of life, particularly those looking for an alternative to the Judaeo-Christian orthodoxy of the time. It is important that the contributions of women are not only remembered and acknowledged, but also celebrated. The reader will find that some well-known contributors, such as Venerable Myokyo-ni continue in print. Others included in the book are in danger of being forgotten almost entirely, Beatrice Lane Suzuki, for example, spent her married life in the shadow of her husband, DT Suzuki, editing, correcting and devoted to his work, but was someone who had a contribution to make and deserves more attention, and to be remembered.

A selection of graphic works by artists, such as Louise Janin and Aileen Humphreys, who expressed their insight through drawing and painting have been included. Poetry and the crafts have an important place in the Buddhist story and so the work of some overlooked poets from Japan such as Kaga no Chiyo-jo and the potter Rengetsu are here too.

All schools and traditions of Buddhism are now represented in the Western world. No matter the school or tradition, what is common to all is that they draw their inspiration from the journey that Shakyamuni Buddha took. His emancipating insight is there for all, regardless of race, sex, social status or level of education, if we follow the 'ancient path' that he 'rediscovered'. Many of the women included here come from these diverse backgrounds, and have walked far on the Buddha's path. Buddhism is, after all, not simply a 'way' to the ending of suffering, but in the process the 'way', if walked, establishes true emotional intellectual independence. This enables a big 'Yes' to everything that life brings, and thus making good use of it, this is the fruit of any true spiritual path. One lives guided by that invisible, unknowable centre, the source of all, which in Buddhism is depicted as wisdom and compassion. All these women have been an example for us to learn from, and all have contributed in their own unique way.

Desmond Biddulph CBE,
President, The Buddhist Society

INTRODUCTION

This book came into being because I was inspired by words written in the Metta Sutta:

> Even as a Mother protects with her life her child, her only child,
> In such a way with a boundless heart
> We should cherish all
> Living beings;
> Radiating goodwill over the entire world:
> Upwards into the skies, downwards into the depths;
> Outwards without limit,
> Unburdened by hatred, ill will and holding fixed views.[1]

The Buddha Dharma answers every human question there is, just as a mother answers her child. Women have this great capacity to instinctively love all living things. The middle way was the first teaching by the Buddha after his enlightenment and is the name of the journal of The Buddhist Society, from which these texts are collected. The collection offers a rich feminine perspective on a wide range of Buddhist teachings. I want to share it to provide encouragement and insight in our practice. I want the reader to rejoice in the accomplishments of the women who have written these texts and share the history of their contribution to the Buddha Dharma.

The artists, poets, explorers, scholars, Roshis, Lamas, practitioners, psychoanalysts and lay teachers in this collection are all extraordinary women. Through their work, they have given us a greater understanding of the Buddha Dharma and have led fascinating lives, which often connect together in a most curious way. Many other women contributors from *The Middle Way* could have been added and there may be an opportunity to do so in the future.

This anthology has been a journey to very different times and places – from east and west – and has been a rare opportunity for me to research these inspiring women, only some of whom I have met in person.

I imagined myself entering Japan with the pioneering American Miriam Salanave to study Buddhism when barely any foreign women travelled there. I imagined trekking with the extraordinary Alexandra David-Néel in Tibet on horseback, living with the beautiful Li Gotami in the hills of India photographing and painting; meditating with the dignified and graceful Ruth Fuller Everett Sasaki in Zen temples and centres in Japan and New York; writing with the much-overlooked Beatrice Lane Suzuki in Japan, editing and translating for her husband DT Suzuki; leading with the incandescent Freda Bedi in Burma and India with His Holiness The Dalai Lama calling her Mummy; serving with the devoted Ayya Khema in Sri Lanka as a nun and starting monasteries in Australia and Germany; concentrating on Koans with the brave young Maura Soshin O'Halloran in Japan, beating the temple drum and walking barefoot in the snow with a begging bowl, determined to finish her Koan practice, before she later died in a traffic accident in her twenties.

I imagined sketching with the remarkable Louise Janin in London creating ground-breaking drawing and sculpting in her studio, and with the gifted Hassuko, known as Aileen Humphreys, painting and silver-smithing in her London home where she lived with her husband Christmas Humphreys, the founder of The Buddhist Society. I practised Zazen with the indomitable Venerable Myoko-ni, laughing and joking while setting up the two Rinzai Zen Buddhist training centres, Shoboan in London and Fairlight in Luton. I threw pots on the wheel with the profound Otagaki Rengetsu in Kyoto, losing everything and everyone dear to her, crafting her famous ceramics to earn a living and becoming a Buddhist nun at the age of thirty three. I heard the extraordinarily beautiful Mihoko Okumura with DT Suzuki inspiring the Beat Generation by bringing Zen Buddhism to the attention of the west. I worked with the tireless Lama Zangmo teaching Tibetan Buddhism; watched the devoted Ajahn Sundara and Sister Candasari teaching the Theravada Buddhist Tradition whenever asked; I imagined building over forty schools for refugee children with His Holiness's sister, Jetsun Pema or Amala, the mother of Tibet, bringing the dharma with us where ever we went.

These are only a few of the women who have taken me on their journey in this collection. Each contribution has been equally valued and appreciated.

My hope for all women is to be free from persecution, discrimination and poverty to enable them to travel in the Buddha's path. A mother's love has the potential to create a peaceful home and a peaceful world for everyone to share a sense of oneness, which is essential for this planet to survive in our turbulent times.

1. The Karaniya Metta Sutta, Suttanipata [SN 1.8] Khuddakapatha [Khp 9]

Darcy Flynn

EDITOR'S NOTE

The articles and essays in this anthology are reprinted from previously published texts in the journals of the Buddhist Society, *Buddhism In England* 1926-1945 and renamed *The Middle Way* in 1945 - through today, following the editorial principles below.

Corrections are made to misspellings and missing words where they are obvious.

Slight changes are made to the punctuation to correct obvious errors or non standard and misleading punctuation.

The spelling, hyphenation, capitalisation and italicisation of a few specialised terms has been altered if required.

In most cases capitalisation of words follow the original texts despite their inconsistency.

In a few rare cases corrections and deletions are made to content where obvious.

Otagaki Rengetsu (1791–1875)
Buddhist Nun, Artist, Potter, Poet, Calligrapher

Darcy Biddulph and Aminah Borg-Luck, 2018

Otagaki Rengetsu was a Japanese Buddhist nun who lived at a time of considerable social change during which Japan began a process of shifting from feudalism to an era of modernisation and Westernisation. It is believed that she was the daughter of a geisha and a nobleman, but was adopted in infancy by the samurai Otagaki Teruhisa and his family. As was very common with upper-class girls in those times, when she was roughly eight years old she was sent to Kameyama Castle, Kyoto, where she served as a lady-in-waiting, as well as learned traditional arts. She was trained in jujitsu, naginayatsu, keyetsu and kusarigama, all martial arts, as well as dance, sewing, and the Japanese Tea Ceremony.

Rengetsu's (or, Nobu, by birth name) early life was marked by tremendous loss. When she was only a teenager, both her stepmother and stepbrother died, and before her mid-thirties she went on to lose two husbands and all of her children. She had had piercingly direct experience of the truths about the nature of reality taught by the Buddha and saw a way to transcend her grief through the practice of Buddhism. At the age of 33 she renounced worldly life, ordained as a nun in the Pure Land tradition at Chion'in Temple and took the name Rengetsu, meaning 'Lotus Moon.'

Alongside her spiritual pursuit, she went on to become a highly accomplished waka poet, painter, ceramicist and calligrapher. As much as she may have used her art to engage with life's deep questions, her work was also undertaken out of a very practical necessity: on the death of her father in 1832 Rengetsu had to find a way to support herself. While she remained humble, even dismissive, about her own skill, she was a very well-respected artist. Some accounts speculate that every household in Kyoto once owned a piece of her pottery, and decades after her death strips of illuminated paper with handwritten poetry were sold in the city.

Her ware, known as Rengetsu-yaki, demonstrates her incredible precision and dexterity which must have required great focus and attention. She inscribed her ceramic work with poetry in calligraphic script directly onto wet clay, often on very small surface areas. Her technique was self-developed and the pieces she made were highly unique. Teapot for Steeped Tea bears the following poem:

> May the pine wind flowing,
> Flowing,
> Through the house,
> Brush away the dust,
> Of the ages

Rengetsu also produced many paintings; sometimes just working with ink on paper, and at others using colour and silver as well. These, too, include poetry in her flowing calligraphy and were typically made into hanging scrolls. Hakuzosu the Fox-Spirit below depicts a fox dressed in the clothing of a Buddhist nun; the poem is about a deceiver lurking in Kyoto's Sagano fields at twilight and, employing a clever pun, may point to the theme of one's nature.

Buddhist themes are woven throughout Rengetsu's poetry and her compositions are characterised by tenderness, grace and also playfulness. She composed in the traditional waka form (out of which the widely known haiku form emerged), wherein poems are made up of 31 syllables arranged in five lines over 5-7-5-7-7 syllables. Despite the economy of this form her poetry is full of feeling and powerfully expresses not only her spiritual reflections, but also her wrenching experiences of loss and even social concerns.

> It is with the names of two rival warriors,
> Who strove,
> In crossing its current,
> To be the first in the field,
> That the waters of the river Uji have ever flown.
> Refreshing is the torrent
> Of April rain
> (America),
> Promising blessing
> Upon the thirsty land.
> Thinking of
> The cold bodies
> Left on the road – Someone's dear sons
> Never to return.

All day the wind blows
Rustling through the pines,
Yet my dull ears don't hear;
When the rustling wind ceases to blow,
Comes consciousness of something missed.
How I love the flower fair,
Ever blooming its first delight,
And in the morning
Sun so bright
Falling bravely, pure as air.

In Frank Brinkley's 1901/2 book, *Japan: Its History, Arts and Literature*, it is noted that Rengetsu composed the following lines within the hour before her death at the age of 84. Her poem reminds us a little of the encouraging verses uttered by nuns of the Buddha's own day who practised diligently to cultivate the Noble Eightfold Path and arrive at the supreme happiness of the extinguishment of suffering.

Tsuyu hodo mo
Kokoro ni kakaru
Kumo mo nasbi
Kyo wo kagiri no
Yugure no sora
Without the shadow
Of a cloud
To darken my soul,
The sun of my life sets
In a clear evening sky.

Darcy Biddulph is an author who also writes under the name of Flynn. She is editor of the quarterly journal, *The Middle Way*. Aminah Borg-Luck has worked for SuttaCentral, The Buddhist Society, Tate Encounters Research and Anukampa. Originally published in *The Middle Way*, vol. 93, no. 2, August 2018.

The Butterfly painting by Otagaki Rengetsu

Posthumous depiction of Otagaki
Rengetsu writing

The Fox Spirit

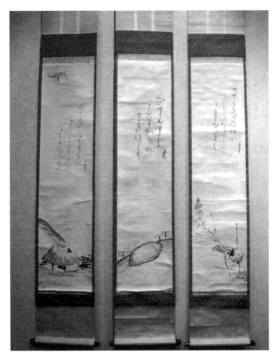

Calligraphy and 3-scrolls by Otagaki Rengetsu

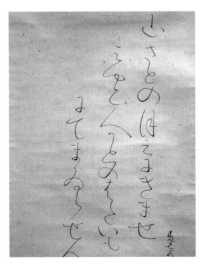

Calligraphy by Otagaki Rengetsu

Ink painting by Otagaki Rengetsu

Ceramic tea pot by Otagaki Rengetsu known as Rengetsu ware

Ceramic Bowl by Otagaki Rengetsu

CAROLINE AUGUSTA FOLEY RHYS DAVIDS
(1857–1942)

*Translator, scholar and President
of the Pāli Text Society.*

Caroline Augusta Foley was born on 27 September 1857 in East Sussex, England, shortly after the death of five of her siblings within one month from diphtheria. A vaccine was not developed until 1920 and only three of the eight Foley children survived until adulthood. She was home schooled by her father, the vicar of Wadhurst, who was a graduate of Wadham College, Oxford, as had his father, who was also a clergyman and a descendant of the college's founder Nicholas Wadham (1531–1609). Founded in 1601, Wadham College had become a focus for secular study in the sciences and became the meeting place for the Oxford Philosophical Club, of which Sir Christopher Wren was a graduate and which eventually led to the creation of the Royal Society. Wadham did not accept women as undergraduates until 1974 and Caroline's father ensured that she read Philosophy, Psychology and Economics at University College London, which was founded as a university with a secular charter, in contrast to the Oxbridge Colleges, which had a strong Christian element in their charters.

Caroline had a brilliant scholastic career, winning the John Stuart Mill Scholarship in Philosophy and the Joseph Hume Scholarship. The German orientalist Reinhold Rost (1822–1896), a Sanskrit scholar and student of Indian philosophy, who later became Head Librarian from 1869 to 1893 at the India Office Library and Secretary of the Royal Asiatic Society, was an important influence in her life. His successor at the India Office Library, CH Trawley became skilled in Greek Latin and German and a well-known translator of Sanskrit classics. It was however her psychology tutor, George Croom Robertson (1842–1892), who was Professor of Philosophy of Mind and Logic and a supporter of women's suffrage, who sat on the national committee to support women in attending university, at whose behest she met her future husband, Dr Thomas William Rhys Davids.

In 1894 they were married, after which she became his close collaborator in Pali and Buddhist research, and later his successor in that field. Christmas Humphreys wrote of her:

'She was, in fact, the last of a great line of pioneer translators; by whose efforts the Buddhism of the Southern School has become available to Westerners. She was never in fact a Buddhist, though often asked to represent Buddhism at conferences of comparative religion, and she was never an attractive writer, being unable, it would seem, to present her scholarship freed from the scholastic chrysalis in which they had matured. But the nuggets of gold were there for those who sought them, and in all humility, I suggest that generations yet unborn will recognise her as the vital and historic link between mere scholarly translation and Buddhism as a living religion in the West.'[1]

She became Lecturer in Indian Philosophy at Victoria University of Manchester from 1910 until 1913 and Lecturer in the History of Buddhism at the School of Oriental and African Studies from 1918 until 1933. From 1907 she was also the Honorary Secretary of the Pāli Text Society, which her husband had founded in 1881 to transcribe and translate Pāli Buddhist texts.

Caroline and her husband had three children. After their son died in the First World War in 1917 Thomas, her husband, died in 1922, Caroline turned to Spiritualism. She became particularly involved in various forms of psychic communication, such as Clairaudience, with the dead. This doubtless gave rise to her doubts regarding anattā (the central Buddhist doctrine of 'no soul, no I, no self' – the doctrine of non-self). Later in life she rejected the concept of anattā as an 'original' Buddhist teaching, but remained 'a loyal and devoted follower of the 'enlightened one.'[2]

In 1923, the year after her husband's death, she took his place as President of the Pāli Text Society until her own death in 1942. Her publications include *Kindred Sayings on Buddhism* (1930), *The Milinda-questions: An Inquiry into its Place in the History of Buddhism with a Theory as to its Author* (1930) and *What was the original gospel in 'Buddhism'?* (1938).

Notes

1. *The Middle Way*, Christmas Humphries.

2 *The Middle Way*, Christmas Humphries.

Mind in Buddhism

Caroline Rhys Davids, 1934

In 1914 I published a little book on *Buddhist Psychology* for the Quest Series of manuals.[1] (*B. 236*). In 1924 I published a new impression of this, only adding a few newer impressions and corrected convictions in a supplement. After yet another ten years I have been asked whether, in case the book did not as a whole express my present opinions, I preferred it should be put aside, and a general restatement published, as far as, in a brief sketch, this could be done.

Of course I prefer that. The historic study of Buddhism, in no matter what branch, is a very new study. New materials have been coming every year to hand; nor are materials, now for some years made accessible, studied as they should be by those who write and speak on Buddhism. What such give us is mainly (a) discourses on formulas, (b) 'individual reflections' which 'try to convince us philosophically...'[2] Now formulas are church-made fossils. And philosophical reflections too often ignore the changing values inseparable from the long historic growth of a world religion like Buddhism. Moreover, they are usually based on inadequate knowledge of its records.

I do not pretend that my knowledge of Buddhist records is as a whole adequate. But since 1914 such knowledge as I then had of those records, which are earlier than any others we yet have, is greatly increased. If I have altered much in what I now write about Buddhism, it is because I know it better, and not because I am drawing more on, I will not say my imagination, but on fancy. No man of science, no historian can get further in research without imagination. By it they must construct where yet they know only in part; by it they must recreate and make alive a dead past. No, it is better knowledge about early Buddhism that has altered what I have to say. It is this which makes it better on the whole, that the manual of 1914 should be replaced by a better manual.

Here meanwhile I set down in brief what 'mind' was coming to mean for India when that which we of today call 'Buddhism' was a new mission of the 'men of the Sakyas'.

Mental Analysis of a New Interest

I drop the word 'psychology' because it is a term of this new world of ours, and only that. In my youth indeed we never heard it. We spoke of Mental Science, Philosophy of the Mind, and even Mental Physiology. It indicates a specialisation in analytic, scientific procedure unknown before. Much more was this the case in ancient India. And if the word 'psychology' in somewhat of a misfit for this modern procedure, it is a far worse misfit for what the teaching about 'mind' came to effect in the Buddhist teaching about the 'man'. There is today too much reading the new into the old. By this I am not saying, that Buddhism did not bring a new view into an older view of things. Emphatically it did, both in what it tried to do, and in what it did.[3]

But preoccupation with mind was a new phenomenon for the thought of India generally, and this is not yet recognised as it deserves to be. This new interest arose in or rather before the seventh century BC. Buddhism came to be strongly affected by it, and through it came to use words for it in quite a new way. For example, the form of the stem *bhaj*, 'distribute', used only for portions of food, or other matter, came, in Buddhist sayings, to be used for the breaking up of, for details in, things unseen, such as ideas, opinions. Such meanings had come to be needed, and so language was adapted to supply the need.

Just what do I mean by this new Indian phenomenon? We cannot hope to understand the line of evolution taken by early Buddhism unless we make due allowance for this new sort of attention to the mind.

I do not mean a new use of the word 'mind' in speech-idioms. The Vedic hymns and applied utterances (*samhitas*) use *manas*, 'mind,' much as we do today. Thus we read, 'Which prayer, O Agni, is to be the choice of thy mind?' 'By what strong mind may we arrest the Maruts (wind gods)?' 'What a man reaches with the mind, that he expresses by speech.'[4] If the Buddhist Sayings merely carried on this way of speaking about mind, there would be no new things to records about 'Buddhist psychology.' Again, when we come to the Ritual Sayings (Brahmanas), there is much mention of *manas*; but it is the man as expressing, as manifesting 'the self' (India did not say 'himself'), as, that is, by way of, mind, speech, eye, ear, breath, work (*karman*). Nowhere do we find any attempt made to resolve the *manas* into constituent parts.

In the early Upanishads we come upon the new note. Not only, as in the Vedas, is mind spoken of as an instrument of the man, praying or what not; the mind is now spoken of as a wherewithal to act upon the body. In the next place, mind is coming to be viewed in the new light of a manifold, a varied 'more' (*bhuyas*) in the man. Thus, while it is the self or man who 'seizes hold of' and animates the body, it is 'with the mind' (*manasa*) that he does so; with the mind he sees, hears, feels, etc. And then, 'in the self', we read, 'there is surely more than "name"'; (this word in ancient India – and where not else besides? – meant all of man that was not visible shape, *rupa*); 'there is speech; nay more, there is mind ... nay, more, there is intention (*samkalpa*) ... there is thought (*citta*) ... there is musing (*Dhyana*) ... there is intelligence (*vijnana*) ... there is memory (*smrita*) ...'

Here are two very marked New Words in Indian thought: mind as instrumental medium between body and the man; mind as an ascertainable plurality. In the former, we do not find the word instrument or tool; it was practically non-existent; it was not then our world of instruments. Nor do we find the word 'will'; man's will was there, but he had not differentiated it from mind. As to that, we, with our grand word 'will,' may yet be heard saying: 'I have a mind to do it.' There was the word *kama*, not yet debased as it became under Buddhist monasticism to mean only sensuous desires, but it never meant more than the vague generic term 'desire'; it never appears harnessed to bodily efficiency as it is when we say, e.g. with Jesus: 'I Will! Be thou clean!' (Luke, v.13). For it Buddhism did not find a worthier word, not at least until centuries later. But Buddhism did link man with body through mind in a volitional way, even without the fit word.

In the latter, 'New Word' we see a crude effort to unfold a Many in the mind. Recalling that the root idea in 'mind' is measuring (*minati*), we may call it seeing ways of measuring in detail. And the new interest in this was not looked at without apprehension, for we find the teacher Kaushitaki, in the Upanishad so called, warning his pupils: 'Seek not to know speaking, feeling, thinking, doing; it is the speaker, the feeler, the thinker, the doer who is to be known.'

Proto-Sankhya

It is reasonable to assume, in this new interest, the work of some one man with a new message for his land and age. Had India taken earlier to writing, as did China, Egypt, Assyria, we might know much about him. As it is, he is but a name: Kapila, the 'tawny one.' To him and his 'school' is ascribed this analytical doctrine, which came down to be known as *sankhya* (Pali, sankha, sankhana), meaning literally 'seeing well,' and secondarily, in computing, naming, numbering. It has come down in a number of aphorisms of quite uncertain date, but centuries older than the exegeses in which they are unfolded. In these aphorisms, whereas the man or self is kept aloof, apart from matter, a very prime reality, but not 'computable' (since he is sole computer), he is also kept apart from mind, this being held to be as divisible as is body; divisible into parts and functions, such as the senses, and much more, and existing, even as body exists, for the man, and only explicable as bringing enjoyment (or experience) not for itself, not for the many parts, but for the user, the enjoyer, the man.

Here then was the new phenomenon: man was no more just *nama-rupa*: soul (or inner world) and body. He had not one, but two parallel servants or sets of servants, or instruments. I do not find it recognised by us as a new phenomenon. My own first recognition of it may be seen in my *Gotama the Man* (1928) (B. 240). When it is recognised, we can then see that its great expansion in Buddhism, in a way calculated to bring great help to Buddhism as a religion, was not a purely Buddhist product, but was the influence exercised on Buddhism by a vogue of the day. Brahman (or early Hindu) teaching heeded the warning of Kaushitaki, and no doubt of other teachers; it harnessed proto-Sankhya into its service; it held up the analytic cult in a man's training as complementary to the opposite stress in culture which it called Yoga; it held the balance. Buddhism also started to do the same. It called *sankhana* and *bhavana* (making become: the imaginative, constructive side) as 'the two strengths' (*balani*).[5] But the analytic 'strength' won, and the whole trend of Buddhism was led by it, in a way Kapila will never have foreseen.

Let me not be misunderstood – that there must be some connexion between those Sankhyan and Buddhist analyses of man's inner world was brought forward some 38 years ago by Jacobi commenting on Garbe's *Sankhya Philosophie*. But neither of them seemed to see the long growth there was in both Sankhya and Buddhism. Hence the conclusion they came to was not happily worded. It was that 'Buddhist philosophy' was 'derived' from 'Sankhya.' For them 'Buddhist philosophy' involved the whole of what we may call the religious message of Buddhism. There is a world of difference between the two. That which alone deserves the name of a Buddhist philosophy dates from our era. It may be said, in some measure, to be due to influences partly derived from the Sankhyan preoccupation with mental analysis. I refer chiefly to the writings of the Buddhists Nagarjuna, Vasubandhu and Ashvaghosha. But between these and the Sakyan religious mission of the sixth century CE. lay some nine centuries of evolution in Buddhist standpoints, ideals and ecclesiastical and scholastic development. It should be clear, then, that if we take the world Buddhist philosophy in this stricter sense, it cannot well be derived from the proto-Sankhya of the seventh century CE or again, that is we use the word philosophy in a large general sense for 'culture', we must carefully distinguish, as those thinkers did not, the different periods of Sankhyan and Buddhist 'culture' in deriving the one from the other.

Parallel between Body and Mind

Confining ourselves just here to the first age of Buddhism (from Gotama to Asoka), let us ask ourselves to what extent those first Buddhist teachers were influenced by this growing interest in mind as distinguishable from the 'man', and to what extent, if any, did it form an integral part of their gospel.

The answer, if we find one, will of course not cover the whole question of the 'mind in Buddhism.' But for me it is of vital importance to seek it. And it is so because of the strange credulity with which we writers on early Buddhism make such a mere pundit of the great founder, not to mention his chief co-workers. Great world religions are not the inspirations of the makers of categories and formulas. Charles Eliot's 'Buddha', for instance, is just a pundit. And Dr Stcherbatzky, in his voluminous *Buddhist Logic* [B. 955] (Vol.1), is content to believe that the founder taught, 'a very minute analysis of the human Personality,' namely, the doctrine of the so-called five *skandhas* (Pali, *khandha's*), one of bodily, four of mental phenomena. By 'Personality' he means the *pudgala* (Pali, *puggala*). Now I am convinced – and I have studied early Buddhism, in a way, at first hand, as Dr Stcherbatzky has not – that both the term *puggala* and the *skandhas* doctrine played no part in original Buddhism. We see the term *puggala*, quite foreign to the religious literature of the sixth century CE. creeping into the Suttas (at times in the compromise *purisa-puggala*), betraying as it comes the degraded concept of the man which was spreading over Buddhism. And we can discern the *skandha*-gag inserted into teachings which knew only the man with the body and the mind, or the 'beminded body.' The learned author's credulity appears yet more glaring when he goes on to say: 'This is the first main feature of early Buddhism: its soul-denial.'

If by 'early Buddhism' were meant the new ecclesiasticism of the centuries succeeding that of the founder's lifetime, I have not much quarrel with the tragic statement, albeit even then it is crude and inaccurate. But let us keep 'the Buddha' out of this Buddhism! Or, if the title 'Buddha' (unknown to the Pali prose records of the first and second Councils) be claimed as just a symbol of the after-men's teaching, let us hear only of Gotama as the real Sakyamuni. If we use the torch of history, let us at least be historical!

Far too much and too long have later dogmas been made to pose as the genuine message of the founder of primitive Buddhism. To assign these dogmas to their true place in history, to discover what was that real message – these are crying needs which must be worthily satisfied before we can write easy guidebooks on this subject. Let us then seek an answer to my question.

Let us take the second Suttanta of the First Collection: the 'Samannaphala'[6] Possibly this had attained something of its present connected continuity as an oral discourse (probably not its final and present form) when the first Council was held, for it is one of the only two discourses which are there referred to by name. In it I see emerging the view, that 'mind', while it is not body, is as distinguishable from the man as is the body. It is considered as a sort of mental body.

The solitary muser, having emptied himself of all hindrances, wins to one or more of eight inner experiences. In the first he values the relation of the body to the self. This is pictured as a jewel strung on a cord, taking on the tints of the cord as would a colourless diamond. The self is here called not *atta*, or *puriso* (man), much less *puggalo*, but *vinnana*, literally awareness, intelligence. This is very old teaching, usually met within Pali when the body perishing at death is contrasted with the surviving 'man,' or again, when the body is referred to as a station or perch for the imperishable 'man.' In the second experience, he 'imagines' (literally, fashions; there was no word for imagination) another body, having shape (*rupi*) but mental, fully organised. Just as a man could draw out a reed from the sheath, a sword from the scabbard, a snake from its sloughed skin, distinguishing the one from the other.

This is all. Writers have hitherto thrown no light on this apparently useless reflection. But if we recollect the stirring of a new interest in 'mind' as an invisible organism, in a way parallel to the bodily organism, both in procedure and in limitations, surely the quaint passage becomes full of significance. In the possibly not much earlier Katha Upanishad, the injunction is to distinguish, as it were 'draw out,' the inner self (*antar-atman*) from the body, 'like an arrow shaft cut from a reed.' Here it is *manas* that is to be drawn out in idea.

It may be said: It doesn't take us very far. True, but it takes us back to the dawn of a new 'more' in the man, to the discerning of a new inner order he had not before got at. Life was for him made wider, deeper. Nor for him alone. I cannot forget the exhilaration I felt in my youth, when the first reading of – was it Carpenter's *Physiology of Mind?* – revealed to me the wonder of this inner orderly procedure. There is nothing of magic in the paragraph, as I (not to mention others) used to think. The word used for body: *kayo*, means actually a group or aggregate of any kind, even as our word 'body' may be used. We have here a definite advance on the older Indian teaching of man as somehow 'in' body. We have a second body which 'he', the muser, 'applies and bends down thought' (*citta*) to discern.

The New Need of Control

The realising of mind as a sort of body, and so as a servant, complicated life for the religious teacher. It was no new thing to teach control of body, but control had now to be extended to governance of mind. And it is noteworthy that the leading and trusted co-worker Sariputta the brahman is especially associated, in the Suttas, with this new stress. He and his colleagues are shown discussing what would most add lustre to the glory of the moonlit night in the woodland. He elicits opinions, but gives thereupon as his own: 'He who has the mind (*citta*) under control, and is not under the control of the mind. Just as man takes from his clothes-chest and puts on just the suit he requires, even so is such an one.[7] In four contexts do we find him made to say this.

The Upanishad parable of the Katha is more like Plato's. The man drives the chariot of the body with its prancing horses of sense. He is the experiencer (*bhoktri*); the mind is the reins and the driving, and reins must be held firm.

In all three teachings one thing at least is clear: the man or self is held distinct and very real; he is not merged in mind. (Even where in another Pali book the driver is mind, the king-warrior stands beside the driver.) Mind-ways are instruments to be at man's disposal. The clothes are not the man. They wear out, are sloughed off; he persists.

And the injunctions to control of mind cease to be trite when we remember how new they then were; what a fresh emphasis, coming from a new outlook, lies in them.

Terms for Mind

Our late James Ward rightly said, in his 'Psychology' (*Encyclopaedia Britannica*): 'In psychology words are things.' They are in it what things seen, heard, weighed are to material research. Let the reader therefore bear with a word of discussion hereon. So far reference in Pali has been to three terms for mind: *manas, cittas, vinnana.* The last I rendered by 'self.' The discourse would lose its point, did we render it by mind (or consciousness), since this is the subject of the next experience. Morever, though neuter in gender, it is defined in current idiom as he-who-speaks, he-who-experiences (*vado vedeyyo*) in the masculine gender. The two phrases are about man and his body, man and his mind. And the second is a 'More' in experience come to be put into words.

I may be reminded by the, alas, too few who know their Suttas, 'Does it not say that these three mean one and the same?' *Iti pi mano*: this is mind, this is thought, this is intelligence.[8] Could anything be plainer?

No, nor could anything be more plainly stated than the equation between the three Persons in the Christian Trinity, as now established in formula. But there was a day, a long day, when this was not yet an established teaching. Beneath the established identity in the Suttas, too, we see an earlier diversity. And this diversity led to each of the three tending to be used in different contexts. Note, too, that the line quoted by my imagined critics occurs once only, and in such a way as to suggest a later inserted gloss. The Sutta deals with just the man weighing which, if either, it were for a moment plausible to identify with himself, with 'the self'; the body or the mind (*kayo, cittam.* Not *nama-rupa*, note! Nor *rupa* and four mind-*skandha's*). Surely body, since that at least does perdure for some decades; thought is as shifty, as flighty as a monkey leaping from bough to bough; a new leap every moment. The conclusion of the matter, one would think, will have been that warning of the Second Utterance: neither of the two is the man or self; both are just tools, useful, but limiting man's divine development. Actually the moral drawn is purely monkish standpoint, and leaves us wondering how far the editorial hand has here been busy?

Here is no space to go into the older distinction in idiom of the three exhaustively. I can but give one or two instances where *manas* and *citta* seem to have borne a distinct natural difference.

Not only above is *citta* likened to an ape. Restless preoccupation with impressions from without in the uncontrolled mind inspired the vivid little poem by one Valliya (*Theragatha*) [B. 247]: –

'Within the little five-doored hut an ape
Doth prowl, and round and round from door to door
He hies, rattling with blows again, again.
Halt, ape! Run thou not forth! For thee
'Tis not herein as it was wont to be.
Wisdom doth hold thee captive. Never more
Shalt roam from hence (in freedom as of yore).

Dhammapala's exegesis confirms us in holding the figure to be that of the *citta*, receptive of, susceptible to impressions. *Citta*, too, is the term ascribed to Sariputta's teaching above.

Now *manas* is not used with such a deprecatory stress. We see it made the referee, the valuer of sensations. We see it as the type-word of psychical action (*mano-kamma*) as distinct from vocal and bodily action. We see it used for deliberate, as distinct from impulsive, reaction in the word *manasikaro*, a word which came to stand as equal with our 'attention.' Reaction in act, again, is given to *manas*, not in *citta*, as in the entirely Upanishadic sayings of the ancient Dhammapada:

'If with corrupted mind (*manasa*)...' or again: 'If with a pious mind a man do speak or act...'

Very different in outlook is the line put in to overlie the two couplets, these being, as 'twin verses', in keeping with the rest of the chapter – but to that I will return.

Of the special significance of the third term for mind, vinnana, I have spoken of it (when not ironed out) to mean as much as, and no more than, the other two I have spoken of. As such, it came down to be defined as meaning, for instance, 'one is aware of a taste as acid, sweet, alkaline, etc.' Yet that India should have had a specific term for man as surviving – and that after all still holds the field, as life's great crisis, however much we bury our heads in the sand about it – would not make her unique. Persia, too, had her specific term, the word *urvan*, meaning as some hold, 'the chooser.' That India had a rival term should open our eyes to a date in her religious values, when the matter of man's birthright in the worlds, man's right-of-way in the worlds bulked as largely, as vividly, in her religious preoccupations as we know it did in those of ancient Persia. Very early Buddhism shows this living interest. The Sutta Collections are full of it, but they also show it as waning.

And with that waning the distinctive meaning of *vinnana* waned, so that we find this inconsistency in what is told of the founder – he is shown psychically seeing an evil man of another world (*Mara*) seeking the *vinnana* – the just released 'soul' or 'man' of a monk-suicide, and there is no suggestion that what is sought is in itself an illusion. He is also shows elsewhere sharply rebuking a disciple for believing that the *vinnana* is anything more than a mental result of preceding mental conditions (*Majjhima*, No.38); that it is no persisting 'speaker' and 'experiencer.' We cannot see the founder consistent in holding to both standpoints. But if we see, in the two suicide Suttas,[9] an older tradition, in the Sutta of the sharp rebuke a later composition betraying a striking growth in preoccupation with 'mind', explanation becomes possible. *Vinnana* in the latter has ceased to be the *urvan* of the Persian; it has become merely a mental phase. These Suttas leave us in no doubt about the matter. It is too easy a solution to reject the former pair as 'mythological' and take only the last Sutta seriously. On the one hand, the latter is so obviously a later, more scholarly, more deliberately compiled scripture, the work of the revising editor. On the other hand, there are the scattered allusions to *vinnana* as gaining a 'platform,' a bodily 'support' (*thiti, patittha*) in this (bodily) encasement or that.

One more *vinnana*-context should be noticed. It is once or twice listed as a sixth element, with earth, water, fire, air, space.[10] I do not think we should read any 'cosmic consciousness' into this context. The Commentaries pass it over, or just say: *vinnana* means *nama*, the other five are *rupa*. (That space should be *rupa*, not the absence of it, is interesting). For me the term *vinnana* here means 'man', 'mankind', as completing the constituents of the known universe.

Two more terms for mind deserve brief comment: *sanna, panna*, both variants of the root *na*, to know. The former we find illustrated (as is that worsened *vinnana*) by our 'perception,' whether by this we mean the modern specific recognition of a sense-group, e.g. an orange, or the looser term for any 'coming-to-know.' Both ranges of meaning appear in Pali. *Sanna* is the act of recognising by way of the name. And when, in the furthest reach of abstract musing a man was said to attain to 'neither *sanna* nor not-*sanna*', the idea appears to have been, that he had awareness of a name with unawareness as to the thing named. This seeming paradox should be as familiar to us as to the early Buddhist. We may have names for That Which or Whom we have as yet no adequate conception. We can only conceive a More; we give It the name of the Most: *summum bonum*, supreme heaven, Deity, Consummation.

Panna, like *vinnana*, has a history, and it is also a tale of depreciation. In early Buddhism, until at least the compilation of the first book of Abhidhamma, *panna* was as important as, shall I say, such a term as 'growth in grace,' will have been for the Christian. But in the classic manual, *Compendium of Philosophy* [BB. 67] of probably the 11th century, it is cited only to be dismissed in a line. Just as, in *vinnana, the vi-* means our 'dis-' in e.g. discriminating, the *san-* in *sanna*, means inclusiveness and continuity, as in our 'syn-' and 'con-,' so in *panna* the *pa* (Sanskrit: *pra*) means a forward force, e.g, *pa-kkamati*, to pass on, advance: our *pro-*, e.g. progress.

This connexion with growth appears in an interesting observation, ascribed to Sariputta (*Majjhima*, No. 3): 'What is *vinnana* is to be understood (*parinnatabbam*); what is *panna* is to be made-become (*bhavitabba*).' When this Sutta was compiled, *vinnana* had evidently fallen to the status prescribed in Sutta No. 8, as cited above. But *panna* still retained its high Indian status. And that was no mere phase of mental proficiency or progress. It meant growth, becoming more, in the very man, self, spirit. It meant essentially spiritual growth. Our own psychology is so preoccupied with the man's tool, the mind, or rather with 'minding,' that it has neglected the one thing that supremely matters, the procedure in growth of the minder. The same thing had already happened ages ago in Buddhism. In the Abhidhamma list of terms defining *panna*, a list far exceeding all other such lists, that for energy along being commeasurable, and making a bad second at that, the terms are a mix-up of words for intellectual and spiritual proficiency. The man was becoming merged, by that time, in mind. To be *pandita* (adjective, which in the Suttas is equal to *pannavant* (having wisdom) came eventually to mean just 'clever' and 'learned' (the old *sutavant*); and so we come down to 'pundit.' Preoccupation with mind had annexed the word, but had outlived the older tradition of sanctity attaching to it.

The tradition died hard. There had been formulated, we know not when, the triad: *sila, samadhi, panna*: morals, mind-training, wisdom. Morals the base, like the firm earth; *samadhi*, the various ways of mental study, including *jhana*; *panna*, or growth on a higher plan than either of these. And we find that, for the, as I hold, lonely last tour of the aged founder and Ananda, in the absence of a listening recorder, a little set piece on these three is put into his mouth as his last sermons – O the pathetic absurdity of it for the Man of Way! – and so sturdy was the tradition that nine centuries later, Buddhaghosa made them his framework of his *magnum opus*. In this work,[11] *sila* is exclusively monk-morality, for he was addressing only his little world-within-world. To *samadhi* we shall return. The *panna*-section he begins with mind exclusively, so had the subject encroached on what had been purely spiritual, and passes on to examine a scholastic world whence the 'man' was judged to have been entirely excluded as reality by the mind.

Originally published in *Buddhism in England*, vol. , no. , Sept–Oct 1934.

Notes

1.   I quote from pp.54 and 68 of this year's *Buddhism in England*.

2.   On this distinction see my *Outlines of Buddhism*, 1934.

3.   *Rig-Veda*: I, 76, 1; I, 171, 2; I, 165, 2; *Taittiriya-samhita*, V, 1, 33.

4.   *Gradual Sayings*, I, p.47, f. (*B*. 1,204)

5.   See *Dialogues of the Buddha* (B. 286), Vol.I, No. 2 .

6.   *Further Dialogues*, I, No. 2.

7.   *Samyutta-Nikaya*, ii, 95).

8.   Both in *Samyutta-Nikaya*: Godhika and Vakkali.

9.   In *Majjhima*, latter Suttas.

10. Translated as the *Path of Purity*, by Pe Maung Tin (B. 1,046–8).

11. *Vishuddimaga* by Buddhaghosa, *Path of Purification*, Caroline Rhys Davids, Pali Text Society, London 1920, 1921

ALEXANDRA DAVID-NÉEL

(1868–1969)

Adventurous trailblazer who left a huge legacy of exciting, exotic and scholarly work in 30 books devoted to her travels and to Tibetan Buddhism.

The causes and conditions that led to the extraordinary life of Alexandra David-Néel are to be found in the lives of those who influenced her in her childhood and youth. Her parents were part of a group that included passionate idealists, intellectuals, learned professionals and free thinkers, people who were able to imagine beyond the boundaries imposed by the bourgeoisie way of life of the time. It is of little surprise that Alexandra David-Néel led the life she did.

Born in 1868 in France to Belgian-French parents, her mother Louise Eugénie Alexandrine Marie Borghmans (who was known as Alexandrine) was a Belgian Roman Catholic and her father, Louis David, a Huguenot French Freemason, liberal journalist, teacher and republican activist.

Her father opposed the *coup d'etat* of Louis-Napoleon Bonaparte on 2 December 1851 that followed the 1848 revolution, and was forced into exile as a consequence. In Brussels, he met and married Alexandrine, where they published a republican journal together.

After the couple returned to Paris, their daughter, Alexandra was born in Saint Mandé, Val-de-Marne on 24 October 1868.

In 1869, a year later, under the influence of the historian and statesman Victor Duruy, a woman was awarded the baccalaureate degree for the first time and women were admitted to the Sorbonne and to medical schools. It was the dawning of a new dispensation for women, and one that opened many doors for Alexandra.

As a result of the execution of the leading Communards of the Paris Commune in 1871 the family moved back to Belgium, where Alexandra's brother was born in 1873, but died six months later when she was five years old.

In her early life, Alexandra was influenced by reading books including *The Lives of The Saints* (1579) and Jules Verne's *Voyages Extraordinaires*, a series of bestselling adventure novels that includes *Journey to the Centre of the Earth* (1864), *Twenty Thousand Leagues Under the Seas* (1870), and *Around the World in Eighty Days* (1872). She was inspired to seek a life of self-sacrifice through her reading of the jataka story in which the Buddha throws himself into the path of a hungry tigress so that she can eat him in order to feed her cubs, as well as by the lives of the saints, whom she emulated through fasting and austerities.

In addition to her reading, Alexandra was also inspired by Élisée Reclus (1820–1905), a close friend in her father's circle, who was banished from France to Bruges for his republican activism and was a friend of the Russian anarchist Pyotr Kropotkin. Reclus was a Universal Geographer, anarchist, vegetarian, naturist, and part of the 'anti-marriage movement' – although married, he opposed the bondage of marriage that many women endured. He was an outstanding figure of his time, father of the animal rights movement, nature conservation and social ecology, a man of letters and a true pioneer in a turbulent time who doubtless had a powerful influence on Alexandra's imagination as all her interests seem to have come from him.

Before she was eighteen years old, Alexandra travelled extensively on her own, running away at the age of fifteen while on holiday and crossing from Holland to England, and later, without permission, traversing the St. Gotthard Pass to the Italian lakes. At seventeen she entered the Conservatoire royal de Bruxelles to study piano and music, where she received a first prize for singing and became interested in the Theosophical Movement, first studying its principles before joining the Scottish Rite of Freemasonry, of which Reclus was a member and with whom Alexandra spent a considerable amount of time.

Alexandra visited the Musée Guimet (The National Museum of Asian Arts-Guimet), which had opened in Paris in 1889, and, inspired by what she had seen and learned, began to study Art History and Eastern thought and became a Buddhist – events that she noted in her diary published under the title *La Lampe de Sagesse – The Lamp of Wisdom* – in 1986. She also decided to become an orientalist and enrolled at the École pratique des hautes études to learn Sanskrit, Tibetan and Eastern Philosophy. It was here that she became friends with Sylvain Lévi, the French orientalist, with whom she remained in contact until his death in 1935. At this point in her life Alexandra became depressed and considered suicide.

In 1891, at the age of 21, on the death of her godmother Elisabeth Morgan, a fellow Theosophist, she inherited a considerable sum of money, which enabled her to travel extensively in Sri Lanka (known then as Ceylon) and India where she studied with Swami Bhaskarananda Saraswati in Benares (now Varanasi) and travelled as far as the Nepal-Sikkim border. After running out of money and returning to Europe, Alexandra joined the European Section of the Theosophical Society in London on 7 June 1892. Shortly after joining, she returned to Paris where she became a member of the Ananda Lodge. In a letter to the English writer and historian GRS Mead, dated 10 December 1892, she wrote that she had broken off relations with her family because of her refusal to renounce Theosophy.

She then returned to Belgium and contacted Annie Besant, who was now head of the Theosophical movement, for advice on meditation. She became involved with the anarchist movement to the extent that she was noticed by the police. Her parents' financial problems required her to return to singing and piano, from which she had previously earned money. Alexandra sang in various opera companies, in particular the Opera Hanoi in French Indochina (now Vietnam) for the 1895–96 and 1896–97 seasons, as the principal singer under the stage-name Alexandra Myrial. She performed in various operas including Verdi's *La Traviata* (1853) as Violetta as well as works by Victor Massé, Charles Gounod, Léo Delibes, Georges Bizet and interestingly *Thaïs* by Jules Massenet, a work that deals with the protagonist's conflict between her various identities as scholar, performer, lover and religious renunciant.

In 1897, she lived in Paris with the composer and pianist Jean Haustont and wrote the libretto for a lyric-tragedy entitled *Lidia*, which they composed collaboratively. The following year, in 1898, Alexandra's first book, *Pour La Vie* was printed by Haustont and was followed by an anarchist pamphlet in 1889 with a foreword by Reclus. Poverty forced her to take up work with the Athens Opera from November 1899 until January 1900.

In July that year, while working in Tunisia with the Municipal Opera of Tunis she met a distant cousin, Phillippe Néel de Saint-Sauveur, who was the chief engineer of Tunisian railways and they become lovers.

Following a visit by Haustont in 1902 she gave up singing and became director of the Tunis Casino. On 4 August 1904, at the age of 36, she married Phillippe, who was aware of her lack of interest in children and a domestic life. On 21 December that year, her father died and left her 20,000 francs, which was at the time a considerable sum.

Reclus died in 1905 and Alexandra returned to Belgium to pay her respects. The following year she returned to London and met and became friends with the translator and scholar Caroline Rhys Davids and her husband and founder of the Pāli Text Society TW Rhys Davids. She also worked with Meh-ti to learn Chinese philosophy. She also met DT Suzuki, who she later visited in Japan.

With her father as well as her mentor, Reclus, gone, Alexandra became depressed and purposeless and returned to France once again to resume her studies under Lévi at the École pratique des hautes études. In 1910 she published *Contemporary Buddhist Thinkers* and lectured at the Theosophical Society in London and Paris. In 1911 she published *Modern Buddhism and the Buddhism of the Buddha.*

In 1910, she declared herself a *poseur* and an 'armchair Buddhist'. After her husband, Phillippe, suggested that she visit India to learn and perfect her language skills and offered to pay her expenses for a year, she set out in 1911 on a journey that would take fourteen years, throughout which she inundated Phillippe with letters and articles for publication.

During her stay in India, via Sri Lanka, she met notables including Sir John Woodroffe (also known as Arthur Avalon) who was the High Court Judge of Calcutta and an openly practising Tantric Yogi of the Kali-worshiping sect, whose most well-known works are *Shakti and Shákta* (1918) and *The Garland of Letters* (1922), a description of the chakras and the cosmogeny of Advaita Vedanta or non-dualistic Vedanta. She also met Sri Aurobindo Ghose, a founding member of the National Congress of India, who, following a conversion experience later founded Pondicherry Ashram and Integral Yoga. Despite his opposition to partition he was nevertheless one of the founding fathers of modern India.

While Alexandra was in India, the Indian police made secret enquiries to France and she was placed under surveillance by the government of India due to her anarchist affiliations and the fact that the French authorities considered her a known 'extremist'.

In 1912, she met the thirteenth Dalai Lama in exile in Sikkim and travelled throughout northern India with the blessing of the Maharaja of Sikkim, who befriended her, and whose son she later advised on the reform of Buddhism, which aligned the dharma with the discoveries of modern science and other profound changes.

Alexandra then became the disciple of the highly revered teacher, the Third Lachen Gomchen under two conditions: absolute obedience and no trips without permission. She remained with him taking instruction, much of it in solitary retreat, until 1916, during which time the 15-year-old lama, Aphur Yongden, entered her service.

On the invitation of the Panchen Lama, she entered Tibet and Shigatse. On her return to India, she discovered that the British Authorities (The Government of India) were not pleased with her wanderings without proper permits and they demanded she leave the country. In February 1917 she found herself in Japan, in Kobe, where she met Ekai Kawaguchi, who had previously travelled to Lhasa disguised as a Chinese Monk and who she had met before, in 1912 in exile in Sikkhim, when she had received an audience with the Dalai Lama.

From late 1917 until 1923 she travelled extensively with Yongden, covering 2000 miles in her journey from Japan, through China on foot, mule and horse to Lhasa, which she reached in 1924.

Following her return to France in 1924, she gave a series of conferences sponsored by her old friend Sylvain Lévi. Over the following year, she published many books, including *My Journey to Lhasa* in 1927.

She found herself something of a celebrity and settled in Digne-les-Bains, in the Basses Alpes district of France. Her book *Magic and Mystery in Tibet* was published in 1929, but she then left for China at the age of 69 in 1937 to study ancient Taoism, a journey that would last until 1946, during which time her husband died in 1941. She continued to publish many books and returned to France in in 1946 to Samten Dzong (meditation fortress) in Digne-les-Bains. In 1955, her lifelong companion and adopted son Lama Yongden died.

During her extensive travels with Lama Yongden to remote areas of India and Tibet, she met many prominent Tibetans, including the 13th Dalai Lama and the Panchen Lama. She learned Tibetan and Sanskrit, translated many texts, received many honours awards and titles of Lama and Doctor and was known as Yeshe Tome; 'Lamp of Wisdom'. Her international fame came with the publication of *My Journey to Lhasa* (1927). Most importantly, she resolved the conflicts of her early life, and fulfilled the dreams of her childhood, combining religion, travel and philosophy into a unique life. She was also a contributor and admirer of *The Middle Way*. She died at the age of one hundred in Monaco, shortly after applying to renew her passport. Her house in Digne-les-Bains is now a museum. Her ashes were taken to Benares (now Varanasi) in 1973 by her personal secretary Marie-Madeleine Peyronnet and scattered with those of Lama Yongden.

Does Buddhism Respond to the Needs of Today?

Alexandra David-Néel, 1932

The world of today is almost unanimous in declaring that the essential aim of science is to contribute to the good of humanity and that scientific discoveries must manifest results of practical value. This excellent way of regarding the purpose of science should likewise prevail in all that relates to religious and philosophical studies in general, and Eastern philosophies in particular. It is very regrettable that a number of scholars should persist in considering the study of oriental philosophies as simply a cultured pastime, suitable for occupying the leisure of a small intellectual aristocracy, but incapable of any useful end. Now the present condition of the world does not permit of us spending our time in intellectual diversions devoid of practical social results. If the study of Eastern philosophies can only procure for us that kind of pleasure, it would be as well to leave them alone for the moment. All our charts are required for urgent work at this time of universal confusion.

It is a mistake, however, to think that oriental studies are lacking in practical interest. Among the various doctrines elaborated by Indian and Chinese sages there are some which offer very profitable suggestions for the solving of certain social and moral problems that are at present preoccupying the mind of man. It would be extremely profitable to study them all from this point of view, and one cannot do better in a Buddhist review than to examine what the Buddha's Doctrine really is, and in what way it can be useful to us.

What is Buddhism? A religion? A philosophy? Perhaps both together, perhaps neither the one nor the other.

A religion? Buddhism creates in those who have embraced and understood it, fervour, spiritual joys, even ecstasies, which equal and surpass in intensity those experienced by the adepts of all other religions in whatever age. There exists a Buddhic mysticism, but it is a rational mysticism that comes from the brain instead of having its source in disordered emotions over which no control is exerted.

If Buddhism can be termed a religion, it must be admitted at once that it is a religion for intelligent followers who at no time consent to give up the right of exercising their intellectual and critical faculties.

Now, is it possible for a teaching to be called a 'religion' when it does not speak of God, nor of divine revelation, when it has no dogma, prescribes no ritual, nay – much more, expressly condemns belief in the efficacy of religious rites, but advocates a complete liberty of examination and thought?

This appears scarcely possible. In truth, a Buddhist religion can be found only where the primitive Buddhic doctrine has been corrupted by the masses who were incapable of raising themselves to its height.

Is Buddhism then a philosophy?

Without doubt, if we bear in mind the many philosophers who have acknowledged the Buddha as their Master. There have existed, and still exist at the present day, schools of philosophy that have derived their doctrines from that of the Buddha, interpreting and developing it in many different ways. However, in the original Buddhism all speculations are rejected. No theories are set forth concerning the First Cause or analogous subjects. The Buddha declares that it is unprofitable to engage in hypotheses regarding questions such as the following:

Is the world finite or infinite in space, is it finite or infinite in time?

Does the being who has attained the Nirvanic state continue to exist or does he cease to exist, or again, does he exist and not exist at the same time?

All discussions on subjects of this kind only end, the Buddha thought, in giving out the fruit of our own personal cogitations. And he expressed his thought by saying: 'One fool declares: "All exists, all exists" ... Another fool declares: "Nothing exists, nothing exists" ... And both are fools, because for the one who knows according to wisdom there is neither existence nor nonexistence.'

That is to say, that beyond the pairs of opposites, between which our limited mind moves as between the walls of a prison, there may be a domain where the coexistence of these opposites is possible and where, perhaps, they resolve themselves into fundamental unity.

But even though it can be impregnated with the most profound wisdom, can we liken a teaching to a philosophy what has in it no place for either metaphysics or speculation. Each one is at liberty to decide this question for himself.

In reality, Buddhism is essentially a method: a practical method, at once spiritual and material, for combating suffering and for obtaining deliverance from it. It is for this reason that Buddhism is always up to date.

As a rule, religions and philosophies are intimately connected with the personality of their founders; they are dependent on it. It is difficult to imagine Islamism without the Prophet Mohammed and it is quite impossible to imagine Christianity without Jesus.

This is not the case with regard to Buddhism. According to a declaration of the Buddha, the appearance of Buddhas such as he, in the world, is of no importance as to what concerns the doctrine which they promulgate. This does not derive its value from the divine or venerable character of the Master who preaches it, it is based upon undeniable facts, which it is possible for each one to verify if he will but take the trouble.

Among these facts, the statement of which forms the basis of the Buddhist teaching, I will point out: the impermanence of all things and the composite nature of personality. According to Buddhism the latter is an unstable aggregate and not at all a stable and permanent unity.

A Tibetan one day described to me in very picturesque imagery what was a person, an individual.

'A person is an assembly' he said. 'This assembly consists of many *dramatis personae* who have come from different directions, animated by different inclinations and tending to different ends. Sometimes one of them gets up, gives a discourse or accomplishes an act, then reseats himself and remains silent, motionless, while another in his turns speaks and acts. Other times, several of these personages get up together, support each other in their discourses and combine activities. But often, too, those who get up are not in agreement one with the other, they dispute fiercely, quarrel and anathematise each other. Occasionally the assembly grows very tumultuous, all the members rise together and fight frenziedly'. 'That,' he said, 'is a person, and such is each one of us.'

This picture is exact. The members of this assembly are the representatives, in us, of past activities. They are the hereditary and atavistic tendencies embodied in the particular constitution of our physical organism. They are the tendencies produced by our education, by the material surroundings and mental atmosphere in which we live; finally they are the numerous tendencies, the manifold impulses coming from sources that remain wrapped in mystery for the majority of us.

All these heterogeneous elements move within us. They bring about those sudden strange changes of front in our opinions and conduct and, when in collision, cause those painful inner conflicts from which we suffer.

It is truly the tumultuous assembly depicted by the Tibetan.
The Buddha proclaimed his doctrine for the first time near Benares, at Isipatana.

He had asked himself: 'What is it that leads to wisdom, to peace? What is it that can overcome the evils from which we suffer?' The first words of his first discourse answer: "It is right views."

It is well-known that the one who mistakes the poisonous toadstool for the edible mushroom suffers terribly, or even dies because of his error; also that the child, not knowing the nature of fire, burns itself in trying to seize the dancing flames on the hearth.

Are not the fatal effects of error as plainly visible in those trifles of everyday life as in the decisions of governments which entail immeasurable consequences for the whole of humanity?

There are few people who will not recognise the value of right opinions and the necessity for them, though, no doubt, many will think that there is no need for Buddhism to teach them anything on the subject.

But meanwhile, it is usual for each one to believe his opinion to be right and his point of view correct. Likewise for each one to consider, as equally excellent, the acts that he accomplishes himself or that he encourages and approves of in others, always keeping as standard his own opinion and point of view.

It is precisely with this mode of thought that the Buddhist teaching is at variance. When the latter makes the holding of 'right views' the basis of its ethical system and of its spiritual training, it warns us that we must guard against taking any idea as being correct before having submitted it to a minute examination.

The following passage from the *Kalāma* Sutta clearly indicates the teaching on this subject:

'Some young men had come to tell the Buddha that, in their country, the philosophers were so numerous and expounded such diverse theories that they did not know in which of them to believe.

Whereupon the Buddha advised them thus:

"Put not your faith in traditions merely because they are old and have come down to us through many generations. Do not believe anything upon the ground of common report or because people talk a great deal about it. Believe not a thing merely because someone lays before you the written testimony of some one or other of the sages of old time. Do not believe anything that you have imagined thinking you have received the inspiration from a god. Believe nothing upon the authority of your teachers or priests.

"Whatsoever, alter personal experience and investigation, is found to agree with your own reason and tends to serve your own well-being as well as the well-being of all other living things – that cleave to as truth and shape your life in accordance therewith.'"

And elsewhere, in a dialogue between the Buddha and some of his disciples, which is recounted in the *Majjhima Nikāya*, the Master concludes thus:

'If now, knowing this and perceiving this, would you say: "We honour our Master and through respect for him we repeat what he teaches?" – "We should not, Lord."

'That which you believe, that which you affirm, O disciples, is it not only that which you yourselves have recognised, seen and grasped?' – "It is so, Lord."

The Buddha was not afraid to trust the human mind nor was he afraid of appealing to human reason. He did not crush man by demonstrating to him his insignificance, his lack of power; he did not enjoin him to be humble. On the contrary, he counselled him to be daring.

Shortly before his death he said to those around him:

'Whosoever, either now or after I am dead, shall be a lamp unto themselves and a refuge unto themselves, shall betake themselves to no external refuge, but holding fast to the truth as their lamp, and holding fast as their refuge to the truth, shall look not for refuge to anyone besides themselves – it is they, among my disciples, who shall reach the very topmost Height.'

Does this mean that each one of us would do well to go about in life yielding to his every impulse?

Certainly not. Right views are something quite other than the absurd ideas which spring up in our brain under the effect of passing impressions.

Is it not generally known that a person's mood can vary according as to whether the sun shines or the rain falls. Do we not know also that the course of our ideas and the actions which are produced by them can change according as to whether we are in health or out of health; as to whether we hear a jazz tune, the spirited strains of a military march, or sacred music played on a cathedral grand organ?

How then could the opinions arrived at by the mind, as well as its judgments, be correct and just, if, in this way, it unconsciously yields to passing influences from outside?

That which is true remains true whether we be well or ill, whether we be in church or in the crowded marketplace.

Right views, as they are understood in Buddhism, are those which have been submitted, in all their details, to a prolonged and impartial examination.

In the Buddhist method, perfect awareness is pointed out as the means by which to attain to knowledge, therefore, to acquire right views. It is a question of scrutinising one's feelings, of discovering the causes which one obeys when one desires, loves, approves, rejoices, etc., and also when one rejects, hates, blames, grieves, etc. It is a question of not abandoning oneself to unreasoned indignation or enthusiasm.

Briefly, it is a question of being conscious, reasonable, well-balanced beings instead of poor little puppets pulled in every direction by numberless strings of which they are unaware.

When in Buddhism we find advocated such a line of conduct, does its teaching not answer to a real need? The need of modern thought, which maddened, disordered, rushes at random in a thousand directions without being able to attain to the equilibrium and composure, which are the necessary basis of all individual and national right action?

It is not essential for people to call themselves Buddhists, but what is essential, and none can deny it, is the cultivating of right views, the rooting up of error wheresoever it appears.

The Buddhist teaching insists on this necessary work, which we too often forget and at which we do not labour sufficiently either in ourselves or around us. It invites us to convince ourselves that ignorance and false ideas are the sources of all evil and proposes to us as an ideal: the march towards Light, towards Knowledge, which is also the march towards Happiness.

This is a Message that answers the need of every age and, perhaps, more especially that of our own time. For this reason, although it be 25 centuries old, it is yet useful to repeat.

This text was originally published in *Buddhism in England,* May–June 1932.

Mahayanist Theories in Tibet

Alexandra David-Néel and The Lama Yongden, 1938

The theories discussed below are some of those which I have heard taught and expounded in centres little known – one might say unknown – in a still mysterious land: Tibet.

Mahayana, the 'Great Vehicle' (in Tibetan, *Thegpa chenpo*) is an appellation that covers an infinity of doctrines. The first thing necessary to understand, when one wishes to study Mahayana, is that one does not find oneself confronted by a unique doctrine, but facing a multitude of philosophical schools differing considerably from one another, or even professing theories that are completely contradictory.

In my opinion, Mahayana contains the highest Buddhist philosophy. Certain of its schools seem to have reached the logical conclusion of ideas which are only sketched in the sutras of the Theravadins. On the other hand, however, we find denominated as Mahayana the coarsest degeneration of Buddhism. In fact, under the label of Mahayana we find even catalogued as Buddhist, doctrines that have absolutely nothing Buddhic about them, such as that of the salvation through the grace of Amitabha, even as Christians preach salvation by the grace and the vicarious atonement of Jesus Christ.

The term Mahayana has sometimes been represented as meaning 'great vehicle' in the sense of a conveyance of large dimensions, capable of receiving a large number of travellers, and of transporting them all together towards a happy land. This grotesque conception has, to certain people, seemed marvellous. Above all, it seemed to them to realise an ideal of the most efficacious charity: therefore they began to look down on the Theravada depicting it as a small carriage that could only carry a few passengers. Such definitions are not found in Tibet.

In Tibet, Mahayana is considered as the Great Vehicle, great being understood in the sense of 'superior,' or 'higher.' Instead of receiving everyone without distinction, the Mahayana as Tibetan philosophers understand it, is the vehicle which only a spiritual elite can reach. One must not see in this an egoistic ostracism. No one bars the door of the superior vehicle, but the traveller must be capable of opening it himself, and one must understand that it is his intelligence and energy which permit him to obtain access. However, it must be remembered that the concept of a superior path likewise exists among the Theravadins. They also establish a distinction between that which they call *lokya* 'of the world' and *lokuttara*, 'beyond the world.' Thus they distinguish correct views 'of the world,' *lokya sammāditthi*, from correct views 'beyond the world,' *lokuttara sammāditthi*, and the same for each branch of the Eightfold Path. Accordingly, all physical and mental activities function on two planes, the *lokya* and the *lokuttara*. In Mahayanaist teaching, great importance is attributed to the *pāramitas*, generally translated as signifying 'excellent virtues.' Tibetans reckon six of them, namely: giving, morality, patience, assiduity-endeavour, meditation, knowledge-intelligence. But, impressed with the idea of *lokuttara*, in a greater degree even than the Theravadins, they have translated differently the Sanskrit term. With them, *pāramita* is not 'excellent' but *pharol tu phyinpa*, that is to say, 'that has gone beyond.'

Whether, grammatically speaking, they are right or wrong is of little importance: what interests is this clear affirmation of a spiritual path. It has nothing to do with the doctrines and codes. They are based on conceptions connected with the world which are born of the world, and therefore, can only lead to continued 'turning in the round of existence.'

This round, this samsara, is considered by Tibetan philosophers as a pure illusion, a dream that the mind itself creates. And they believe that it can be escaped from by passing 'beyond' – 'upon the other shore' as the Theravadins say.

But this 'beyond' is not a place, this 'other shore' is nowhere but in our minds. It behoves us to pass beyond those narrow, prejudicial, erroneous conceptions which we have of charity, morality, patience, effort, meditation, and the whole mass of our limited learning which we consider knowledge with a capital K.

All those who are acquainted with Buddhist doctrines know that at their base is found the negation of an existing ego, an uncompounded and permanent entity, either in the person or in anything whatsoever that we can imagine. In spite of the difference in philosophical theories, all Buddhist sects agree perfectly upon this point. *Sabbe dhamma anatta* – 'all things are devoid of an ego' say the Pali texts and Tibetans desiring undoubtedly to fortify this statement repeat it twice to avoid any quibbling: 'There is no ego in the individual. There is no ego in anything.'

Let us listen to a Tibetan philosopher describing the person, or individual, even as it has been described to me.

'A person,' said the learned Tibetan, 'resembles an assembly, a council composed of several members, sometimes one of them rises from his seat, pronounces a discourse, expresses a wish, advocates one or other form of action, and then sits down, leaving his colleagues to decide upon the motion he has proposed. Sometimes two or three members of the Council rise together, hold forth in unison, mutually defending their propositions, supporting them by various arguments drawn from their different experiences. But it also happens that several members of the Council rise simultaneously to be heard and violently contradict one another, obstinately resisting, quarrelling and fighting. The Council is sometimes very turbulent.

Certain members of this assembly are, at times, forcibly expelled by their colleagues, others voluntarily withdraw, while newcomers penetrate the Council Chamber, either by forcing the door, or slipping through at a moment when they have been left open. One also observes some councillors growing anaemic or declining, weakening, becoming inaudible, while others increase in vigour and, no longer timid as they once were, present their motions vociferously, making their colleagues tremble.

The members of the Council are instincts, tendencies, desires, ideas, concepts, beliefs. They come out of a distant past, descendants and heirs of causes whose line is hidden in the eternity of time. Physical and mental affinities have grouped them momentarily, but the group is not indissoluble. On the contrary, every moment alters its composition.

Thus are explained the contradictory impulses which we feel, our changes of opinion or of conduct. All this is nothing but the manifestation of different members of the Council.'

Learned Tibetans adhere to the peculiar Mahayanaist doctrine which is expounded in the *Prajña Pāramita*, the great philosophical work ascribed to Nāgārjuna. Now, in the *Prajña Pāramita* it is written: 'Like images seen in a dream, so should we consider all things.'

The world which appears to us, the Tibetan masters say, is within us, not without us. It is made up of subjective images that we ourselves create. All that we see, all that we feel, resemble that which we see or feel in a dream state. In our dreams we suffer, we rejoice, we live in opulence or we are clothed in rags. We meet all sorts of people, we perform all kinds of actions and when we awake, all this phantasmagoria disappears: we are men or women who have spent the night in bed. Well, say the Tibetan philosophers, when we awake in our bed, another phase of the dream begins, but it is always a dream.

If you try to embarrass the philosopher who asserts this by saying that the proof of the reality of what you see lies in the fact that other people see the same thing, he will be able to answer you: 'How,' he will ask, 'can you prove that these other people exist? You, yourself are the only witness, these "people" are perhaps nothing else than subjective images projected by your own thoughts. They affirm that they see what you see, because you speak through their lips, they resemble the "people" whom you converse with in your dreams.'

One finds analogous theories in India and China. A celebrated Chinese philosopher named Chuang Tse said: 'Last night I dreamed that I was a butterfly, and now I ask myself: Am I a man who has dreamed he was a butterfly: or am I a butterfly who, at this moment, is dreaming that he is a man?'

One will be tempted to invoke memory as a testimony and say: 'I am certain that I am not a butterfly, for I remember perfectly that, yesterday, I was a man and performed actions that are proper to man alone, and I remember that last year and during many other years the same thing happened.'

To this reasoning some learned Tibetans will answer: 'Tell me, please, when you know that you have performed these actions in the past?' The question seems strange indeed, but after having reflected, one must admit that it is at the present moment that one 'knows' this. Then, after certain explanations, the Tibetan will conclude that since it is at the present moment that one knows this, he will affirm that he had performed these actions, is conscious of having done them, it is possible that it is a question of ideas that have only now been born in the mind. He has the idea that he did this or that, but only the idea exists.

Perhaps this may make the interlocutor angry and he will reply to this tiresome reasoning: 'As a proof that I was a tailor here is a coat that I sewed: to prove that I was an architect, here is a plan, and a house that was built upon this plan. To prove that I was married, here is my son who is 20 years old.' But the imperturbable Tibetan will smilingly reply: 'But, my friend, in your dreams you have already been a tailor, an architect, the father of a family and all kinds of other characters and you have seen the fruits of their activity: all that you say applies to subjective images projected by your mind which is full of ideas. You, yourself are only an idea present in my mind. I have no infallible proof that you exist. I can only know that I have an idea of this, the impression that it is so. This idea, this impression comes from a cause, but it is not absolutely certain that this cause is really the existence of this man, who argues with me, as I imagine to be.'

Buddhist teaching includes theories relating to rebirth and rejects the belief in reincarnation. How could it, after having denied the existence of an uncompounded and permanent ego, admit reincarnation? One would ask: reincarnation of what? But the force of habit, and attachment to the powerful illusion of personality, conceived as an uncompounded entity, has made the majority of Buddhists hold to the ancient Hindu belief; the reincarnation of the *jiva* or spirit which, 'just as a man casts off worn-out clothes and puts on others which are new, casts off worn-out bodies and enters others which are new.' [Bhagavad Gita ii. 22]. However, if we consult more enlightened adepts in Buddhism, we shall hear of theories regarding rebirth that exclude reincarnation.

I shall limit myself to my subject: Tibetan ideas. We have already seen that religious Tibetans consider a person to be an aggregate of various elements and not made up only of two parts: soul or spirit and body. They hold that all these elements persist. Not one of them dies nor is otherwise destroyed: each transforms itself and continues to live in the guise of its successive transformations. Tibetan masters adhere to the original doctrine of five skandhas but each of these five they see as subdivided in many ways. According to their theory, we never meet with an indivisible unit, a simple atom of homogeneous substance. Everything is compounded, is an aggregation, and no sooner has one seized and separated the elements of those aggregations than each of them appears as a complex, capable of being in its turn divided into several elements.

Thus, consciousness is viewed as including five dimensions, each one representing the particular consciousness corresponding to one of the five senses. A sixth consciousness corresponds to intellect, to ideas and, as a subdivision of this latter, is reckoned as a consciousness of the illusory 'self,' that which 'I' voyage in the bardo during the time that elapses; between the death (in the ordinary sense of the word) of a person and his rebirth. During this period the consciousness of the eye, the consciousness of the ear, etc., are reborn separately.

It is impossible for me to undertake here explanations which would need more space than I have at my disposal. I shall only point out that one finds traces in the Upanishads of this belief in the dispersion of the elements composing a person, some going into herbs, some into water, some into the ether, etc. – the final question put by Artabhaya being: 'When all these constituent parts of the man are separated where does man himself go?' [Brihad Aranyakopanishad]

'Man himself,' the purusha of the Upanishads, may be assimilated to this 'I' consciousness which Tibetans send travelling in the horde. How will it be reborn? One is almost obliged to say reincarnated, for with the bardo theory, we are already far from the doctrines clearly denying reincarnation.

Let us consult Tsong Khapa, the founder of the sect of the Gelugspas (also called Yellow Hats sect), an important authority in Tibet, for he is the animal ancestor of the present state clergy. In the *Lamrim* (his principal work) he writes: 'The fact of rebirth is brought about by the physical and mental actions that the deceased has accomplished during his lives. These are the principal causes (*Egyu*). The most important of the secondary causes (*Ekyen*) is the parents who, through their union, supply the material body that makes rebirth possible.'

The 'I' consciousness – which is to be reborn – is made of notions derived from the eye consciousness, ear consciousness, and the consciousness of the ideas. To be conscious of one's self, the Tibetans say, is to remember impressions that were produced by sensations or perceptions. Conception, according to Tsong Khapa, is brought about by the desire of this consciousness (in Tibetan *rnam par Shepa*) to gain taste sensations produced by the senses, this being impossible since this consciousness is no longer united to a physical body. Driven by his passion for life, lived in union with a body, the *rnam shes* seeks a 'place of birth' (a womb). When causes proceeding from past lives are to bring about birth as a male, the *rnam shes* feels attraction for a woman, its desire influences her and leads her to seek sexual union. The *rnam shes* takes advantage of this to reincarnate at the moment of conception. If a feminine birth is to take place, the *rnam shes* feels attraction for a man and the latter is incited to seek union with a woman.

We should note that, according to this theory, the movements of the *rnam shes* are not arbitrary. It acts according to the impulses produced by the elements of which it is made. As I have already pointed out, in this philosophical system, no 'simple bodies' exist made of 'indivisible atoms,' if I may use these expressions by way of analogy. The *rnam shes* is a complex, subjected to the law of affinity, it is swayed by attractions and repulsion that are determined by the nature of the elements composing it.

From this point of view, the undeniable fact of heredity, explained with difficulty, sometimes even denied by some followers of the Theravada, is no longer in opposition to the popular doctrine of karma. I say popular, for Tibetan philosophers expound other doctrines regarding karma or as is said in Tibetan, *las rgyu hbras* – 'the fruit caused by the action.' The new being will resemble his parents for it is precisely under the influence of physical and mental tendencies corresponding to those of his parents that he has been driven to seek rebirth as their child. There is already a pre-natal resemblance, but resemblance does not mean complete identification. If certain elements existing in the 'group' called the 'I consciousness' correspond to those that exist in the 'groups' forming the 'persons' of the father and mother chosen by it, or at least are in sympathy with them, the *rnam shes*, nevertheless, contains other elements also. These may differ considerably from the elements that constitute the 'persons' of its chosen parents; they may be absolutely antagonistic to them. At the moment of 'choosing' perhaps these elements, of an opposite nature, were not so active – in the *rnam shes* – as those that determined the 'choice' or, according to certain opinions it may have happened that they sought complementary elements, or even, have yielded to attraction of contrast. They can later manifest themselves as extraordinary divergences of temperament, such differences as are sometimes observed between parents and children. This term 'later' may apply to a distant epoch.

According to the same doctrine, we carry, latent within us, the germs of many possibilities that remain unmanifested, but although for a time inactive, their influence is nevertheless felt by the *rnam shes* in quest of parents to provide it with a body. A *rnam shes* attracted by tendencies of courage, daring, existing in the person who will become his father, may in his new incarnation be governed by contradictory influences that put to sleep the similar tendencies that existed in itself; but these dispositions, though dormant, may remain alive and attract a *rnam shes* animated by analogous inclinations, if nothing impedes the manifestation of these inclinations. We shall, then, have a grandson resembling his grandfather and, perhaps, not at all his father.

It is interesting to examine these theories, but we must beware of thinking that they constitute the last word on the matter, among philosophers in Tibet. The final teaching sweeps away any idea of the duration of life from birth to death. This we find, however, expressed also in the *Visuddhi Magga*, a book much esteemed by the Theravadins, in the words: 'The existence of a being does not exceed the duration of a single thought. As soon as this thought causes to an end, the being also finishes.'

This applies to the change that has occurred in the 'group' that constitutes the being, who, at the end of the thought, is no longer the same being that existed before the thought arose, nor the same that existed during the actual time the thought was being thought. It seems that here it is not a question of 'members of a council' voicing their opinion, then becoming silent again, though remaining present, as in the allegory previously quoted. The author of the *Visuddhi Magga* appears to believe in the definitive exit of an element of the 'group.'

Certain contemplative Tibetans conceive this 'group,' see it, they say, as a kind of vortex. The elements composing it are continually escaping, drawn away by other attractions, while also other elements are continually incorporated in it, tearing themselves away from other vortexes. This conception I heard explained by means of an illustration.

Suppose, said the Lama, that from countless blazing fires, sparks and red-hot cinders leap up, some of them fall into neighbouring fires while others, more violently projected, cross the space and land in far distant blazes. The exchange of sparks is perpetual, no single fire exists that can pretend to burn with its own fire. No 'self' exists that is not made up of 'others.' The dissolution followed by rebirth of the elements forming the 'group' called 'person' takes place, not only after that which the ignorant call 'death,' but is occurring every instant. 'Birth' in its sense of a first beginning, and 'death' in its sense of a final ending, do not exist. That is what Nāgārjuna expressed when he declared: 'No birth, no death; no coming, no going.'

I understood that it was a question of a perpetual dance of atoms which nothing creates, nothing destroys and which, sometimes here, sometimes there, continually change their form and their partners, but I ventured a question: 'Sparks presuppose fuel that has fed the fire, what is this fuel?'

The reply was: 'The Buddha placed ignorance at the beginning of the chain of interdependent causes that produce the beings of our world. Nāgārjuna resumed these 12 in three causes, namely: ignorance, desire and act. Desire leads us to act to satisfy ourselves, to get hold of the desired object or to repulse that which we deem undesirable. The act produces a pleasant or a painful sensation and the sensation awakens the desire to act in order to re-experience this pleasant sensation or avoid the return of the painful sensation. And so the round of desire and action goes on dominated by ignorance which creates false conceptions regarding objects of desire and motives of action. The 'fuel' could be imagined as a first cause. This is one of the subjects that the Buddha wisely set aside and against which he warned his disciples when saying: "Do not ask if the samsara is eternal or if it has a beginning and will have an end." All theories regarding a first cause or an ultimate end that we can elaborate, are, perforce, based on our limited perceptions, and, consequently, cannot but be erroneous. Moreover, the round with its 'fires' are 'images seen in dreams' as the *Prajña Pāramita* asserts, what reason could we have to hunt for the origin and nature of a fuel that only exists in our imagination? In truth, the samsara is within us, and not outside of us.'

The most imperative advice that the *Prajña Pāramita* gives us is: 'Do not imagine anything.' What counts is the awakening, the liberation from the dream, then all vain questions and discussions cease. With this statement, we return to the fundamental theme of Tibetan Mahayanaist philosophy.

This text was originally published in *Buddhism in England*, March–April 1938.

Alexandra David-Néel and The Lama Yongden

CARMEN BLACKER

(1924–2009)

An eminent scholar of Japanese culture and an inspiring teacher, who encouraged closer understanding between Britain and Japan throughout her life.

Carmen Blacker was born in Kensington, London on 13 July 1924 to Maude Pilkington and Carlos Blacker, a decorated war hero in both world wars, who was a psychiatrist, eugenicist and promoter of family planning.

Carmen's interest in Japan was inspired during her childhood, to the extent that she bought a book on Japanese grammar. During the Second World War, she worked on Japanese problems at Bletchley Park, having been recruited at the School of Oriental and African Studies where she had continued her study of Japanese language and literature.

She was introduced to the illustrious scholar and translator Arthur Waley and kept in contact with him until his death in 1966. Carmen graduated from the School of Oriental and African Studies in 1947 with a degree in Japanese and from Somerville College, Oxford in 1949. After the Second World War, she helped to re-establish The Japan Society London, which had been shut during the war. For many years, she was an active member of its Council, she gave lectures to the Society and also to the Asiatic Society of Japan, of which she was a member for many years. She also contributed to The Buddhist Society Summer School, as well as to its journal.

In the early 1950s she studied at Keio University in Tokyo. She was a lecturer in Japanese at Cambridge University from 1958 until her retirement in 1991. Japanese studies would not have survived there without her efforts to attract and support students. In the 1980s, she averted the closure of the Japanese Department and helped to establish a Chair in Japanese Studies.

She visited Japan almost annually, was occasionally a visiting fellow at prestigious North American universities and taught folklore at Ueno Gakuen

University in Tokyo. Her contributions to the study of Japanese religion and folklore were significant and penetrating. *The Catalpa Bow: A Study in Shamanistic Practices in Japan* (1975) resulted from her many travels around Japan observing and participating in rituals and folk practices. Her last work, *The Straw Sandal*, published in 2008, was a translation of a fantastic story by the eighteenth-century Japanese writer Santō Kyōden.

Carmen Blacker was never formally a Buddhist, but much in the Japanese forms of Buddhism attracted her. She regularly attended Buddhist conferences in Britain, was a friend of Christmas Humphreys and Myokyo-ni and was a loyal supporter of The Buddhist Society. She frequently attended its Summer School when Sōkō Morinaga Roshi, who she considered a friend, was a speaker.

For her services to scholarship and to Anglo-Japanese relations she was awarded the Order of the Precious Crown by the Japanese government in 1988 and received the Minakata Kumagusu Prize in 1997. She was president of the Folklore Society from 1982 to 1984, was elected a fellow of the British Academy in 1989 and was awarded an OBE in 2004.

She experienced a great deal of opposition as a woman in academic life and contributed considerably to the attempts of scholars and practitioners of both sexes to understand and engage actively with the heart of Japanese and Chinese religious thought.

Carmen brought together a number of disciplines within the orbit of her interests including religion, folklore, language and culture, and thus hugely enriching Buddhist scholarship. She died on 13 July 2009.

Originally published in *The Middle Way*, vol. 84, no. 3, November 2009.

MIHOKO OKAMURA

(1934–2023)

Secretary and companion to DT Suzuki from 1953 to 1966, editor for The Eastern Buddhist *from 1969 to 1998, lecturer, editor, translator, Honorary Director of the DT Suzuki Museum, Kanazawa, Japan and councillor of the Japan Folk and Crafts Museum.*

Mihoko Okamura was born in Los Angeles, California in 1934.

Okamura was secretary to DT Suzuki from 1953 to 1966, following her family's release from Manzanar War Internment Camp in California close to Mount Whitney. She met DT Suzuki in New York while he was lecturing at Columbia University. During this time and in the period that followed she met major figures in Buddhism, including Christmas Humphreys, Ven. Myokyo-ni, John Cage, Alan Watts, Erich Fromm, Karl Jaspers Huston Smith, Carl Jung and other well-known philosophers, artists psychologists and academics.

After DT Suzuki's death, she was present during his final illness at his home in Kamakura in 1966. Following his death, she worked as an editor for *The Eastern Buddhist* founded by DT Suzuki and his wife Beatrice from 1969 to 1998 and as a lecturer at Ōtani University in Kyoto from 1992 until 2006.

Okamura was instrumental in the building of the DT Suzuki Museum in Kanazawa, Japan, a beautiful building designed by the architect Taniguchi Yoshio to reflect the spirit of Zen Buddhism and a fitting building to commemorate the life and work of DT Suzuki. It includes a contemplative space that is open on four sides, as well as the collected works of DT Suzuki in Japanese and English for visitors to read and reflect on.

Okamura was the translator for two of the potter Bernard Leach's books, *The Unknown Craftsman* (1972) and *Hamada, Potter* (1990) subject of various TV features including a recent documentary. Okamura resides in Kyoto, Japan with her husband.

The Early Memories of Daisetz Teitaro Suzuki

(1870–1966)

Carmen Blacker and Mihoko Okamura, 1964

Editorial foreword: We are greatly privileged to publish this article which its author, now 94, was good enough to enable Miss Mihoko Okamura and Dr Carmen Blacker to prepare from notes taken at repeated interviews for this special issue of The Middle Way. *The Buddhist world is so indebted to Dr Suzuki for the range and depth of his Buddhist scholarship that it is possible to forget that he writes at all times with the spiritual authority of his own experience. The early life of such a man must be of the greatest interest to the readers of his 20 works in English, but he has always answered requests to speak of it with that great humility which is literally his second name; he was named 'Daisetz' by his master Soen Roshi, and such is his outstanding quality today. For this occasion, however, he was persuaded to reveal a little of his early days, and his intensive search for truth. In thanking him for this unique contribution to our special issue, we humbly acknowledge the enormous debt which is owed to him by all in the West who have found inspiration in the way of Zen.*

My family had been physicians for several generations in the town of Kanazawa.[1] My father, grandfather and great-grandfather were all physicians and strangely enough they all died young. Of course, it was no very unusual thing in those days to die young, but in the case of a physician under the old feudal regime it was doubly unfortunate, since the stipend his family received from his feudal lord was cut down. So my family, although of samurai rank, was already poverty stricken by my father's time, and after his death when I was only six years old, we became even poorer owing to all the economic troubles which befell the samurai class after the abolition of the feudal system.

To lose one's father in those days was perhaps an even greater loss than it is now, for so much depended on him as head of the family – all the important steps in life such as education and finding a position in life afterwards. All this I lost, and by the time I was about 17 or 18 these misfortunes made me start thinking about my Karma. Why should I have these disadvantages at the very start of life?

My thoughts then started to turn to philosophy and religion, and as my family belonged to the Rinzai sect of Zen it was natural that I should look to Zen for some of the answers to my problems. I remember going to the Rinzai temple where my family was registered – it was the smallest Rinzai temple in Kanazawa – and asking the priest there about Zen. Like many Zen priests in country temples in those days he did not know very much. In fact he had never even read the *Hekiganroku*[2], so that my interview with him did not last very long.

I often used to discuss questions of philosophy and religion with the other students of my own age, and I remember that something which always puzzled me was, what makes it rain? Why was it necessary for rain to fall? When I look back now, I realise that there may have been in my mind something similar to the Christian teaching of the rain falling on both the just and the unjust. Incidentally, I had several contacts with Christian missionaries about this time. When I was about 15 there was a missionary from the orthodox church[3] in Kanazawa, and I remember him giving me a copy of the Japanese translation of Genesis in a Japanese style binding, and telling me to take it home and read it. I read it, but it seemed to make no sense at all. In the beginning there was God – but why should God create the world? That puzzled me very much.

The same year a friend of mine was converted to Protestant Christianity. He wanted me to become a Christian, too, and was urging me to be baptised, but I told him that I could not be baptised unless I was convinced of the truth of Christianity, and I was still puzzled by the question of why God should have created the world. I went to another missionary, a Protestant this time, and asked him this same question. He told me that everything must have a creator in order to come into existence, and hence the world must have a creator, too. Then who created God, I asked. God created himself, he replied. He is not a creature. This was not at all a satisfactory answer to me, and always this same question has remained a stumbling block to my becoming a Christian.

I remember, too, that this missionary always carried a big bunch of keys about with him, and this struck me as very strange. In those days no one in Japan ever locked anything, so when I saw him with so many keys I wondered why he needed to lock so many things.

About that time a new teacher came to my school. He taught mathematics, and taught it so well that I began to take an interest in the subject under his guidance. But he was also very interested in Zen, and had been a pupil of

Kosen Roshi,[4] one of the great Zen masters of that time. He did his best to make his students interested in Zen, too, and distributed printed copies of Hakuin Zenshi's work *Orategama*[5] among them.

I could not understand much of it, but somehow it interested me so much that in order to find out more about it I decided to visit a Zen master, Setsumon Roshi, who lived in a temple called Kokutaiji near Takaoka in the province of Etchu. I set off from home not really knowing how to get to the temple at all, except that it was somewhere near Takaoka. I remember travelling in an old horse-drawn omnibus, only big enough to hold five or six people, over the Kurikara pass through the mountains. Both the road and the carriage were terrible, and my head was always bumping against the ceiling. From Takaoka I suppose I must have walked the rest of the way to the temple.

I arrived without any introduction, but the monks were quite willing to take me in. They told me the Roshi[6] was away, but that I could do zazen in a room in the temple if I liked. They told me how to sit and how to breathe and then left me alone in a little room telling me to go on like that. After a day or two of this the Roshi came back and I was taken to see him. Of course at that time I really knew nothing of Zen and had no idea of the correct etiquette in *sanzen*. I was just told to come and see the Roshi, so I went, holding my copy of the *Orategama*.

Most of the *Orategama* is written in fairly easy language, but there are some difficult Zen terms in it which I could not understand, so I asked the Roshi the meaning of these words. He turned on me angrily and said, 'Why do you ask me a stupid question like that?' I was sent back to my room without any instruction and told simply to go on sitting cross-legged. I was left quite alone. No one told me anything. Even the monks who brought me my meals never spoke to me. It was the first time I had ever been away from home and soon I grew very lonely and homesick, and missed my mother very much. So after four or five days I left the temple and went back to my mother again. I remember nothing about my leave-taking with the Roshi, but I do remember how glad I was to be home again. A most ignoble retreat.

Then I started teaching English in a little village called Takojima on the Noto peninsula – that peninsula protruding into the Japan Sea. There was a Shin temple there with a learned priest who showed me a textbook of the Yuishiki school called Hyappo Mondo, *Questions and Answers about the Hundred Dharmas*. But it was so remote and abstruse that, though I was eager to learn, I could not understand it at all well.

Then I got another position, teaching in Mikawa, a town about five *ri* (15 miles) from our home in Kanazawa. Again I missed my mother very much and every weekend I used to walk all the way back to see her. It took about five hours and it meant my leaving the house at about 1 a.m. on Monday morning in order to be at the school on time. But I always stayed at home until the last minute as I wanted to see my mother as much as possible.

I might add, by the way, that the English I taught in those days was very strange – so strange that later when I first went to America nobody understood anything I said. We always translated everything absolutely literally, and I remember being very puzzled by the way one says in English 'A dog has four legs', 'A cat has a tail.' In Japanese the verb to have is not used in this way. If you said, 'I have two hands,' it would sound as though you were holding two extra hands in your own. Sometime afterwards I developed the idea that this stress in Western thought on possession means a stress on power, dualism, rivalry which is lacking in Eastern thought.

During the six months I spent in Mikawa my Zen study stopped. But then I moved to Kobe, where my brother was working as a lawyer, and soon afterwards he sent me to Tokyo to study, with an allowance of six yen a month. In those days a student's board and lodging for a month cost about three yen 50 sen. The university I chose to study at was Waseda, but one of the first things I did on arriving in Tokyo was to walk down to Kamakura to study Zen under Kosen Roshi, who was Abbot of Engakuji at that time. I remember that I walked all the way from Tokyo to Kamakura, leaving Tokyo in the evening and arriving in Kamakura early the next morning.[7]

The *shika* monk, the guest master, took me to have my first introduction to the Roshi with ten sen 'incense money' wrapped in paper and offered to him on a tray. The guest master impressed me very much. He looked just like the pictures of Daruma[8] I had seen, and had very much a Zen air. The Roshi was 76 years old when I first met him. He was a very big man, both in stature and personality, but owing to a recent stroke he had difficulty in walking. He asked me where I came from, and when I told him that I was born in Kanazawa he was pleased and encouraged me to go on with my Zen practice. This was probably because people from the Hokuriku district round Kanazawa were supposed to be particularly patient and steady.

The second time I met him, in a special interview, he gave me the koan[9] *Sekishu*, 'the sound of one hand'. I was not at all prepared to receive a koan at that time. In fact as regards Zen my mind was like a piece of blank paper.

Anything could be written on it. Each time I went to *sanzen*, he just put out his left hand towards me without speaking, which puzzled me very much. I remember trying to find reasonable answers to the koan of the sound of one hand, but all these Kosen Roshi naturally rejected, and after going to *sanzen* a few times I got into a kind of blind alley.

One interview with him impressed me particularly. He was having breakfast on a veranda overlooking a pond, sitting at a table on a rather rough little chair and eating rice gruel which he kept ladling out of an earthenware pot into his bowl. After I had made my three bows to him he told me to sit opposite him on another chair. I remember nothing that was said at that time, but every movement he made – the way he motioned me to sit on the chair, and the way he helped himself to the rice gruel from the pot – struck me with great force. Yes, that is exactly the way a Zen monk must behave, I thought. Everything about him had a directness and simplicity and sincerity and, of course, something more which cannot be specifically described.

The first time I attended his *teisho* lecture was also unforgettable. It was a solemn business, starting with the monks reciting the Heart Sutra and Muso Kokushi's last words[10] – 'I have three kinds of disciples' and so on – while the Roshi prostrated himself in front of the statue of the Buddha, and then got up on his chair facing the altar, as though he were addressing the Buddha himself rather than the audience. His attendant brought him the reading stand, and by the time the chanting was finished he was about ready to start his lecture.

It was on the 42nd chapter of the *Hekiganroku*, the one where Ho-koji visits Yakusan, and after the interview Yakusan tells ten monks to see him off down the mountain to the temple gate. On the way the following conversation takes place: 'Fine snow falling flake by flake. Each flake falls in its own proper place.'

This struck me as a strange subject for Zen monks to talk about, but the Roshi just read the passage without a word of explanation, reading as though he were entranced and absorbed by the words of the text. I was so impressed by this reading, even though I did not understand a word, that I can still see him sitting in his chair with the text in front of him reading, 'Fine snow falling flake by flake.'

All this happened in 1891, when he was 76 and I was 21.

I remember that year, too, attending the ceremony of Toji at the winter solstice, when the monks all pound rice to make rice cakes and have a general carousal which goes on all night. The first of these rice cakes was always offered to the Buddha, and the second to the Roshi. Kosen Roshi was very fond of rice cakes dipped in grated *daikon*[11] sauce, and in fact he would eat any amount of them. On that occasion he demanded a second helping, which his attendant monk refused to give him, saying that it was not good for him to eat so much. The Roshi replied, 'I shall be quite all right if I take some digestive medicine.'

On 16 January of the following year, 1892, the Roshi suddenly died, and as it happened I was present at his death. I was in the ante-room next door to his with his attendant monks, when suddenly we heard the sound of something heavy falling in the Roshi's room. The attendant monk rushed in and found him lying unconscious on the floor. Apparently just as he was coming out of the washroom he had a stroke, fell and hit his head on the chest of drawers. That large body falling on the floor made a big noise. A physician was immediately summoned, but when he arrived and felt the Roshi's pulse he said it was too late. The Roshi was already dead.

Kosen Roshi's successor as Abbot of Engakuji was Shaku Soen.[12] At the time when Kosen Roshi died he had just come back from a visit to Ceylon to study Theravada Buddhism and was already a rising personality. He was not only very brilliant intellectually, but had also received his *inka-shomei*, or certificate to become a Roshi, while he was still quite young – an unusual thing in those days when it took about 15 years to reach so advanced a stage. After receiving his *inka* he went to Keio university to study Western subjects, which was again an unusual thing for a Zen priest to do. Many people criticised him for this step, including Kosen Roshi, who told him that Western studies would be of no use to him at all. But Shaku Soen never took any notice of other people's criticisms, and just went quietly on in his own way. So altogether he was a remarkable person, with rather unconventional tendencies.

At Kosen Roshi's funeral he was the chief mourner and performed all the ceremonies, and in the spring of 1892 he was installed as the new Abbot and I started to go to *sanzen* with him.

He changed my koan to *Mu*, as I was not getting on very well with the sound of one hand, and he thought I might have my *kensho* quicker and earlier with *Mu*. He gave me no help at all with the koan, and after a few *sanzen* with him I had nothing to say.

There followed for me four years of struggle, a struggle mental, physical, moral and intellectual. I felt it must be ultimately quite simple to understand *Mu*, but how was I to take hold of this simple thing? It might be in a book, so I read all the books on Zen that I could lay my hands on. The temple where

I was living at the time, Butsunichi, had a shrine attached to it dedicated to Hojo Tokimune,[13] and in a room in that shrine all the books and documents belonging to the temple were kept. During the summer I spent nearly all my time in that room reading all the books I could find. My knowledge of Chinese was still limited, so many of the texts I could not understand, but I did my best to find out everything I could about *Mu* intellectually.

One of the books which interested me particularly was the *Zenkan Sakushin*, 'Whips to drive you through the Zen Barrier,' compiled by a Chinese master of the Ming dynasty called Shuko. It was a collection of writings on Zen discipline and of advice given by various masters on how to deal with the koan. One of the examples I found in this book I thought I must try to follow. It said, 'When you have enough faith, then you have enough doubt. And when you have enough doubt, then you have enough *satori*. All the knowledge and experience and wonderful phrases and feelings of pride which you accumulated before your study of Zen – all these things you must throw out. Pour all your mental force on to solving the koan. Sit up straight regardless of day and night, concentrating your mind on the koan. When you have been doing this for some time you will find yourself in timelessness and spacelessness like a dead man. When you reach that state something starts up within yourself and suddenly it is as though your skull were broken in pieces. The experience that you gain then has not come from outside, but from within yourself.'

Then in the way of moral effort I used to spend many nights in a cave at the back of the Shariden[14] building where the Buddha's tooth is enshrined. But there was always a weakness of willpower in me, so that often I failed to sit up all night in the cave, finding some excuse to leave, such as the mosquitoes.

I was busy during these four years with various writings, including translating Dr Carus's *Gospel of Buddha* into Japanese, but all the time the koan was worrying at the back of my mind. It was, without any doubt, my chief preoccupation and I remember sitting in a field leaning against a rice stack and thinking that if I could not understand *Mu* life had no meaning for me. Nishida Kitaro[15] wrote somewhere in his diary that I often talked about committing suicide at this period, though I have no recollection of doing so myself. After finding that I had nothing more to say about *Mu* I stopped going to *sanzen* with Shaku Soen, except for the *sosan* or compulsory *sanzen* during a sesshin.[16] And then all that usually happened was that the Roshi hit me.

It often happens that some kind of crisis is necessary in one's life to make one put forth all one's strength in solving the koan. This is well illustrated by a story in the book *Keikyoku Soden*, 'Stories of Brambles and Thistles', compiled by one of Hakuin Zenshi's disciples, telling of various prickly experiences in practising Zen.

A monk came from Okinawa to study Zen under Suio, one of Hakuin's great disciples and a rough and strong-minded fellow. It was he who taught Hakuin how to paint. The monk stayed with Suio for three years working on the koan of the sound of one hand. Eventually, when the time for him to go back to Okinawa was fast approaching and he had still not solved his koan, he got very distressed and came to Suio in tears. The Master consoled him saying, 'Don't worry. Postpone your departure for another week and go on sitting with all your might.' Seven days passed, but still the koan remained unsolved. Again the monk came to Suio, who counselled him to postpone his departure for yet another week. When that week was up and he still had not solved the koan, the Master said, 'There are many ancient examples of people who have attained *satori* after three weeks, so try a third week.' But the third week passed and still the koan was not solved, so the Master said, 'Now try five more days.' But the five days passed, and the monk was no nearer solving the koan, so finally the Master said, 'This time try three more days and if after three days you have still not solved the koan, then you must die.'

Then, for the first time, the monk decided to devote the whole of whatever life was left to him to solving the koan. And after three days he solved it. The moral of this story is that one must decide to throw absolutely everything one has into the effort. 'Man's extremity is God's opportunity.' It often happens that just as one reaches the depths of despair and decides to take one's life then and there that *satori* comes. I imagine that with many people *satori* may have come when it was just too late. They were already on their way to death.

Ordinarily there are so many choices one can make, or excuses one can make to oneself. To solve a koan one must try standing at an extremity, with no possibility of choice confronting one. There is just one thing which one must do.

This crisis or extremity came for me when it was finally settled that I should go to America to help Dr Carus with his translation of the *Tao Te Ching*. I realized that the rohatsu-sesshin[17] that winter[18] might be my last chance to go to sesshin and that if I did not solve my koan then I might never be able to do so. I must have put all my spiritual strength into that sesshin.

Up till then I had always been conscious that *Mu* was in my mind. But so long as I was conscious of *Mu* it meant that I was somehow separate from *Mu*, and that is not a true *samadhi*. But towards the end of that sesshin, about the fifth day, I ceased to be conscious of *Mu*, I was one with *Mu*, identified with *Mu*, so that there was no longer the separateness implied by being conscious of *Mu*. This is the real state of *samadhi*.

But this *samadhi* alone is not enough. You must come out of that state, be awakened from it, and that awakening is Prajña. That moment of coming out of the *samadhi* and seeing it for what it is – that is *satori*. When I came out of that state of *samadhi* during that sesshin I said, 'I see. This is it.'

I have no idea how long I was in that state of *samadhi*, but I was awakened from it by the sound of the bell. I went to *sanzen* with the Roshi, and he asked me some of the sassho or test questions about *Mu*.

I answered all of them except one, which I hesitated over, and at once he sent me out. But the next morning early I went to *sanzen* again, and this time I could answer it. I remember that night as I walked back from the monastery to my quarters in the Kigenin temple, seeing the trees in the moonlight. They looked transparent and I was transparent too.

I would like to stress the importance of becoming conscious of what it is that one has experienced. After kensho[19] I was still not fully conscious of my experience. I was still in a kind of dream. This greater depth of realisation came later while I was in America, when suddenly the Zen phrase *hiji soto ni magarazu* – 'the elbow does not bend outwards' – became clear to me. 'The elbow does not bend outwards,' might seem to express a kind of necessity, but suddenly I saw that this restriction was really freedom, the true freedom, and I felt that the whole question of free will had been solved for me.

After that I did not find passing koans at all difficult. Of course other koans are needed to clarify kensho, the first experience, but it is the first experience which is the most important. The others simply serve to make it more complete and to enable one to understand it more deeply and clearly.

Originally published in *The Middle Way*, vol. 9, November 1964. Republished in *The Middle Way*, vol. 1, August 2016.

Notes

1. Kanazawa is the capital of the Ishikawa Prefecture in the middle of the West coast. For 300 years it was under the jurisdiction of the feudal clan of Maeda, and Dr Suzuki's ancestors were physicians to the Lord Maeda's court.

2. *Hekiganroku*, usually translated 'The Blue Cliff Records'. One of the most important textbooks of Zen. See *The Blue Cliff Records*, trans. Dr RDM Shaw. Michael Joseph, 1961.

3. The Greek Orthodox Church.

4. Imagita Kosen Roshi was the predecessor of Soen Shaku Roshi at Engakuji, Kamakura, where he is buried. Dr Suzuki has written a biography in Japanese.

5. *Orategama*, 'My little iron kettle', is a collection of letters written by Hakuin Zenji (1685–1769) to his disciples. *See The Embossed Tea-kettle*, trans. Dr RDM Shaw, Allen and Unwin, 1963.

6. The Roshi is the master of the Zen monastery who takes pupils in *sanzen*, personal interviews and supervises their zazen meditation.

7. From Tokyo to Kamakura is thirty miles.

8. Daruma is the Japanese name for Bodhidharma (Sk.) or Tamo (Chin.), the first Patriarch of Ch'an or Zen Buddhism who arrived in China from India in 520 CE.

9. A koan is a word or phrase which cannot be 'solved' by the intellect. It is given by a Roshi to his pupil to help him gain insight into reality, which lies beyond the reach of dualistic thought.

10. Muso Kokushi's Last Words may be found, see Suzuki, *Manual of Zen Buddhism*, at page 182 of the First Edition.

11. A *daikon* is a very long and large white radish. A popular vegetable in Japan.

12. Shaku Soen is known to the West by the name of Soyen Shaku as the author of *Sermons of a Buddhist Abbot*, Chicago, 1906. He was the favourite disciple of Imagita Kosen (See Note 4) and was only 25 when he received his master's 'seal' (*inka*). In 1893 he attended the World's Parliament of Religions in Chicago. He later travelled in Europe.

13. Hojo Tokimune was the Regent who in 1282 founded Engakuji, the Zen monastery north of Kamakura where Dr Suzuki lived for many years in the sub-temple building, Shoden-an.

14. The Shariden building in Engakuji (see Note 13) is the only surviving example of Sung dynasty temple architecture. It is quite small and severely plain. Although damaged in the great earthquake of 1923, it was later restored.

15. Nishida Kitaro (1870–1945). The great modern Japanese philosopher and an intimate friend of Dr Suzuki's since early youth. See *A Study of Good*, trans. by VG Viglielmo, Tokyo: Japanese National Commission for UNESCO, 1960.

16. Sesshin. A period of intense meditation lasting one week.

17. Rohatsu sesshin. *Ro* refers to the month of December, and *hatsu* or *hachi* means the eighth. 8 December is traditionally regarded as the date of Buddha's enlightenment. Everyone makes

a special effort at this sesshin, which begins on 1 December and ends early at dawn on the 8th, to become enlightened. Usually they go without sleep the whole time long in their earnest endeavour.

18. This would be the Rohatsu-sesshin of 1896.

19. *Kensho*. 'Seeing into the Self-nature' can be described as the first glimpse of *satori* or enlightenment.

D.T Suzuki and Mihoko Okamura

BEATRICE ERSKINE LANE SUZUKI
(1875–1939)

Scholar, editor, theosophist, co-founder of The Eastern Buddhist, *wife of DT Suzuki and graduate of Radcliffe College, Boston.*

Although it is often said that 'under a great tree nothing grows', this is certainly not the case with Beatrice Lane Suzuki, who, despite being married to DT Suzuki, the world-famous Zen scholar and celebrity, made a significant contribution in her own way to the 'Zen Boom' in the west. Nowadays however, her name is almost forgotten and her contribution unacknowledged.

The American academic, James Dobbins, has recently published material that has thrown considerable light on Beatrice's mother, whose official origins were said to be the Scottish aristocracy, and the following owes much to his original research, which rewrites the history of these two remarkable woman, mother and daughter. Their biographies need to be considered together, as Beatrice's life and her interests were almost inseparable from those of her mother, whose humble origins would not have predicted a place for her daughter in the history of the transmission of Buddhism to the west, nor would her mother, Emma, have imagined the role that she too was to play.

She was born Beatrice Elizabeth Greene Lane in Newark, New Jersey in the United States. Her mother, Emma Augusta Slocum, was born in 1846 in Providence Rhode Island. Beatrice's grandfather, William H Slocum, who was born in California in 1820, was a jeweller and a shoemaker, before becoming a farmer.

Emma married Thomas J Lane (1839–1906) a shoemaker from nearby Lynn, Massachusetts in 1867 in an Episcopal ceremony after meeting him in the early 1860s. Emma became a leader within the labour movement and became very active in progressive politics, during which time she was mentored by

William Batchelder Greene (1819–78), who was founder of the Labour Reform League as well as a Unitarian minister, philosopher, transcendentalist, promoter of free banking, a soldier and Beatrice's biological father. Emma's daughter Beatrice was born in 1875 and Emma separated from Thomas Lane in around 1879. Emma then married a German American immigrant, a doctor named Johann Albert Hahn (1852–1920) in July 1885. They had met while Emma was enrolled in Boston's College for Physicians and Surgeons as a medical student. They separated in 1901 and divorced in 1905 on the grounds of desertion.

Beatrice was sent for a year to Germany to study and worked and trained for three years while staying with Hahn's relatives in Newark, New Jersey. After attending Cambridge Latin School in Massachusetts from 1893, Beatrice entered Radcliffe College, a prestigious women's liberal arts college in Boston affiliated with Harvard University, where she remained from 1894 to 1898. In 1898, Emma took a sudden interest in Theosophy, as described in a letter from Hahn to Beatrice. All her education was financed by her stepfather Johann Albert Hahn. At Radcliffe she studied with the great William James, the brother of the novelist Henry James, and one of the most original thinkers of his time, who delivered the Gifford Lectures 1901–02, in which he suggested that the purpose of religion is the 'maintenance and sustaining of human happiness' – the very same goal of Buddhist practice. These lectures were later published as *The Varieties of Religious Experience*. Other influences included the philosopher and historian Josiah Royce and George Herbert Palmer, translator of *The Odyssey*. No doubt, it was through her teacher William James, who had been a Theosophist since 1882, that Beatrice also became a Theosophist, as did her mother Emma the following year in 1893. During her student days she was able to drop Hahn as a surname and emerged from college without it. It was through mother and daughter's shared interest in Theosophy and other religions that Beatrice met her future husband, DT Suzuki, when Shaku Sōen, a Zen Buddhist monk and teacher, gave a talk with DT Suzuki acting as interpreter to the Vedanta Society, on the occasion of the Buddha's birthday on the 8th April, in New York in 1906.

DT Suzuki subsequently visited and stayed with Beatrice and Emma on their farm in Stamford, Connecticut, on two occasions in July and subsequently in August following a talk that he gave at the Green Acre conferences in Eliot, Maine, in 1907, before Beatrice and DT Suzuki undertook a long-distance courtship. They married in 1911 in Yokohama, Japan and Beatrice became a Japanese citizen.

Beatrice and DT Suzuki, and her mother Emma, who later joined them, became members of The Theosophical Lodge in Tokyo and Beatrice and DT Suzuki later founded The Eastern Buddhist Society in 1921. They settled down and Beatrice adopted a son, Alan Masaru Suzuki (1916–71) and joined the Japan Humane Society, an animal rescue centre.

They all lived together for a number of years and there are references of their lives together by those who visited. Eventually her mother had to move out. Not long after, in 1927, her mother died, thus ending what must have been an intense lifelong symbiotic relationship and leaving Beatrice quite isolated. Beatrice published *In memoriam: Emma Erskine Lane Hahn (1846–1927)* in the same year.

Beatrice was instrumental in translating her husband's writing, as not only did she have a deep knowledge and practice of Buddhism but was also able to edit his work to make it accessible to Western audiences; William James, whose main interest was the religious mind of man, had, after all, been her teacher. Soon after meeting each other, it had become immediately apparent that Beatrice's editing skills would be of great assistance to both Shaku Sōen and DT Suzuki.

Beatrice's main interest was Shingon Buddhism and she contributed many articles on the subject to *The Eastern Buddhist* journal that she founded with her husband. The first issue appeared in May 1921 and included an article by Beatrice entitled, *What is Mahayana Buddhism?*

In 1963, DT Suzuki was nominated for a Nobel Peace Prize and became a driving force in bringing Mahayana Buddhism and particularly Zen, to the West, an undertaking that would have been impossible without Beatrice's education and superior grasp of idiomatic English. Her editorial skills were also considerable, and, excellent though DT Suzuki's command of the English language was, it is doubtful that without Beatrice at his side this would have been possible.

She was much overshadowed by her husband and time has yet to recognise and acknowledge the place in the transmission of Buddhism to the West that she deserves. Her involvement with Buddhism was likely an aspect of her 'religious liberalism' and an expression of her espousal of the 'progressive social values' of her American upbringing and without a doubt of her mother's strong influence, and her education under such world-leading figures as William James. A biography of her life, which has not been translated into English, was written in Japanese by Kachiko Yokogawa after her death. Her letters are a testimony to her as a loyal and loving wife, who often struggled to keep cheerful in a one-sided relationship, living in a foreign land and spending long periods alone while her husband travelled and enjoyed the limelight.

Her book *Mahayana Buddhism*, published by The Buddhist Society in London with a foreword by Christmas Humphreys in 1938, the year of her death, contributed to the study, understanding and transmission of Mahayana to the West. The publication *Buddhist Temples of Kyoto and Kamakura*, selected from her contributions to *The Eastern Buddhist*, was published posthumously in 2013.

Her health failed and she died 27 years before her husband. She is buried in the graveyard behind Tokei-ji temple, founded in 1285, within the Engaku-ji jurisdiction, an ancient refuge for battered wives, which is sometimes known as the 'divorce temple', or 'running and jumping temple'. Kitarō Nishida, DT Suzuki and Reginald Horace Blyth are also buried there, but Beatrice's grave is often forgotten by those visiting.

Beatrice Lane Suzuki with D.T Suzuki and their son.

Zen at Engakuji

Beatrice Lane Suzuki, 1936

Kamakura, the ancient capital of the Hojo Shoguns, seven centuries ago, is 14 miles from Yokohama. Now it is a peaceful town devoted to fishing and harbouring visitors and city dwellers, noted as a summer and winter resort. There are a number of temples, the most important of them belonging to the Zen sect, and of these Engakuji and Kenchoji are still, as in historic days, seats of Zen learning and practice. Each maintains a *sodo*, that is, a home for monks to work and study and meditate, presided over by a Zen master.

Engakuji, set in an ideal site – a valley filled with great cryptomeria trees – was founded in 1282 by Shogun Hyojo Tokimune, and its first Abbot and Teacher was the famous priest Bukko Zenji. From that time to this Engakuji has been renowned for its *sodo* and *zendo*, and a series of remarkable masters, one of the recent ones being the well-known priest Shaku Soyen, who attended the Parliament of Religions in America in 1893 and who visited and lectured in America and England a few years later.

Engakuji, so beautifully situated before the earthquake of 1923, had many fine buildings, almost all of which except the great gate were demolished, and although some have been rebuilt, Engakuji is not yet its former self. The Shariden, erected to hold a relic of the Buddha, is a fine example of the Chinese architecture of the Sung Dynasty. It is a national treasure and after the earthquake it was restored by the government.

I have said that Engakuji possesses a *sodo* and a *zendo*. Readers of Dr Suzuki's books on Zen will know what is meant by this. A *sodo* is a home for monks where they live a community life spending their time in work and study and meditating and sleeping in the *zendo*. The *zendo* at Engakuji is about 35 by 65 feet, and 30 or 40 monks can be accommodated although generally there are about 24, 12 on each side. The space for each monk is 3 x 6 feet, and here he sits while meditating, and also sleeps.

The monks are presided over by a head monk. They take turns in giving service, sometimes as cook, sometimes as attendants on the master, again keeping accounts or receiving visitors. The Roshi, their master at Engakuji, lives in a separate little house very near the *sodo*. It is he who directs their meditation and their Zen life generally.

Some years ago I had the privilege of living within the temple of Engakuji, sitting for meditation in the *zendo* under the direction of the Master, who, at that time, was the Rev Tenshin Hirota, although I had already received some instruction in Zen from the Rev Soyen Shaku when he was in America. The Rev Tenshin permitted me to sit in the *zendo* with the monks and to attend the *sanzen* interviews. I was given a koan, that is a problem upon which to settle my consciousness.

I was able to take part in a number of the *sesshin* periods, including the December one, when each student makes strenuous efforts to master his koan. I had a special mat assigned to me and clad in a black robe in order to look less conspicuous as a woman and Westerner, I took part in every detail of the monkish discipline during the Sesshin periods, and I came to know the Engakuji *zendo* in all seasons and aspects. Eventually I was given my Zen name of Seiren, and counted as one of the Roshi's disciples. Even now the memory of those days is happy and comforting. This leads me to speak of Zen methods of meditation.

In regard to posture, any posture will do which keeps the spine straight. Sitting, standing, lying down, walking are all possible. I know one man who did almost all his meditation while pacing up and down and received his *satori* while walking thus. In fact, the koan is to be with one no matter what the position or occupation. But in the *zendo*, the monks sit with their legs crossed in front of them. Women, when meditating, sit with their legs behind, resting the body upon the feet in the usual Japanese sitting posture. Western people are told that they may use a chair.

In regard to breathing, teachers differ, some saying practically nothing about it while others lay considerable stress upon it. The idea seems to be to make the breaths as long and slow as possible; there are no short breaths. The breathing is to be slow and rhythmical and the force must be put into the exhaled breath when the abdomen is expanded and not contracted as in done in many methods of breathing.

The usual koans given to beginners are *Sekishu*, 'What is the sound of one hand?' and *Mu*, 'nothingness', although some teachers give others, but these two are perhaps the most popular. The koan is to be taken into consciousness and made one's own mentally, and in every other way, until it becomes such a part of oneself that it finally reveals its meaning. At the *sanzen* interviews, the impressions and views which the monk or pupil has are given to the master who will demolish one by one his ideas, thoughts and feelings upon the subject. The koan is a mystery until its meaning is revealed and is not to be discussed with others, only with the teacher and with him alone. Lectures are given every day during the special *sesshin* periods. A *sesshin* is a special meditation week in each month when more than the usual time is given up to strict meditation, and during which the other work of the monks is curtailed. Zen is unlike all other meditation methods. It cannot be compared with Hinayana or with mystic or New Thought contemplation. It is something quite separate and apart and its aim is enlightenment and enlightenment only.

We are attached to so many things in this life, but the time comes when we wish to be delivered and become masters of ourselves free from the three poisonous passions of anger, lust and folly. Then it is that we turn to Zazen. But without a proper teacher the way is difficult, almost impossible. 'A little learning is a dangerous thing.' So it is with Zen.

To take part in a *sesshin* at a *sodo* is a great help for a beginner and the interviews with the teacher are necessary. Without them, the Zen practiser is quite at sea, like trying to steer a boat without oars. For Zen, as I said before, is quite unlike any other method of meditation or contemplation and it is therefore very easy to go astray or to remain stationary. The teacher's suggestions are needed as pointers to the road. To experience Zen, it is necessary for a man to enter another world which is a world of neither space nor time. In that world he acquires a new point of view which illuminates for him all existing worlds.

Many persons have asked for exact and definite instruction as to Zen meditation. But all that can be said is that the koan is to be always with one and made the centre of one's consciousness. This is the whole system of Zen. It is not to be reasoned upon, and yet unconscious conditions should not be allowed to supervene. The ideal is to understand the mind as it is, that is Reality. The quiet sitting, the slow and rhythmical breathing and the centring of the mind and entire personality upon the koan will bring about a state of consciousness which is entirely different from the ordinary one, and it will be found to be filled with vital energy and peace. The Zen practiser should not be disappointed if he finds the koan difficult or even impossible to solve, for from his effort to do so he will have gained a power and serenity which nothing can take away. Different persons get different experiences from their Zazen practice and inevitably some will get much more than others.

To put the Zazen practice into a nutshell is to keep the koan continually before the mental vision, without strain, but persistently and with the full force of the will. This constitutes Zen discipline.

Originally published in *Buddhism in England*, July–August 1936. Republished in *The Middle Way*, vol. 4, no. 94, 2019.

Beatrice Erskine Lane Suzuki, 1915

Characteristics of Mahayana

Beatrice Lane Suzuki, 1938

I. CAUSATION, KARMA, NON-EGO

Mahayana, like Hinayana and Primitive Buddhism, accepts the three fundamental principles:

1. All is transitory
2. All is suffering
3. All is egoless.

And based upon these, the so-called Four Noble Truths:

1. All existence is suffering
2. Suffering is caused by desire
3. The extinction of desire leads to extinction of suffering
4. The way to the extinction of suffering is the Eightfold Noble Path, the steps of which are Right Views, Right Aspiration, Right Speech, Right Behaviour, Right Livelihood, Right Effort, Right Mindfulness and Right Concentration.

Suffering results from rebirth, which is due to Karma working according to the law of cause and effect. Karma controls the universe as well as individuals, and is due to ignorance (*avidya*), which involves a series of rebirths. The doctrine of ignorance is expressed in the following formula of the Twelve *Nidanas* or Causal Chain.

1. In the beginning there is Ignorance (*avidya*);
2. from Ignorance comes Action (*sanskara*);
3. from Action comes Consciousness (*vijnana*);
4. from Consciousness, Name-and-Form (*namarupa*);
5. from Name-and-Form, the Six Organs (*sadayatana*);
6. from the Six Organs, Touch (*sparca*);
7. from Touch, Sensation (*vedana*);
8. from Sensation, Desire (*trsna*);
9. from Desire, Clinging (*upadana*);

10. from Clinging, Being (*bhava*);
11. from Being, Birth (*jati*); and
12. from Birth comes Pain (*dukkha*).

Vasubandhu explains it thus. According to his *Abhidharmakosa*, the formula runs: 'Being ignorant in our previous life as to the significance of our existence, we let loose our desires and act wantonly. Owing to this karma, we are destined in the present life to be endowed with consciousness (*vijnana*), name-and-form (*namarupa*), the six organs of sense (*sadayatm*) and sensation (*vedana*). By the exercise of these faculties we now desire for, hanker after, cling to these illusive existences which have no ultimate reality whatever. In consequence of this 'Will to Live' we potentially accumulate or make up the karma that will lead us to further metempsychosis of birth and death.'

From the problem of ignorance we come to consider non-atman or non-ego. This doctrine of non-ego is difficult to understand, and different interpretations of it are given by different Buddhist writers. It simply means that beings and things have no ego entirely of their own. To have any true individuality they must be united in the Dharmakaya. This will take place through enlightenment, when the true meaning of non-ego will be revealed. It means the elimination of selfishness, for there is only one true self, the Dharmakaya, and there can be no sense of separateness from it. But what the True Self is can only be found out through the experience of enlightenment. Anything predicated of it is only theory and a maze of words, and while many books have been engaged in discussing it the wise Mahayanist leaves it to intuition to disclose it.[1]

II. THE BUDDHIST DOCTRINE OF KNOWLEDGE

There are, according to Mahayana thinkers, different forms of knowledge. According to the Yogacara School of Asanga and Vasubandhu there are three forms: Illusive (*parikalpita*), Relative (*paratantra*), and Perfect or Absolute (*parinishpanna*). According to the Madhyamika School of Nagarajuna, there are two: Conditional or Relative Truth (*Samvritti-satya*) and Transcendental or Absolute Truth (*Paramarthasatya*). It is the object of all Buddhist teaching to lead beings to Absolute Knowledge (*prajna*).

We shall consider first the three forms. Buddhism lays much stress upon illusion, and teaches that many of the troubles of life are due to their illusory aspect, because the idea of egoism belongs to this form and promotes all ignorant beliefs and practices, religious and otherwise. A favourite example given by the Mahayanists is the analogy of a rope and a snake. We are deceived by the similarity between them and often take the rope for a snake. Without inquiring further as to the real existence of the snake, we frequently assume it to be real and act accordingly, thinking that everything is in reality what it seems to be.

The second form of knowledge is relative, sometimes spoken of as accommodated truth, which asserts that we cannot know absolute truth in our practical everyday life, and therefore that relative truth is sufficient for the field of human experience. It is conditional, empirical, pragmatic, and serves for ordinary life. Most philosophical and religious teachings belong to this category, religion being accommodated to our ability of mind. Buddhism believes that even 'if its own doctrines as are not the result of direct spiritual experience belong to this form of knowledge, the doctrines, scriptures and ceremonies of all religions, including its own being regarded as relative or accommodated. For this one of knowledge the Japanese use the word *hoben* ('expediency,' or 'device') which is the accommodated truth for the benefit of the unenlightened.

As relative knowledge is for the unenlightened, absolute knowledge is for the enlightened. It is a matter of experience, and efforts to explain it belong to the realm of relativity. It is the perfect or absolute knowledge or enlightenment which leads to ultimate salvation or Nirvana.

To continue the analogy of a rope and a snake: an unenlightened man walks over something long and thin in the moonlight and, taking it for a snake, is terribly frightened. This is illusion. For when he examines it more carefully, he finds it to be a piece of rope. Ordinarily we go no further, being satisfied with this relative knowledge. But the rope is made of straw, its existence is dependent on it, it is not an absolute entity, and there is no finality in it. Therefore, it is not real knowledge, and no enlightenment comes out of it. Unless we go beyond the realm of relativity and experience what lies behind the world of the rope, or that which makes the existence of the universe possible, no true salvation is possible.

This, however, does not mean that rope, as rope, has no use in our practical life. Relative knowledge has its value as long as our relative existence continues. The mistake only arises when we take relative knowledge for absolute knowledge. The point is to use the rope for tying up bundles, but not for crossing the stream of birth and death.

The Madhyamika School, instead of three forms of knowledge, proclaims two kinds of truth, Relative or Conditional Truth (*Samvritti-satya*) and Transcendental or Absolute Truth (*Paramarthasatya*). Here the terms 'truth' and 'knowledge' are interchangeably used, and Nagarjuna's relative truth includes the illusion and relative knowledge of the former school of thought.

Relative truth concerns the conditions of this phenomenal world, which have to be taken as real for practical purposes, but we must know absolute truth if we want to see things as they really are.

Nagarjuna asserts that those who do not know the distinction between the two truths do not understand the meaning of Buddhism. The Madhyamika calls the highest truth 'Void' (*sunya*), in that nothing connected with relativity can be predicated of it, but Void does not mean nothingness; it is only void or empty of all relative terms and descriptions. In other words, it is absolute, that is, all that can be said of it fails to give any correct idea of it. In fact it is no idea at all, as it is to be intuitively grasped and not logically represented. The intuitive understanding of Void constitutes Enlightenment.

III. TATHATA, NIRVANA

1. THE MAHAYANA DOCTRINE OF TATHATA (SUCHNESS)

Absolute knowledge constituting Enlightenment is the knowledge of the Absolute which is absolute truth. In Buddhist terminology it is the knowledge of Suchness (*Tathata* in Sanskrit and *Shinnyo* in Japanese). 'Suchness' may sound strange to the Western mind, but Buddhists think it most expressive. What is Suchness? It is to see things as they are in themselves, to understand them in their state of self-nature, to accept them as themselves. This seems easy, for when we see a flower before us we know it is a flower and not an inkstand or a lamp, but our knowledge is always coloured with all kinds of feelings, desires, and imaginations, and no such knowledge is pure and free from subjective 'defilements.' Mahayanists go even further and declare that this knowledge itself is the outcome of the self-asserting subjectivity of the knowing mind. To the Buddha's mind the flower is the inkstand and the inkstand is the lamp.

To see things as they are, i.e. in this state of suchness, means to go back to a state of mind before the division of the knowing and the known takes place. The dividing mind is the result of discrimination, and discrimination is going to the other end of suchness, which is grasped only when no discrimination takes place. The knowledge of suchness is therefore the knowledge of non discrimination. When we discriminate a world of dualities ensues, and this polarisation clouds the mirror of Prajna. Finally, the Dharma or Reality is lost sight of and the mind is 'defiled.' The Dharma is to see things as they are, in a state of *Yathabhutam*, which is another word for suchness.

The *Prajnaparamita* sutras are the earliest works of the Mahayana school in India, in which most of the major ideas of the school are expounded. In these sutras the Buddha is often referred to as the Tathagata (*tatha + agata* or *tatha + gata*), which means 'one who thus comes or goes.' Whether he is the one who is come or gone does not concern us here, for the question is about the term 'thus' or 'such' – *tatha*. What makes up the essence of the Tathagata is this suchness, for without it he is not such as he is, that is, he is no more Tathagata. But this suchness does not belong to him only; it is possessed by all his followers, in fact by all beings, and it is something that neither comes nor passes away; nor is it subject to destruction, nor to obstruction, nor to discrimination. As long as all beings hold it within themselves they partake in the suchness of the Tathagata, that is to say, they are neither born nor dead. In this the Tathagata and all beings are one and not two. When we talk about all beings being born we imagine that they follow the way of matter or mind, but the truth is that such things are born and pass away in the suchness of the Tathagata, while this suchness remains itself through the past, present and future. When, however, reference is made to the oneness of suchness in the Tathagata and all beings, we must not picture this suchness as existing by itself, as something separate from all beings, as enjoying its own existence as suchness, for 'Suchness to be regarded as suchness is no suchness,' says the author or compiler of the Prajnaparamita sutras.

From this one can see that by the suchness of the Tathagata is meant his Truth, his Reality, whereby he is what he is. When suchness means 'being so' it is Truth; when it suggests an idea of substance or self-nature it is Reality, and is sometimes found with *bhuta* prefixed. *Bhuta-tathata* may, however, be taken to mean being 'truly such.'

Our ordinary knowledge is never able to take hold of suchness, for its nature is to discriminate, to divide, to dwell on dualities, and suchness is just on the other side of it. The suchness of the Tathagata is the suchness of all beings, and these suchnesses are one and not two, says the *Prajnaparamita*, but at the same time suchness is no more suchness when it is so designated and regarded as something separate, existing by itself as the One, because in this case suchness is discriminated, and thereby becomes an object of ordinary knowledge. We cannot, therefore, form a picture of suchness in the way that we conjure up an image of an atom as something infinitely small, like a grain of the sand in the Ganges. Suchness is not in the world of the senses, nor is it an idea created by logical conventions. It is something unthinkable, unrepresentable, unnamable, indescribable. For this reason, when the *Prajnaparamita* begins to talk about it, it is full of contradictions and negations.

2. SUNYATA AND PRAJNA

Suchness thus seems to be the most appropriate term to point to the presence of something in our experience with the world whereby all ordinary knowledge finds its validity. The Mahayanists were not, however, fully satisfied with the term, for they wanted to incorporate it in the system of thought to be traced back to the mind of the Buddha himself. They therefore called it 'Void' (*sunyata*). *Sunyata* is thus *tathata* and *tathata* is *sunyata*. Void is suchness and suchness is void. The term void has been in use in Buddhism since the beginning of its history, but its meaning had not been defined beyond its being identified with nothingness or emptiness, in the sense of absence of contents. The Mahayanists made it mean the same thing as suchness.

It is the most daring declaration to state that all particular objects which we see about us, including ourselves, are void, of Void, from Void, with Void, and in Void. They stand in every possible prepositional relationship to Void. When Void is understood in the sense of emptiness and made to stand in contrast to fullness or substantiality the gravest fault is committed. Against this the Mahayanists had constantly to fight because our ordinary way of thinking is to divide, to polarise, to set one thing or idea against another. It is the most unfortunate event in our life of thought that we have inherited a stock of language with the meanings given to it by our ancestors, and that when we have a new idea which was never thought of by the latter we have 'to fill the old bottles with new wine.' It is for this reason extremely difficult to make Western readers realise what void means in its Buddhist sense, for they have never come across this way of seeing things in their history of thought. So let us repeat and state that Void is not to be confused with nothingness, contentlessness, mere negation of existence.

The Mahayanists assert that Void is not an object of intellection but of *Prajna*, that is, it is to be understood intuitively. There is no use arguing about it: the point is whether you have it or not. If you have it not, no amount of argument, no array of reasonings will convince you of it. Once *Prajna* is awakened, however, you will know instantly what Void is, and however logical and unassailable the philosopher's dialectical march may be, you will never be disowned of what you have taken hold. This is the meaning of the following phrases so frequently met with in the Mahayana Sutras: 'Do not think of exercising *Prajna*, nor think of not exercising *Prajna*, nor think of doing anything with *Prajna* in any possible way you can think about it; for then you will not be exercising *Prajna*.' The *Prajnaparamita* thus concludes that *Prajna* is the mother of all Buddhas and that *Prajna* is all-knowledge. This latter statement means that *Prajna* is the source of all knowledge, that knowledge ordinarily so called is born of *Prajna*, though *Prajna* itself is not the object of knowledge.

Here we notice two aspects of *Prajna*: *Prajna* in itself and *Prajna* in its relation to knowledge. In a similar manner, the Mahayana speaks of Suchness as having two aspects. It will be better to say that our intellect compels us to put this qualification on suchness or void. The first is unchangeable suchness or void in itself, and the second is conditionable suchness or no void. The following quotations from the *Awakening of Faith* traditionally ascribed to Asvaghosha will clarify the points so far made about the Mahayana conception of Suchness. Asvaghosha, from his psychological point of view, has Mind for what is designated here as unchangeable suchness, and speaks of the Mind as suchness and the mind as birth-and-death, which corresponds to conditionable suchness.

'The Mind as Suchness means that the world of multitudes in its general all-inclusive aspect is one, and that the Mind as such is the principle of order which keeps things regulated. The Mind is essentially not subject to birth and death. All objects infinitely diversified come to be distinguished only because of our wrong ways of thinking. When freed from them, the world in its multitudinousness disappears. All things, therefore (which appear so varied to our minds) are primarily beyond the realm of discursive understanding, nameability, or comprehensibility; they are intimately of sameness, suffer no transformation, and are not subject to destructibility. They are of the One Mind, and therefore to be designated as suchness ...'

Asvaghosha now goes on to describe more fully the nature of Suchness. 'As far as Suchness itself is concerned, it is the same in all beings, it knows no increase in the Buddha and Bodhisattvas, and no decrease in other beings; it was not born in the past, it will not pass away in the future; it remains constant and unchanged. From the first it contains in itself all virtues and there is nothing wanting in it. That is to say, it has in itself the great light of *Prajna* whereby the entire universe is illumined to its furthest end; it has the knowledge of Truth; it is the mind retaining its original purity; it is eternal, blissful, self-ruling, and free from defilement; it is cool and refreshing, unchanged and unfettered. It thus fulfils all the Buddha-virtues, surpassing in number the sands of the Ganga, and these virtues are not separable (from Suchness itself). They are with it, uninterrupted by it, they are united to it, they are beyond the ken of thought. Being thus self-containing, Suchness knows nothing wanting. It is therefore called the Tathagata-garbha, 'womb of Tathagatahood,' and the Tathagata's Dharmakaya.'

'A question may be asked, when Suchness is regarded as always retaining, when in itself, the nature of the sameness, free from all differentiating features, how is it possible to describe it as in possession of such a variety of virtues?'

'The answer is: while it truly contains all these virtues there is no differentiation in them, they are all of sameness, of one taste, of one Suchness. Why? Because of non-discrimination (which characterises Suchness), there is neither that which discriminates nor that which is discriminated. Therefore, Suchness is non-dualistic.'

'If non-dualistic, where does differentiation come in? It is due to our Karma-consciousness whereby things are presented to us in the aspect of birth and death.'

'How does this presentation take place? All things are primarily of the Mind only, in which there is no awakening of thoughts. But mentation somehow moves in the wrong direction, and there is the rising of thoughts whereby the world is perceived in all its multitudinousness. Thus ignorance is talked about. When the Mind remains in and with itself and has no rising (of thought) it is the great light of *Prajna*. When there is the rising of perception in the Mind some things are perceived while other things remain unperceived; but the Mind in itself stands outside perception and for this reason it universally illumines the world. When the Mind moves, its knowledge ceases to be true as it deviates from itself; it is then neither eternal, nor blissful, nor self-seeking, nor free from defilement; on the contrary it burns, it suffers pain, it becomes subject to decay and change, it is no more free; and then there will be all kinds of errors and defilements. Contrariwise, when the Mind moves not, there will be all kinds of pure virtues manifested. So when the Mind is stirred and perceives things before it as objects of thought, it will find in itself something lacking. Just because no thoughts are stirred in the

One Mind it is the repository of virtues innumerable, pure and meritorious, and because it is thus self-contained and wanting nothing, it is called the womb of Tathagatahood, that is, the Dharmakaya.'

From these quotations from Asvaghosha, who is representative of the Mahayanists of India and whose doctrine has been one of the greatest factors which have moulded the thought of Chinese and Japanese Buddhists, we can see in what relationship the idea of Suchness stands to the Mind, *Prajna*, Enlightenment, Void, Womb of Tathagatahood, and Dharmakaya, and further to ignorance, discrimination, the rising of thoughts, the recognition of an objective world, and defilements so called. The Mahayana does not deny the world objective and subjective, for it is Suchness as it is. It becomes the opportunity of defilements when it is discriminated in the direction of dualism and not in the direction of Suchness. Dualism is asserted as soon as a thought rises and its absolute validity is upheld, which is known as wrong attachment. Enlightenment takes place when dualism is recognised in the light of Suchness. This leads us to the consideration of Nirvana.

3. NIRVANA

Nirvana as Void has been one of the thoughts constantly subjected to misunderstanding by the Western critics of Buddhism. It is to be stated at the outset that Nirvana has been used in two senses and that when they are confused Nirvana loses its meaning in the philosophy of the Mahayana.

What are the two senses of Nirvana? The word originally meant 'extinction,' as when we speak of a fire which has burned all the fuel. As all the conditions that have made the existence of a fire possible have ceased, the fire itself is extinguished. This is a state of Nirvana. Likewise, when all the evil passions rising from egoism and consequently from dualism are subdued or uprooted, the mind regains its original purity and grace and becomes altogether free from worries and other annoyances. This is Nirvana. Here Nirvana stands against Samsara, birth and death, because it is due to the working of Samsara and our attachment to it that we become victims of mental disturbances and defiling influences. Samsara is dualism, as it is the thought of birth and death, and as long as we are attached to this thought and remain unaware of the truth that there are no such things as birth and death, and that we are really all of Suchness, eternally abiding in the self-sameness of the One Mind, we are never free and never at peace with ourselves as well as with the world. So we come quite frequently across such sentences as, 'Avoid the pain of birth and death and seek the bliss of Nirvana,' or 'Nirvana is realised only when the root of the evil passions is removed.'

When the Mahayana developed, a new interpretation of Nirvana was adopted. Nirvana was no longer something to be sought outside Samsara, that is, it did not stand against Samsara. When the idea of Suchness opened up a wider outlook for the Mahayanists, Samsara as well as Nirvana found their places in Suchness itself, and Nirvana was Samsara and Samsara, Nirvana. Thus we read in the *Awakening of Faith* that, 'Because of the Tathagata-garbha there is Samsara and again because of the Tathagata-garbha there is Nirvana'; again, 'The self-nature of the five Aggregates is unborn and therefore knows no death, because they are primarily Nirvana'; and again, 'The Bodhisattva once awakened to the Bodhicitta is altogether free from cowardice ... Even when he learns that Nirvana is obtainable only after a continued life of ascetic mortifications through innumerable eons he is not at all discouraged, for he knows that all things are from the very beginning Nirvana.' All these thoughts are in agreement with the doctrine of Suchness as expounded above.

Nirvana is thus Samsara, and no more a transcendental entity to be sought after death or to be reached after crossing the stream of Samsara, birth and death. We who are supposedly living a life of eternal becoming are Nirvana itself. All that we need do, therefore, is to find ourselves. This idea of Nirvana has revolutionised the whole trend of Mahayana thought. While the old usage has not yet died, we must accommodate ourselves to the new situation if we wish correctly to understand the Mahayana.

The sutras will be quoted to show the various interpretations given to Nirvana until in the Mahayana it came to be identified with the highest truth or reality, the Dharmakaya itself, and then with Suchness and Enlightenment.

In the *Agamas* (corresponding to the Pali Nikayas) Nirvana is said to be the state of a complete extinction in which there is no more greed, no more anger, no more folly, nor all the other evil desires and passions. This is the usual Hinayana understanding of the word. In the *MahavibhashaSastra* the etymological analysis of the term is given with its various religious implications. When the root *va* is taken to mean 'to blow,' 'to move,' 'to walk,' or 'to emit a scent,' Nirvana is the negation of all these qualities, that is, 'no more stirring of passions,' 'the disappearance of form,' 'being freed from the evil paths' and 'the cessation of the nauseating odour.' When *vana* means 'a forest,' Nirvana is 'getting out of the forest of the Aggregates.' When *vana* is considered to be a derivative of the root *ve*, which means 'to weave,' Nirvana is 'the no more weaving of the cloth of birth and death.' When an Arhat reaches the stage of No-learning he is freed from karmic laws, and no more weaves the conditions leading to Samsara. When *vana* means 'birth,' Nirvana is 'no-rebirth,' 'going to the other side of the stream.' When *vana* is derived from the root *vr*, meaning 'to cover' or 'to obstruct,' Nirvana is 'non-obstruction,' 'emancipation, 'freedom.'

In the Mahayana sutras, on the other hand, Nirvana acquires a positive significance; it is no more a negative state but something existing by itself; it is Reality, from which all Buddhas issue. In the Mahayana Nirvana Sutra (Fas. VI) we read: 'It is not quite right, it is inadequate to state that the Tathagata's entrance into Nirvana is like a fire going out when the fuel is exhausted. It is quite right to state that the Tathagata enters into the Dharma-nature itself.' Again, we have in Fas.IV of the same canon: 'When there is no more oil, the light goes out, but it means only the going out of the evil passions; as to the oil-container itself, it remains there. Likewise the Tathagata has all his evil passions extinguished but his Dharmakaya remains for ever.' The Lotus Gospel echoes the same idea when it states that the Tathagata's entrance into Nirvana is one of his 'skilful means,' for he stays here with us for ever to preach his gospel. In other Mahayana sutras Nirvana is identified with the Dharmakaya, or with the Dharmadhatu, where all Buddhas have their being, or with the Buddha's deepest meditation, or with *Prajnaparamita*.

The *Suvarnaprabjasa* (Chinese translation) gives many reasons why we have to speak of Nirvana, and the following are some of them:

1. All evil passions rise from greed, but Tathagatas are free from greed, and this is called Nirvana;
2. As they are free from greed, they are not attached to anything, and as they are not attached they neither come into being nor go out of being, and this is called Nirvana;
3. As they neither come into being nor go out of being, they are of the Dharmakaya which abides for ever, and this is called Nirvana;
4. What is thus above birth and death is beyond description, and this is called Nirvana;
5. There is neither subject-ego nor object world, and all that we

see about us is due to the constant changing of conditions, and what is not changeable is called Nirvana;

6. All evil passions are caused by errors and have nothing to do with the Dharma-nature, which is the master neither coming into being nor going out of being. This is known to the Buddha and called Nirvana;

7. Suchness alone is real and all the rest are not. By Suchness is meant Reality, which is the Tathagata and called Nirvana;

8. In Reality there is nothing of falsehood subject to argumentation,and this is understood by the Tathagata alone and called Nirvana;

9. What is unborn is real, what is born is unreal, and the ignorant are drowned in the ocean of birth and death, while the Tathagata is above it, which is called Nirvana;

10. What is unreal rises from conditionality, whereas Reality transcends it and the Tathagata's Dharmakaya is this Reality, which is called Nirvana.

What distinguishes the Hinayana conception of Nirvana from that of the Mahayana is the fact that the latter recognises the existence of a reality which stands by itself, pure and undefiled, perceived only by the transcendental intelligence of the Buddha. The Hinayana has no such metaphysically conceived Nirvana, as it is interested only in the extirpation of the evil passions rising from the individual ego-entity and has not made further inquiries into the philosophical possibility of such experiences. It has stopped short at the negation, whereas the Mahayana wanted to grasp something positive, whereby alone the Buddhist life becomes possible.

IV. TRIKAYA: THE THREE BODIES OF THE BUDDHA.

The heart of the Mahayana lies in the *Trikaya* (Three Bodies of the Buddha) and the Bodhisattva, along with the conception of *Prajna* ('wisdom') and *Karuna* ('compassion').

Soon after the Buddha passed away many of his followers began to think of him as more than a human being. To the Hinayanists the Buddha was a superior human being who attained the perfection of wisdom in this life through the power of his spiritual culture and the accumulated merit of his past lives. 'But the deep reverence which was felt by his disciples could not be satisfied with this prosaic humanness of their master and made him something more than a mortal soul. So even the Pali tradition gives him a supramundane life besides the earthly one.'[2]

The Mahasanghikas conceived of the Buddha as supramundane and transcendent, and their conception passed over to the Mahayanists who thought of the Buddha in three ways, viz.:

1. *Nirmanakaya* (*Nirmana*, 'transformation'; *kaya*, 'body'). As the human Sakyamuni who walked this earth and preached to his fellows and passed away at 80 years of age.
2. *Sambhogakaya* (*Sambho*, 'enjoyment'; *bhoga*, 'to partake'; *kaya*, 'body'). As the Buddha ideal who enjoyed a refulgent body and preached to the Bodhisattvas.
3. *Dharmakaya* (Dharma, 'law', 'substance'; *kaya*, 'body'). As the highest being, comprising all others, the essence of knowledge and compassion, the Absolute.

The Buddha is not three but One. The *Trikaya* are but aspects of the One Buddha. When viewed from the Absolute and Universal point of view, he is the transcendent Dharmakaya; when viewed from the point of view of Ideality, as the human made divine, as it were, he is the Sambhogakaya, preacher to the Bodhisattvas to help them in their work of saving sentient beings: when viewed from the human point of view he is the Nirmanakaya, the historical Sakyamuni who was born in Kapilavastu, obtained enlightenment under the Bodhi-tree, and passed away into Nirvana when his life's work was done.

It must be remembered that Sakyamuni was not the only manifestation of the Dharmakaya in the form of the Nirmanakaya Buddha, for there have been many manifestations of the Nirmanakaya, just as there are many ideals of the Sambhogakaya but only one Dharmakaya, the Absolute Buddha, of which the others are only aspects.

In the *Kayatraya*, Ananda relates the Buddha's discourse on the *Trikaya*. 'Has the Blessed One a body?' Buddha answered, 'The Tathagata has three bodies.' So we can see that the three bodies are three aspects of the one Buddha or Tathagata. They are one in essence, but distinct in their nature and activity.

Nirmanakaya

The Nirmanakaya is the Universal Buddha manifested in the world of sentient beings, adapting himself to earthly conditions, possessing an earthly body yet maintaining purity. He is the representative of the Absolute in the human world, bent on teaching sentient beings in order to relieve them from suffering, and through enlightenment to lead them to salvation. In this way the Buddha teaches and delivers all sentient beings through his religious teachings, whose number is innumerable as the atoms. His all-swaying compassion, intelligence and will cannot rest until all beings have been brought under his shelter through all possible means of salvation. Whatever his subjects for salvation and whatever his surroundings, he will accommodate himself to all possible conditions and achieve his work of enlightenment and salvation.

The Nirmanakaya is generally rendered as a Transformation Body, because this body as used in manifestation by Sakyamuni and other human Buddhas partakes of the characteristics and qualities of mortality, and is subject like that of other mortals to sickness, old age and death. The human Buddha expresses the perfect man, pure, wise and wielding power. He is possessed of all the marks of physical excellence, having strength combined with beauty, and his mind is a union of intelligence and compassion.

Gradually the conception of the Nirmanakaya grew larger and more ideal. The historical Buddha who lived among men but who seemed superhuman to his devoted followers in time assumed more and more the form of the ideal Buddha. As in Christianity we find the glorified Christ, so in Buddhism we find the idealised Buddha.

In Hinayana Buddhism the historical Buddha is revered as a man among men, yet we discern the tendency to idealise him. In Mahayana there is frankly a preference for the ideal Buddha, the Sambhogakaya who preaches to the Bodhisattva as the Nirmanakaya preaches to ignorant mankind. But although the Nirmanakaya Buddha bears a human body he is of the same nature as the Dharmakaya, indeed a manifestation of him, and in this respect divine or, as the Buddhist would prefer to say, of true Buddha nature. The real body of the Nirmanakaya is the Dharmakaya, and all Nirmanakayas are united in the Dharmakaya.

The *Awakening of Faith* says: 'The Nirmanakaya depends on the phenomena-particularising-consciousness, by means of which the activity is conceived by the minds of common people, *Sravakas* and *Pratyekabuddhas.* This aspect (of the Dharmakaya) is called the Body of Transformation (Nirmanakaya).'

Nirmanakaya Buddhas are to be found everywhere and at all times. The Nirmanakaya body is the vehicle for the activity of the Tathagata, and wherever and whenever he sees best to manifest himself as a Nirmanakaya Buddha he does so. This brings us to the conception of the two forms of the Nirmanakaya, the *Ojin* and the *Keshin*, full manifestations and partial ones. The *Ojin* is practically the active Tathagata, but the *Keshin* is an ordinary man who reveals an extraordinary amount of the indwelling Buddha spirit. For example, such men as Shotoku Taishi, the founder of Buddhism in Japan, Kobo Daishi, the Shingon saint[3], Honen Shonin and Shinran Shonin, founders of the Jodo and Shin sects respectively, would be considered as *Keshin*, while Sakyamuni would be regarded as *Ojin*.

The *Keshin* can manifest itself as a Bodhisattva, as a *deva*, an angel or a superior human being. When we find living in this world, at any time, pure-hearted persons who are working solely for the good of sentient beings (not only for human beings but for animal beings as well) there we find *Keshin* Nirmanakaya Buddhas. They are those who are trying to alleviate suffering or giving out high teaching, active workers as well as those who are striving to help by giving the example of exemplary lives, not for the sake of self-merit but with the whole-hearted desire to save others. All these are Nirmanakayas of the *Keshin* type. They are often found in humble positions and their work is sometimes unknown and unappreciated by their fellow men, they themselves perhaps being unaware of their high rank and their superior attainment. To be such a Bodhisattva should be the desire of every devoted Mahayanist.

Sambhogakaya

The Nirmanakaya is a manifestation for the benefit of more or less ignorant beings, such as *Sravakas*, *Pratyekabuddhas* and Bodhisattvas of lower ranks, but the Sambhogakaya is manifested for the benefit of all Bodhisattvas. It is the Sambhogakaya who is the preacher of most of the Mahayana sutras, except the Shingon, which claims to be teaching given directly by the Dharmakaya Buddha.

The Sambhogakaya is sometimes called the Body of Recompense because it enjoys the fruits of its spiritual labours, but later, it was called the Body of Bliss because it is enjoyed by all the Bodhisattvas. The Sambhogakaya is visible to the Bodhisattva. It is a symbol of transcendental perfection and personifies Wisdom. It is the Buddha ideal.

This Buddha Body is a refulgent body from which are emitted rays of light. It has two forms, the first for its self-enjoyment, the second for the teaching of the Bodhisattva. 'This last body is in possession of wonderful spiritual powers, reveals the Wheel of Dharma, resolves all religious doubts raised by the Bodhisattvas and lets them enjoy the bliss of the Mahayana Dharma.'[4]

The Sambhogakaya is an expression of the Dharmakaya and stands between the Dharmakaya and the Nirmanakaya. To many minds, the Dharmakaya is unthinkable, but the Sambhogakaya is thinkable. So to some, the Sambhogakaya takes the form of Amida in his Pure Land, to others, he is the Christian God, to others again, Isvara. He is, on the one hand, the Buddha idealised, on the other, the Dharmakaya personified. There are some who would compare the Sambhogakaya to the glorified Christ, but rather is it like the Christian God, in distinction to the Absolute Godhead. Amida in his Pure Land and God in his Heaven – both are the Sambhogakaya.

The Sambhogakaya is the Eternal Buddha, and many Mahayanists turn to him rather than to the historical Sakyamuni, who is his mouthpiece or shadow. They have been blamed for this, but they retort that they prefer the substance to the shadow, the reality to the image. The Sambhogakaya, they point out, was incarnated in the Nirmanakaya, and when our eyes are open to the glory of the Eternal Buddha we need not look at his human expression. In the days of our ignorance the teaching and example of the human Buddha are helpful to us, but when we see clearly with the eyes of a Bodhisattva, and 'not through a glass darkly,' we look to the refulgent Buddha, the Buddha of Light, of Truth, of Eternality.[5]

Dharmakaya

The general explanation is that the Dharmakaya (*Hosshin*) is the permanent, undifferentiated, comprehending Truth, but the detailed explanation differs according to the different schools of Buddhism. In the *Awakening of Faith*, we read that it is Primary Truth. The Prajnaparamitas take the Dharmakaya as produced by the dharma, the highest being; the Dharmakaya is *Prajna*, the highest knowledge. Eon in the *Daijogisho* says of the Dharmakaya that it is the beginningless body of Being itself. In the *Butsujikyo*, we read that Dharmakaya is the Tathagata's self-nature body, permanent and unchanging, the real nature of every Buddha and every being. The Madhyamika meant by the Dharmakaya the Void which may, however, mean Reality which cannot be expressed in words. The Yogacharas meant the Absolute.

Shingon regards the Dharmakaya as personal, manifesting compassion and activity and saving beings by preaching to them, not only as impersonal and transcendental. It is not formless but is real substance, true and permanent. The Dharmakaya is the sum total of the substance of the Universe. The Dharmakaya manifests itself in the universe in and through all its parts, and this manifestation works actively in law and in form. The Dharmakaya is the inner enlightened body of Buddha. To the ignorant it is formless, but to those who understand, the Dharmakaya has form and preaches the Law. According to general Buddhism the Dharmakaya is absolutely formless and tranquil, but Shingon stresses the supreme enlightenment which expresses itself actively in compassion and thus forms a true personality which the enlightened person can perceive and know.

Reality is probably the best way to describe the Dharmakaya in one word. It is that which must be realised by every being for himself. It is the goal of Bodhisattvas and others, although as a rule only a Bodhisattva can hope to realise it fully. Every being possesses it. It is the real nature of things, and from this aspect of it we can also call it *Tathata, Dharmadhatu, Tathagatagarbha*. Nirvana is its abode. 'Dharmakaya is literally a body or person that exists as principle, and it has now come to mean the highest reality from which all things derive their being and lawfulness, but which in itself transcends all limiting conditions. It is what inwardly and essentially constitutes Buddhahood.'[6]

In the *Lankavatara* the Dharmakaya signifies the Buddha-personality when it is perfectly identified with the Dharma or the absolute truth itself. In the *Awakening of Faith* the Dharmakaya is 'the eternal, the blessed, the self-regulating, the pure, the tranquil, the immutable and the free. Suchness is called the Tathagata's Womb (*tathagatagarbha*) or the Dharmakaya. The activity of the Dharmakaya has two aspects, the first depending on the phenomena-particularising-consciousness by means of which the activity is conceived by the minds of common people, *Sravakas* and *Pratyekabuddha*. The second depends on the activity-consciousness (*karmavijnana*) by means of which the activity is conceived by the minds of Bodhisattvas while passing from their first aspiration stage (*cittotpada*) up to the height of Bodhisattvahood. This is called the Body of Bliss (*sambhogakaya*).'

Some writers on Mahayana give to the Dharmakaya the idea of *Shinnyo*, Suchness, the principle of the cosmos, but writers like DT Suzuki make the Dharmakaya much more personal. He insists that to Suchness is added a living spirit with virtues. This is also the teaching of Shingon. 'The Dharmakaya is a soul, a willing and knowing being, one that is will and intelligence, thought and action. It is not an abstract metaphysical principle like Suchness, but it is a living spirit that manifests in nature as well as in thought. Buddhists ascribe to the Dharmakaya innumerable merits and virtues and an absolute perfect intelligence, and make it an inexhaustible fountainhead of love and compassion.[7]

The *Avatamsaka* Sutra makes a comprehensive statement concerning the nature of the Dharmakaya as follows:

'The Dharmakaya, though manifesting itself in the triple world, is free from impurities and desires. It unfolds itself here, there, and everywhere, responding to the call of karma. It is not an individual reality, it is not a false existence, but is universal and pure. It comes from nowhere, it goes to nowhere; it does not assert itself, nor is it subject to annihilation. It is forever serene and eternal. It is the One, devoid of all determinations. This Body of Dharma has no boundary, no quarters, but is embodied in all bodies. Its freedom or spontaneity is incomprehensible, its spiritual presence in things corporeal is incomprehensible. All forms of corporeality are involved therein; it is able to create all things. Assuming any concrete material body as required by the nature and condition of karma, it illuminates all creations. Though it is the treasure of intelligence it is void of particularity. There is no place in the universe where this Body does not prevail. The universe becomes, but this Body forever remains. It is free from all opposites and contraries, yet it is working in all things to lead them to Nirvana.'

'It benefits us by destroying evils, all good things thus being quickened to growth; it benefits us with its universal illumination which vanquishes the darkness of ignorance harboured in all beings; it benefits us through its great compassionate heart which saves and protects all beings; it benefits us through its great loving heart which delivers all beings from the misery of birth and death; it benefits us by the establishment of a good religion whereby we are strengthened in our moral activities; it benefits us by giving us a firm belief in the truth which cleanses all our spiritual impurities; it benefits us by helping us to understand the doctrine by virtue of which we are not led to disavow the law of causation; it benefits us with a divine vision which enables us to observe the metempsychosis of all beings; it benefits us with an intellectual light which unfolds the mind-flowers of all beings; it benefits us with an aspiration whereby we are enlivened to practise all that constitutes Buddhahood. Why? Because the Sun-Body of the Tathagata universally emits the rays of the Light of Intelligence.'[8]

From all this Suzuki claims that 'the Dharmakaya is the raison d'etre of all beings, transcends all modes of Upaya, is free from desires and struggles and stands outside the pale of our finite understanding.'

Suzuki also puts emphasis upon the intelligent mind and loving heart of the Dharmakaya. Here he approaches the Shingon interpretation.

'The Dharmakaya which is tantamount to Suchness or Knowledge of Suchness is absolute; but like the moon whose image is reflected in a drop of water as well as in the boundless expanse of the waves, the Dharmakaya assumes in itself all possible aspects from the grossest material form to the subtlest spiritual existence. When it responds to the needs of the Bodhisattva whose spiritual life is on a much higher plane than that of ordinary mortals, it takes on itself the Body of Bliss or Sambhogakaya. This Body is a supernatural existence, and almost all the Buddhas in the Mahayana scriptures belong to this class of being.'

'The Mahayanists now argue that the reason why Sakyamuni entered into Parinirvana when his worldly career was thought by him to be over is that by this resignation to the law of birth and death, he wished to exemplify in himself the impermanence of worldly life and the folly of clinging to it as final reality. As for his Dharmakaya, it has an eternal life; it was never born, and it will never perish, and when called by the spiritual needs of the Bodhisattvas, it will cast off the garb of absoluteness and preach, in the form of a Sambhogakaya, 'never-ceasing sermons which run like a stream for ever and aye.' It will be evident from this that Buddhists are ready to consider all religious or moral leaders of mankind, whatever their nationality, as the Body of Transformation of the Dharmakaya.'[9]

We have two conceptions or rather two ways of stressing the one conception:

1. Dharmakaya is Suchness (*Bhutatathata*) the Body of the Law, the Impersonal Absolute;
2. Womb of Tathagata (*Tathagata-garbha*), true knowledge and the source of every individual being, underlying all phenomena, endowed with Love, Compassion and Will, therefore personal.

The Dharmakaya corresponds to the Godhead in Christianity.

The Buddha impressed upon his followers that the true body of the Buddha is not his human but his spiritual body, i.e. the Dharmakaya is his true body. His immediate followers, however, understood this to mean a body of dharmas, but gradually they thought of the Dharmakaya as the essence of all dharmas, hence the essence of existence itself and of Absolute Wisdom. As beings cannot perceive the Dharmakaya except through spiritual experience, it takes the form of the Sambhogakaya for beings of the Bodhisattva type and of the Nirmanakaya for ordinary beings. The Dharmakaya is the representative of *Shinnyo* (Suchness), the impersonal and absolute unity of the Universe.

The Dharmakaya is also the spiritual body of all the Tathagatas.

All this may seem complicated, but in reality it is not. In philosophical Christianity, God is considered in his unknowable aspect as the Godhead, the source of all yet not realisable except through mystical experience. This is the Dharmakaya. That beings may come in contact with him he becomes God as usually known to all Christian believers; this corresponds to the *Sambhogakaya*. But ordinary people need something more tangible and require a living personality. This is the *Nirmanakaya* to Buddhists and Christ to Christians.

If looked at in this way, the mystery of the Three Bodies disappears. In Indian philosophy we find Dharmakaya as both Parabrahman and Brahman, according to the aspect of him considered. *Sambhogakaya* is the same as Isvara, and *Nirmanakaya* applies to the great spiritual leaders of India or may be considered as an Avatar. Instead of three bodies, it may make it clearer to speak of three aspects of the one Buddha: the Historical, the Eternal and the Universal, that is to say:

1. Sakyamuni, the historical Buddha,
2. the Eternal Buddha, as personified by Amida or Akshobhya, and whether considered as Isvara, God or any other Eternal Form,
3. the Dharmakaya as taught by Shingon, unknowable except through spiritual experience and difficult for any but the Bodhisattva to perceive. By meditation or worship on any one of these aspects – and what is worship but a form of meditation – beings may come to realise the Existence of the Infinite for themselves.

To explain the Trikaya in words is difficult, and meditation on the problem will reveal far more than the printed page. But to understand Mahayana Buddhism some understanding of the Triple Body conception is necessary. It underlies all Mahayana teachings and is preached or taken for granted in Mahayana sutras. Whether we read the *Pundarika* or the *Prajna*, the *Lanka* or the *Avatamsaka*, this doctrine pervades all the teachings of these great sutras.

Amida

Amida (Amitabha) the Buddha of Eternal Light and Infinite Life is the form of the Buddha worshipped in the Pure Land schools of Buddhism such as Jodo and Shin.

'When the heart of Sakyamuni, filled with love for all mankind, was about to preach the doctrine of great bliss for the salvation of all beings, his face shone beautifully, and his whole figure became as serene as an autumn cloud, and inspired Ananda to ask Buddha the question as above cited. The word came from Ananda's own lips, but the spirit of the Master was plainly visible in them. The heart of Sakyamuni, which reached the highest pinnacle of purification, naturally moved Ananda, who was his beloved disciple, and made his heart reflect like a looking glass what was going on in the Buddha's heart. Ananda understood the supreme state of 'mutual contemplation of the Tathagatas.' To get a good crop of grain, there must at first be a well-tilled field prepared for sowing seeds. So the appearance of a great spiritual move-ment in the world is to be preceded by well-cultivated minds that are ready to receive the doctrine of a Holy One; for then the latter will find it easy to penetrate thoroughly into their hearts. The time was ripe now, besides the monastic religion of self-enlightenment and penance, for the seed of a religion of salvation by faith to grow and bear fruit in the well-cultivated minds of the Mahayana Buddhists.'

Thus was opened the way to the doctrine of salvation by faith.

'The Saviour of the Shin-shu as the object of faith may be said to resemble to a certain extent the God of Christianity. But Amida's attitude towards sin is what distinguishes the Shin-shu from Christianity. The God of the latter is a God of love and justice, while the Buddha is mercy itself and nothing more. In the world the principle of karma prevails, and the Buddha never judges. The God of Judaism was represented by Christ to be the God of love, yet he is made to judge our sins and mete out punishments accordingly. Amida of the Shin-shu, however, knows only of infinite love for all beings, wishing to deliver them out of the eternal cycle of ignorance and suffering, in which they are found migrating. In Amida, therefore, there is no wrath, no hatred, no jealousy.'

'There is another aspect in the conception of Amida, besides the one we have already referred to; for he is to be interpreted also in the light of the fundamental principle of Buddhism. Amida, as the Tathagata, naturally appears as a person embodying in himself the Absolute Truth, which is also infinite mercy and infinite wisdom.'

'So Amida, our Saviour, is an absolute being transcending time and space, and manifesting himself in the Pure Land, the only purpose of which is to save all sinful beings. In short, out of the absolute Buddha or the Dharmakaya has the Buddha of salvation appeared, and naturally, the spirit of Amida is in deep and intimate communion with the Absolute itself. And on our side, as we are also sharers in the being of the Absolute Buddha, we and Amida must be said to be one in substance, only differing in functions.'

Thus we see that there are two aspects in the idea of Amida. First, Amida is the embodiment of the infinite mercy and wisdom which was obtained, according to the moral law of causation, by perfecting himself through discipline, by performing all that is required of man as a moral being, by accumulating all the merits needed for the salvation of all beings, so that when we believe in him we acquire all those virtues which will immediately be transferred to us and will perfect us. Secondly, Amida is conceived as a person embodying the absolute truth in its highest form, which we also realise in various degrees.

'Practically considered, Amida as our Saviour is infinite in love, wisdom, and power; he is the culmination of our religious yearnings. Those who believe in him are thus saved from ignorance and suffering, gain enlightenment, and find in him a guide of their daily life.'[10]

The general belief in regard to Amida is that he was once a monk who out of compassion for his fellow-beings made vows that he would devote all his own merits which he had gained by many lives of mercy to the saving of others. He established a Pure Land where he could receive those souls who believed in him and called upon his name. Amida is the Sambhogakaya – the Body of Bliss who is spoken of as the accommodated Law-Body for the object of Faith. Yet Amida and the Dharmakaya are really one being, two aspects of the one Buddha; the one, Dharmakaya, from the philosophical side, the other, Sambhogakaya, from the religious. Sakyamuni was the representative of the Dharmakaya for the purpose of preaching the Law and Amida saves sentient beings by means of their faith in him. In the Pure Land sects human life is looked upon as illusory, transitory and miserable through the action of karma, the law of cause and effect. The only way to be released is to call upon Amida in perfect faith and he will save us by calling us to his Pure Land, which is a field for enlightenment. Amida may therefore be conceived of in three ways: as the Dharmakaya absolute and unconditioned, as the Sambhogakaya, the idealised, glorified being who is the object of worship in the Pure Land sects, and as the Nirmanakaya, the historical Buddha Sakyamuni who came to preach the Law.

This text was originally published in *Buddhism in England*, vol. 13, no. 2, July–August 1938, and is an excerpt from *Mahayana Buddhism: A Brief Outline,* which *The Buddhist Society* published in its entirety in autumn 1938.

Notes
1. All these points of Buddhist teaching will not be here explained in detail, as this has been done in many books on Buddhism, with some of which the reader is doubtless already familiar. Moreover in Mahayana they are not so much talked about as simply taken for granted to clear the way for further conceptions, such as enlightenment and salvation.
2. DT Suzuki, *Outlines of Mahayana Buddhism*, p.270.
3. Except by his own followers, i.e. believers in Shingon, who consider Koba Daishi to be more than Keshin, no other than a manifestation on earth of Maitreya, the next Buddha to be.
4. DT Suzuki, *Outlines of Mahayana Buddhism*, p.266.
5. 'The Sambhogakaya manifesting itself everywhere is infinite, boundless, limitless, unintermittent in action and embraces infinite attributes of bliss and merit.' *Awakening of Faith*, by Asvaghosha, pp.101–102.
6. DT Suzuki, *Studies in the Lankavatara*, p.308.
7. DT Suzuki, *Outlines of Mahayana Buddhism*, pp.222–223.
8. DT Suzuki, *Outlines of Mahayana Buddhism*, pp.223–227.
9. DT Suzuki, *Outlines of Mahayana Buddhism*, pp.258–261.
10. Quoted from Shugaku Yamabe's article on Amida as Saviour of the Soul, *Eastern Buddhist*, Vol.I.

MIRIAM SALANAVE

(1876–1943)

A Buddhist pioneer, traveller, pilgrim and writer who worked relentlessly to spread Buddhism and in particular to encourage and support women through Buddhism.

Miriam Witter Salanave was born in 1876 to James W Milner and Joanna Gravilla Milner in Iowa. She was one of four children but spent most of her adult life in California when not travelling. Miriam married Lucien Salanave (1876–1990) in California in 1922; Miriam was 45, Lucien was 35.

At some point she became a member of The Theosophical Society and it was here, through the writings of Madame Blavatsky and Colonel Olcott, that she became interested in Buddhism.

In 1929, she travelled to Japan, where she spent time in two Buddhist temples. She was befriended by Beatrice Lane Suzuki, a fellow Theosophist, who had married DT Suzuki in 1911 in Yokohama. She and DT Suzuki had both been members of the Tokyo Theosophical Society, and later, when Suzuki began work at Otani University, they opened the Mahayana Lodge of the Theosophical Society in Kyoto. Beatrice introduced Miriam to Shingon Buddhism and took her with her to Tō-ji, a Shingon Buddhism Temple founded in 796, to see the ceremony at The Five Story Pagoda and other cultural treasures. Beatrice also introduced Miriam to Zen Temples where she learnt meditation, and it was in Japan that Miriam first became inspired to introduce Western women to Buddhism.

After leaving Japan, she travelled throughout China, Korea and Burma, visiting important temples and pilgrimage sites. In India, she visited the four holy pilgrimage sites of Buddhism, Lumbini, where Buddha was born, Bodhgaya, where he reached Enlightenment, Sarnath, where he gave his first teaching and Kushinagar, where he died. Miriam was the only American woman at the time to be admitted to the Gelugpa Order of Yellow Hats, the dominant school in Tibet, founded by Tsongkhapa (1357–1419) and of which His Holiness the Dalai Lama was the most prominent member.

On her return to California in 1931 she was eager to interest women in the Noble Eightfold Path and in 1935 founded The Western Women's Buddhist Bureau, in San Francisco, which she maintained, in addition to The East-West Buddhist Welfare Mission. She was supported in this by the American writer, Dwight Goddard, who edited *A Buddhist Bible* (1932), who helped her financially and who she referred to as the 'Ashoka of America'. She produced abundant general literature, greeting cards and regular correspondence from both these organisations, in addition to articles, translations and stories, which appeared in various Buddhist journals throughout the world, including *The Middle Way*. At the time of her passing in 1943, she was working on manuscripts, which she intended as the basis of a book, though this remains unpublished.

To quote directly from her writing, 'In Buddhism I find a satisfactory explanation of the complexities and perplexities of this confused world in which I live, filled with apparent injustices and inequalities on every side. In fact, for me, it solves life's riddle and life's mysterious purpose, points out to me – to each one – my own personal responsibility for my acts, makes me realise I am alone, am my own saviour or destroyer, and offers consolation and a comforting hope that by showing me the way out of my difficulties, namely through myself. Among the last words of the Buddha to his cousin and beloved disciple, Ananda, were these "Therefore O Ananda, be a Lamp unto yourself. Be your own refuge."'

In her own way, Miriam Salanave worked for the emancipation of women through the Buddhist teachings. Christmas Humphreys wrote in her obituary in *The Middle Way*, published almost a year after her death, 'She was devoted and sincere, and it can truly be said that she gave her life for the dissemination of Buddhist principles in the two hemispheres. May others arise to pluck her fallen torch, and carry it forward, for it would be a comfort to her.'

Miriam died at the age of 67 in California.

Learning to Die

Miriam Salanave, 1934

'Thou shalt understand that it is a science most profitable, and passing all other sciences, for to learn to die... thou shalt find full few that have this cunning to learn to die...' *Horologium Sapeintae*

The subject of Death is fascinating as any mystery is fascinating. In the words of an adept 'to know the secrets of Death is to know the secrets of Life.'

If we were as absolutely sure as we are of death that sooner or later we were to journey to a far land, there to dwell for some time, a mysterious land and little known, just the anticipation of so exciting a prospect would thrill us whenever we thought of it, and how avidly would we hunt down every available source of information. But the anticipation of a journey to the frontiers of death and beyond, brings no such pleasurable thrills, only dolorific chills. Why?

'... because no religion, with the exception of Buddhism, has taught a practical contempt for this earthly life; while each of them always with that one solitary exception, has through its hells and damnations, inculcated the greatest dread of death.' (From a letter of a Maha Chohan).

Death to most people of the West is terrifying despite the fact we know it to be our ultimate end – 'and we are Death.' So afraid of it are we that we not only avoid speaking of it except when unavoidable, but we try to avoid even the very thought of it. Anyone disposed to seriously discuss the matter is considered despondent – morbid-minded. Perhaps in the past more thought was given to death than now. It was once a rather widespread custom for the ladies, especially elderly ones, to anticipate the melancholy event by preparing their death trousseaux ahead much as girls today prepare their wedding hope-chests, presumably with different emotions, however.

Tomes have been written on the art of being born; the art of living, and on ways and means of cheating death as long as possible, but as Edward Carpenter points out, how singular that nothing has been written from the clinical, physiological or even psychological side of dying. I think he refers only to the modern West for much has been written in the East since early times. Indeed, almost the only literature left by the Egyptians is on the subject of after-death experiences and states in what is called by us the *Book of the Dead*. Contrary to the average Westerner, the average Easterner does not fear death.

The subject is so important and is such a profound one that I approach it with great diffidence, realising too well how incapable I am of doing it anything like justice. But if I should succeed in stirring even a slight interest in this little discussed and rather unpopular subject, my object will have been achieved.

During the time I spent in Japanese Zen monasteries I was present at two funerals; one of a priest at Daitokuji, the other of a laywoman who was laid to rest in the garden of silence at Empukuji. The ritual was the same for both priest and laywoman. A Zen Buddhist funeral is, to one unable to understand what is said, quite like any ordinary Zen ceremony, with one striking exception, the peg upon which this article hangs. The coffin (*Zakwan*), regardless of seasons or weather, invariably remains outside the temple on the wide porch. It is a rude box, rather high and square to fit the body, which is tied up in sitting position – symbolic of the embryo's position, it was told me, death being but a birth into another state of consciousness. Over this rude box is spread a brocaded silk cover. There are no flowers, the decorations being of paper and small flags of the five Buddhist mystical colours. There is no unrefined 'viewing of the body.'

The rhythmic beating of the wooden drums, the rich tones of full-throated bronze bells struck at intervals, the fragrance of burning incense and chanting of the sutras, create a mystic atmosphere, impressive yet tranquil. Returning now to the 'striking exception' at a Zen funeral: During the course of the ceremony, while the officiating priest read the service, suddenly, in the midst of his reading he paused, and seizing his long rod of office beside him struck the floor with a resounding thwack, fiercely shouting the strange word, 'Kwats!' I was so startled and surprised the first I heard the peculiar cry that I involuntarily jumped high off my seat to the amusement of the monks close by and my own confusion. When he repeated the performance a second time and also at the next funeral I attended, I was prepared and waited with lively interest to hear the cry again, And I lost no time in finding out what it meant, my discovery only increasing my interest in the subject of Death. The cry is believed to have a liberating effect upon the deceased.

Professor Suzuki speaks of 'Kwats' in his *Zen Buddhism*, but not in connection with funerals. It is interesting, however, as in my opinion there is a connection. He says the peculiar cry which he does not refine, is a special feature of the Rinzai schools in distinction to other schools of Zen Buddhism; that the famous Zen master, Rinzai, distinguished four kinds of 'Kwats.' He also says that although Rinzai is popularly regarded as the author of 'Kwatz,' there is an earlier record of the peculiar exclamation. The Zen master, Baso, used it with such effect that a disciple's ears were deafened for three days!

Old Zen masters of the past, perhaps more than at present, were given to making exclamatory utterances in reply to questions instead of giving a sensible reply. But those old masters were far from being the crazy fools some in the West imagine them to have been. They had a very definite object in mind when they made such exclamations, or gave strange and obscure answers – *pons asinorum* – or asked unanswerable questions. Their droll and often outlandish acts and irrelevant questions and answers were purposely designed to shock the disciple; suddenly to awaken his spiritual nature or consciousness if possible; to produce that momentary flash of illumination which in Zen is called *satori*, and which is the goal of Zen meditation or *zazen*. The effect of that sudden impact, when the minds of master and disciple fuse, might perhaps be compared to the flash of lightning produced by two clouds charged with opposite electric forces coming together, except that in the case of lightning the clap of thunder comes afterwards; in the case of master and disciple it is reversed; when this takes place the thunder of the master comes before the flash of the pupil. This flash of illumination is only understood by self-experience.

Thus the sudden sharp cry 'Kwats' used by the old Zen master to arouse his disciple's spiritual consciousness from its lethargy, and the sudden sharp cry of 'Kwats' used by the priest at a Zen funeral, seem to be identical in purpose. In each case it is intended to have a liberating effect. Prof. Suzuki traces 'Kwats' back only as far as Baso's time. It may possibly be of still earlier origin. Madame David-Néel, in her book *With the Mystics and Magicians of Tibet* (1931) gives an exceedingly interesting account of Tibetan death customs, and mentions in particular the utterance of a sharp cry shouted by a Lama to a dead person, which strikingly resembles, in my opinion, our Zen funeral 'Kwats.'

The Tibetan word is 'Phat!' and it is shouted by a lama to a dying one or one who has just died. But first, according to Madame David-Neel, comes another strange ritualistic cry, 'Hik,' immediately followed by the all-powerful and explosive cry 'Phat!' The utterance of this sharp exclamation is designed to not only separate the spirit from the body, but also to lead it out through the top of the head, directing it on the right road, for the nature of a man's consciousness just at death very largely determines his after-death state. Please bear these last words in mind as they will be referred to later on.

The effect intended by using the Zen funeral 'Kwats' and the Tibetan 'Phat' used by the lama officiating at a death scene, might perhaps be defined by the words in *The Tibetan Book of the Dead* (Evans-Wentz) as the 'mechanism of a catapult.' 'As a catapult,' says he, 'enables one to direct a great stone at a definite target or goal, so this Doctrine enables the deceased to direct himself to the Goal of Liberation.' There is no reference, however, of any kind, in this last mentioned book, to the word 'Phat.' It is Madame David-Neel who tells of that peculiar cry, and so far as I am aware, no other than myself has noted or at least written of the similarity between the Tibetan 'Phat' and the Zen 'Kwats.' Be that as it may, we have now finished comparing these two strange cries.

Tibetans, it seems, believe – likewise the Hindus – that the spirit of the dying or recently dead leaves the physical body, either just at the moment of passing or shortly after, through any of several exits; the most excellent one being through the top of the skull, the throne of consciousness known to the Hindus as the 'Lotus of a thousand petals.'

The Tibetan word, *Bardo*, according to the famous *Mahatma Letters* 'is a period between death and rebirth – and may last from a few years to a kalpa.' This is the Yellow Hat version, 'the highest and most orthodox Buddhist sect in Tibet.' The *Bardo* of *The Tibetan Book of the Dead* (Evans-Wentz) is, he explains, the version of the Red Hat School, and there is, he admits, a wide difference of opinion between the two schools in many details. But those instanced in this article seem to accord sufficiently for our purpose since we are not here concerned with the various after-death states and *lokas*. Evans-Wentz defines the *Bardo Thodel* as 'Liberation by hearing on the after-death plane,' and says, 'The Great Doctrine of Liberation by Hearing shows how to make the best use of Transference at the moment of death.'

Supposing the chief actor in this interesting drama of death has been properly diligent during life in the pursuit of spiritual knowledge, then he would have already liberated himself to a certain degree, or he would at least understand the rationale, so that the moment of his passing would be greatly facilitated. In any case, however, he is more than likely to forget or incline towards sleepiness or unconsciousness, hence the importance of there being a competent Lama present to give him his cue. This the assisting Lama does by reading the *Bardo Thodel* aloud to him.

Note, please, that the Lama is not there to intercede to any higher power by prayers on behalf of the man; he is present only to help the man to help himself in case he is either ignorant or else has lapsed into a coma due to the nature of his illness. Mark well the self-reliance of this doctrine, Buddhism's outstanding feature. Every Buddhist knows whether in life or death that 'no one saves us but ourselves, no one can and no one may.' Not even the Buddhas themselves can absolve us from our karmic debts – the results of our past acts – 'Buddhas only point the way.'

The dialogue between the lama and the spirit of the deceased reminds one of the passage in the Egyptian Book of the Dead where the dead man pleaded for himself at the judgement: 'I have never given short weight; I have never cheated the widow nor orphan,' and so on. In the *Bardo Thodel*, when he comes to judgment, the Lama tells him it is useless to lie, in case the deceased is tempted to make excuses for himself. The Lord of Death looks into the Mirror of Karma and sees all, for this Mirror of Karma is Memory, and the man is acting as his own judge. The Lama tells him if he is suffering in any way or feels terrified by visions, 'it is not due to anyone else; it is thine own karma.'

When no Lama or close Buddhist friend or relative (in Burma, according to Fielding Hall's *Soul of a People*, a near friend assists) is available to assist at this rite and the man is ignorant yet still conscious, he should then make an effort to visualise as clearly as possible either his teacher or some Buddhist deity or recall a Mantra, not as a means of saving himself, remember, or as a straw to cling to, but only as a means of lifting up his mind to a higher plane at this supreme moment of passing, for as already emphasised, the importance of last thoughts largely determine the man's future. Just how important these last moments are is told in *The Mahatma Letters*.

'That feeling which is the strongest with us at that supreme hour; when, as in a dream, the events of a long life, to their minutest details, are marshalled in the greatest order in a few seconds in our vision (a footnote in this letter adds: That vision takes place when a person is already proclaimed dead. The brain is the last organ to die.) – that feeling will become the fashioner of our bliss or woe, the life principle of our future existence...' (Letter XXc).

In the same letter occurs another interesting passage: 'Guiteau is gone into a state during the period of which he will be ever firing at his President, thereby tossing into confusion and shuffling the destinies of millions of persons; where he will be ever tried and ever hung. Bathing in the reflection of his deeds and thoughts – especially those he indulged in on the scaffold,'

It is the Lama's purpose to prevent if possible that break. In the flow of the stream of the deceased's consciousness, but only one far advanced is able to retain his consciousness throughout the process according to *The Mahatma Letters*. (Our nights of sleep are much the same.) The first 49 days after death are considered so important in Mahayana Buddhism, during which time, in Japan at least, services are held almost daily for the dead – and in Tibet the daily reading of the *Bardo Thodel* – are merely symbolical. Forty-nine is a sacred number, seven times seven, seven being a sacred number. The heavens and hells spoken of are also symbolical.

In *The Tibetan Book of the Dead* it is pointed out that the text of the *Bardo Thodel* makes it very clear by 'repeated assertions,' that the apparitions likely to be seen by the dying one are only reflections of his though-forms. That everything the percipient is likely to see on the *Bardo* plane is due entirely to his own mental content. In other words man's heavens and hells are of his own making.

'We ourselves create our *Devachan* as also our *Avitchi* while yet on earth and mostly during the latter days and even moments of our intellectual sentient lives' (*Mahatma Letters*).

Originally published in *Buddhism in England*, May–June 1934.

Miriam Salanave sitting zazen in Japan.

BUDDHIST WOMEN
POETS OF JAPAN

TEXTS AND TRANSLATIONS

BY WAYNE YOKOYAMA

Kaga no Chiyo-jo. Woodcut illustration by Utagawa Kuniyoshi

KAGA NO CHIYO-JO

1703–1775

The world of haiku is patterned on the world of nature. The four seasons, the flowers, the birds and bees, all appear in good time. This natural rise and fall of the seasons is the basis of the Shin religious culture of the Hokuriku region that nurtured Kaga no Chiyo-jo (1703–1775), the pioneer women poet of Japan. My first exposure to Chiyo-jo took place some years ago when I visited a good friend in the city of Matto whose Shin temple was associated with her. He showed me the dissertation of a French scholar named Dominique Chipot who did extensive research on Chiyo's haiku. Interestingly the area also produced the poet Akegarasu Fusako whose *tanka* are the subject of another essay in our series. The area, now called Hakusan, is thriving with local culture related to Chiyo. It has an annual morning glory festival in her honour. Her famous morning glory haiku also sprouted the regional cultivation of morning glory varieties that the Japanese so love. There is also a museum in her honour whose homepage features a number of haiku in English translation. In the present selection the theme of morning glories and butterflies recurs. In one poem Chiyo sees a butterfly at a Shin Buddhist service where the devotees are loudly chanting the Buddha name. There is also more than one morning glory haiku. The haiku presented here have been augmented to more fully convey the meaning of the poem.

The Morning Glory *Haiku no Chiyo-jo*

Kaga no Chiyo-jo

Oh morning glory!
The truth about flowers is
They prefer not to have people about ...
Once it lets its roots down
A woman's desires are harder to pull out
Than the sumire' violets by the wayside ...
As far as sheer strength goes
I vow not to let the butterfly beat me
This lovely spring morning ...
Oh butterfly!
On the path of women –
Are you in our lead
Or in our tow ...
The nodding dandelion
Sometimes stirs the sleepy butterfly
Awake from her dreamy dream ...
With no voice of her own
To hold back in modesty
The butterfly attends the service ...
Dreaming all along
The butterfly alights on bloom or flower
Taking command of all she touches ...
Time and again the butterfly arises
Coming in and out of view
As she floats through the mist ...
Oh morning glory!
Even the drifting path the butterfly takes
Is just a line drawn on the surface of a dream ...
Oh morning glory!
Life for you 'tis but a midsummer's night
Spent within a dream ...

To live to be a hundred
You have to be fully at one with yourself
As you live life from the heart ...
Ah, Madam Morning Glory!
I see you have imperiously laid claim to the well bucket,
Forcing me to fetch my water elsewhere ...
Oh Ms Butterfly!
What elegant dream are you dreaming
As you fan yourself with your wings ...
At any rate
I leave my fate to the winds –
Like the dry pampas grass ...

Translated by Wayne Yokoyama

Kaga no Chiyo
Calligraphy: Inscription and Haiku, Edo Period, before 1754
Hanging scroll, ink on paper
Eliza S. Paine Fund
2012.86 Worcester Art Museum

YAMADA FUSAKO

1886–1913

Born to an established Shin temple family near Nagoya, Yamada Fusako (1886–1913) received a thorough literary education that included poetry composition. Through her scholarly brother Sasaki Gessho (1875–1926), later president of Otani University, she met Akegarasu Haya (1877–1954) who edited the leading Shin magazine *Seishinkai* ('Spiritual world') for 12 years, from its inception in 1901 until 1913, the year of her death. During these years they spent little time together since he was based in Tokyo while she manned the Akegarasu home temple near Kanazawa. From 1905 to 1909 she contributed over 100 poems to the journal. Her poems of love reveal the Shin spirituality she was nurtured on that gave her the strength to endure the long years of separation.

The present selection is based in part on the original research done by Ama Michihiro, Professor of Japanese Language and Culture, University of Montana, Missoula, on *Voices of Buddhist Women in Modern Japan: Representations of Female Spirituality in the Seishinkai* (in a forthcoming companion volume to *Cultivating Spirituality*, ed. ML Blum and M Conway; Honolulu: University of Hawaii Press).

We wish to thank Dr Ama for his generous permission to use these materials. Portions have been adapted and augmented to more fully convey the imagery of the poems. I also need to express my thanks to Dr Mutsumi Wondra for correcting my initial versions of some of the other poems.

The Love Song of Akegarasu Fusako

Yamada Fusako

That I should be so happily in love with you as this!
Though I dwell on the wasteland of sin
And wander through life lost in delusion,
Oh how I cling to the compassionate hands of our loving Buddha!
The mists draw back to reveal a perfectly peaceful sky.
Oh if only I could turn myself into a butterfly! –
How much I want to see you again, my love ...
Take the hot tears I shed over you, my love,
And rub them down with an ink stick –
To set down my songs of love for you ...
How deeply the Buddha's compassion comes across
Whenever we call the Name together,
Making our days so enjoyable ...
Scoop water from the well of happiness, my love.
And let me share it with those dying of thirst ...
As I am guided by the Buddha's light
It lightens the pain in my heart
To hear the Buddha calling to me ...
While mountain and ocean might
Separate our bodies physically,
In spirit we smile upon one another,
You and me, my dear ...
Wandering about the autumn fields
Together with you, my love,
Listening to the bell crickets chirping
In the shade of the plume grass ...
Turning my face to the clear moon, my love,
All I can think of is you –
Hearing the pounding of the waves,
Alas, how lonely my heart feels tonight!
As pleased as I am to receive this wondrous robe of faith

Turned over to me by the Buddha,
All the same I find it impossible for me
To discard the old garments I am so accustomed to wearing ...
Whenever we are together I always say
I'll be brave and can hold up alone.
But once separated from you, my love,
You the thread of my life, I am lost without you
And look only to the day we meet again ...
Whenever we have to part,
Oh how I pray for the day we meet again!
Parting from you is always so painful for me –
I swear my body literally aches for you ...

Translated by Wayne Yokoyama

KUJO TAKEKO

1887–1928

In the fairy tale version of her life, Kujo Takeko (1887–1928) marries the Baron and lives happily ever after. But as we all know that is not what happens. A photograph taken in London circa 1910 shows her at one of the happiest moments of her life. Even the Baron is smiling, having married one of the celebrated three beauties of the Taisho. But happiness did not last long. Soon she returns to Japan, broken-hearted. She writes poetry, cries, engages in humanitarian work, all the while nursing an aching heart. There is a rumour she was romantically involved with the famous writer Akutagawa Ryunosuke. It is hard to tell if there is any truth to it. But she died six months after he took his life having grown sick of it.

One of our other women poets, Okamoto Kanoko, wrote a novel on the final episode of his life. A museum in her honour was established at Kyoto Women's University which she helped found after seeing one of the women's universities in London. This selection of poems did not make it in time to be included in Kujo Takeko's *Leaves of My Heart*, recently published by ABSC New York. But I was able to publish a version of it in the BSC Honolulu newsletter Metta. The work on the book itself was done some time ago. It was first revised by Dr Mutsumi Wondra and later benefited from further editing by Edythe Vassall. I am indebted to them both, pleased the book has finally come out, and hope too Takeko is now happy.

Whispers

Kujo Takeko:

Whether our lives be blessed or miserable,
All of us receive the sunshine of this bright new day
That fills the heavens from end to end ...
Whatever cares or worries may fill our heart, 'Look to the sky,' I say:
Ah, is the sparkling sun not shining most beautifully today! ...
'Oh, gee, how I miss him!' is what my aching heart sounds like,
As I kick the pebbles around distractedly:
Makes me wonder if he is ever coming home ...
Brushed by my kimono sleeve as I got to my feet,
The scissors fell to the ground
With a clear tinkling sound like a tiny bell ...
Today, was just about to leave the page blank again,
Nothing coming to mind,
When I scrawl out something short in my diary,
Just to write down something, anything ...
When I breathe on it, it leaves a faint cloud,
And when I wipe it away:
Oh how cold the mirror is! ...
As you watch the whirlpool going around and around,
'Tis as if you could duck your head to pass through its vortex,
To appear again on the other side in another world far, far away ...
The new Moon, assuming her basic form, is not there at all:
Not there at all and yet in that form
She happily proceeds down the path set out for her ...
With nothing to occupy myself
And tire me out physically doing this and that,
My heart is just about to roll itself up out of sheer boredom ...
No matter how sad we are, in our heart laden with sadness
There is a delicate mechanism that is designed
To somehow bring us back to life again ...
Resigning myself to never seeing him again,

At the door to my house, finding I have forgotten my key,
I start to cry as if I had gone nearly half mad with grief ...
Forgetting whether we are rich or poor,
All of us sleep in peace and quiet
In the wee hours of the night ...

Translated by Wayne Yokoyama

Kujo Takeko

OKAMOTO KANOKO

(1889–1939)

The noted modern poet Okamoto Kanoko loved to wear pearls and silk dresses. She came from a wealthy family in the Tokyo area. Her marriage to talented illustrator Okamoto Ippei is often described as an unhappy one, but a look at Ippei's 15 volume collection of illustrations and writings does not suggest he was the frivolous sort. The fact they did not divorce and even travelled abroad together to Paris, London, and New York suggests they were devoted to one another and were trying to reach a reconciliation.

One of Ippei's memorable assignments was to accompany Einstein on his 1922 tour of Japan. The amusingly illustrated essay is in Volume One of his collected works. In the same volume are numerous writings on religion. Around age 40, Kanoko gave up poetry and turned to writing novels. She also started to look more deeply into Buddhism, authoring several books on the theme. Long poems such as the one below sometimes appear among her essays. Her final book of poetry was cleverly illustrated by Fujita Tsuguharu (Leonard Foujita) of Paris. Her son Okamoto Taro also accompanied her to Paris where he remained for some years.

Taro's sculpture 'Tower of the Sun' for the 1970 World Exposition in Osaka is symbolic of the emergence of Japan as a major world economy. He also has a 'Tower of Mother'. But what it represents and whether it is somehow related to mother Kanoko is a question I cannot answer. As we see in her poem on motherly love, her artistic son was a source of much vexation for her. In a final poem she reaffirms female spirituality saying, 'Women, we are the Bodhisattva.'

To render the poems below I have taken the liberty to adapt and augment the originals. In the first poem, the most difficult term is nenzuru, literally the verb form of 'the mind now.' To nenzuru is to exist in the state of mind where the world of Buddha opens up to us and engages us on the field of play. I wish to express my thanks to Dr Mutsumi Wondra for revising the first poem in this selection.

The Universe of Motherly Love

Okamoto Kanoko, 1937

The Warped Mind / Higami

The warped mind is
The grime that builds up
In the sump of the heart ...
The heart of the weak person,
That is, those who fake it,
Those who want to show off,
Form these sumps ...
The honest truth about ourselves is
What makes people calm down
And prevents our hearts forming these sumps ...
Just as bared claws are
The payback for bared claws,
Hatred calls down more hate upon itself,
As the grime too builds up more grime ...
The grime is again
Where the bacillus makes its home.
The bacillus is again
What eats away at the heart ...
Thus at first
There is just a heart with a depression in it, a sump,
But then it goes on to rot and be eaten away by decay ...
The heart that has first started to rot and be eaten away by decay
Then goes on to become
A heart that has lost its original form ...
The heart that
Has developed even the first signs of a sump,
That has started to build up even the least bit of grime ...
When we notice that our heart
Has started to accumulate even the least bit of grime

Immediately we have to ...
Immediately we have to
Wipe the grime away,
Iron out the wrinkle in our hearts ...
Let our minds open up to being the Buddha now –
Do that and the wrinkle in our hearts
Will there and then resolve itself ...
This 'Buddha' you speak of –
What is it,
What sort of thing is it?
Buddha is what fills the universe from corner to corner.
It is the honest truth of who we are.
It is the muscle in our arm.
Whenever our hearts
Have grown weak,
Whenever our hearts have developed a sump ...
What we want immediately is
The honest truth of who we are,
We want to feel the muscle in our arm ...
Immediately
Let ourselves call to the Buddha.
Let our minds open up to being the Buddha now,
Yes, let our minds open up to being the Buddha now.
O Buddha dwelling in our minds!
You are the honest truth of what we are!
O Buddha dwelling in our minds!
You are the muscle in our arm!
We beseech you to come forth!
Let our minds open up to being the Buddha now,
Yes, let our minds open up to being the Buddha now.

Translated by Wayne Yokoyama, an author, researcher, scholar, and editor, in Kyoto, Japan. Editor of *House of Silent Night*, published by The Buddhist Society Trust, 2023. Translator of *The Suzuki English diary* for the Matsugoaka Bunko Foundation, and *Cultivating Spirituality* by Mark L. Blum, 2011, *The Nirvana Sutra*, 2013. Translator of *Coffinman: The Journal of a Buddhist Mortician* by Shinmon Aoki, 1993.

AILEEN HUMPHREYS
also known as HASSUKO

(1891–1975)

Buddhist, silversmith, jeweller, gardener, illustrator and co-founder of The Buddhist Society.

Mrs Christmas Humphreys, the Co-Founder of The Buddhist Society and wife of its President, died on 16 December, aged 84.

During the memorial service, which was held at the Society on Saturday 3 January 1976, the President read the following address:

'Let us remember with love the one we knew as Puck Humphreys. Born of Irish parents near York in 1891, she came to London as a young woman to learn the craft of a silversmith and jeweller. During the First World War she served in France as an ambulance driver in the FANYs [First Aid Nursing Yeomanry], being awarded the Military Medal for picking up wounded under fire. After the war she worked as a silversmith in London, with her mark registered at Goldsmith's Hall.

We met in 1922, and soon were saying to each other, 'Hullo, you again!' Both of us had been studying the works of HP Blavatsky, and all that was known then in the West of Buddhism. This combination was the background of what became our joint, inseverable lives. In 1924 we founded the Buddhist Lodge of the Theosophical Society. In 1926 the Lodge became an independent organisation, The Buddhist Society, now the oldest and largest Buddhist organisation in the West. We were married, to a Buddhist service of our own devising, in 1927. During the 50 years of our joint work for Buddhism in the West, no step has been taken, no word written by me without consultation with her, and just before she was taken ill, she was firmly correcting a paragraph in my revision of the Society's Correspondence Course.

Throughout the Second World War, Puck was back in the FANYs as a Captain, working as the Finance Officer for 7,000 women on secret assignment.

As fellow Buddhists we studied books as they appeared, discussed and noted them, and tried to live the Buddhist life together. Her intuition was remarkable, and again and again she leapt ahead of my own understanding. Her copy of Blyth's *Mumonkan* is nigh worn out with handling. She was a person deeply versed in Zen.

As we lay together in the New Year of 1972, waiting for an ambulance to arrive, we spoke of Dr Suzuki's words to Father Merton in their memorable interview in New York, 'the most important thing is Love!' After a pause she suddenly said to me, 'There must be crying before we understand. The heart must break.' She was right. Only then will the inner eyes, unveiled, see the full splendour of the Buddha-Mind, beyond suffering, beyond separation, beyond self.... The Buddha taught that Life is one and indivisible, though manifesting to our eyes in many forms. The body must die but what some call soul or character lives on, and will in time return, purged of imperfections in the life now ended, fortified with virtues gained from past experience. Each pilgrim on the Way is a Buddha in the making, but many lives are needed before this innate splendour is revealed. Life after life we fight the fires of anger, lust and illusion that strive to consume our spiritual heritage, yet though the fight is long, the end is sure.

Originally published in *The Middle Way*, vol. 50, no. 4, February 1976. Adapted for this publication.

Why Not Now?
The Sword of Tempered Speech

Aileen Humphreys, 1932

As Buddhists, we study the Noble Eightfold Path, but how many of us test that path by using it? There is only one sure way of testing the truth of any teaching and that is by living it, and we can be certain that the Path is the right Path by treading it. Then why not begin now? Every moment of time is a moment of choice, but it is useless to choose and then do nothing more. It is true that all the time we are treading a path of some sort through the jungle of Samsara, yet, having seen and chosen the true Path we pass it by, saying to ourselves: 'One day I will tread it, but not now.' This foolishness is due chiefly to lack of coordination between the higher and lower nature, the higher which would tread the true Path when it sees it and the lower which says: 'That may be so, but I am more comfortable wandering in the jungle now. Later on will be time enough to begin my treading of that path.' The spirit is willing, but the flesh is weak.

Having, however, finally decided to tread the true Path, why not begin by

Mr and Mrs Christmas Humphries with Alan Watts @ The Buddhist Society

at least facing in the right direction? Having done this, it may be found that the easiest point from which to start is Right Speech. Think of the revolution in our lives if we walked with truly guarded speech for just one day, yet if we could only begin, how quickly the power would grow! We should never again say: 'If only I had known the facts, I would not have said what I did,' or, 'That was an unjust criticism, but I did not stop to think.' If we used Right Speech such regrets would never arise. We must, however, go further, for if we meditate on this aspect of the Noble Eightfold Path we shall find that not only must we practise Right Speech, but we must refrain from using wrong speech, and learn that most valuable lesson – the necessity of silence. We cannot think if we are talking all the time. How often do we give advice that is not sought, and thrust our point of view upon others without consideration, without understanding? Why not keep silent? Whence this dreadful urge to 'say something'? Words are dangerous things when used thoughtlessly, and a man's life's work may be destroyed by his own or another's ill-considered speech. The power of the spoken word is immense, and we should be wise to remember this before we speak.

The time to tread the Path is now; the place to begin is here; and the best weapon wherewith to arm oneself is the sword of tempered speech.

Published in *The Middle Way*, vol 6, no 9–10, March 1932.

ONLY THE FOOL IS WISE

Only the Fool is Wise

This picture was used for The Buddhist Society's Calendar for 1938, and is described on the back of the Calendar as follows: "The artist Hassuko has used a gorge in the French Alps as the basis of a picture designed to illustrate the famous Zen koan 'Walk On.' Faced with an apparently blank wall of stone, yet road and river, man and beast 'walk on'."

This is a design by Hassuko that was used for The Buddhist Society's 1936 Calendar. It illustrates the famous story known as "Drop it," a slightly different version of which was printed in The Buddhist Society publication *Concentration and Meditation*. The story of this picture is of a wandering seeker of the Way who came to the Buddha, bearing gifts in either hand. Said the Buddha, "Drop it." The visitor let fall one of his gifts. Again the order came: "Drop it." The visitor dropped the other gift. Again the order came. The seeker of the Way was for the moment at a loss; then he smiled, for he had attained Enlightenment.

The Small covers the Great

This picture by Hassuko appeared in The Buddhist Society's annual calendar for the year 1939. It represents a landscape, as seen from Streatley Hill, above Goring-on-Thames, viewed through a hawthorn bush. The koan which it illustrates is one more of those mental nuts which the intellect alone will never crack.

This picture of Hassuko's appeared in The Buddhist Society's 1941 calendar. It is of the bridge which spans the Thames at Streatley, and even as the war planes flew overhead, the artist noted that the shadow of even the swiftest bird is still.

This picture was used in The Buddhist Society's Calendar for 1934, and was specially designed by the Hon. Secretary, Mrs. Christmas Humphreys (Hassuko), for this purpose. She prefers that it shall have no title, leaving each student free to interpret its complex symbolism as they will.

Seek in the Impersonal for the Eternal Man by Aileen Humphreys known as Hassuko, from *The Middle Way*

RUTH FULLER
EVERETT SASAKI
(1892–1967)

An extraordinary woman who opened the way for Westerners to train in Zen Buddhism in the West as well as in Japan. An author and translator, founder of the First Zen Institute and the first foreign Abbess of Ryosen-an sub-temple in Daitokuji, Japan.

Ruth Fuller Everett Sasaki is one of a number of very important figures in the transmission of Zen Buddhism to the West. She was born Ruth Fuller in Chicago, United States on October 31 1892, to Canadian American parents, Clara Elizabeth and George E Fuller. Her father was a successful investor in Canadian grain on the Chicago stock exchange.

Ruth was talented and determined and enthusiastic in the pursuit of her interests; she was very privileged and was partly educated in Europe, studying French and German after graduating from The Kenwood Institute and the Loring School in Chicago at the age of 18.

On April 7 1917, when Ruth was 25 years old, she married Edward Warren Everett, a prominent trial attorney of the law firm Winston, Strawn & Shaw, who was 20 years older than her. On December 30 1918, their daughter Eleanor was born.

In 1924, Ruth visited Clarkstown Country Club in Nyack, New York with her daughter Eleanor for healing and stayed at the Club and lectured there with her husband Edward. The Club was extremely influential and popular with upper class wealthy women and others and it was here that she was exposed to Eastern philosophy and yoga, through Pierre Arnold Bernard, a Tantric Yogi who was known as 'Oom the Magnificent' and was uncle of the explorer and author Theos Bernard, who became known as 'the White Lama'.

Theos, who had visited and trained in Tibet, married the Polish opera singer Ganna Walska. Walska created with Theos, *Tibet Land* later renamed

Lotus Land, an extraordinary 44-acre garden in Santa Barbara California. His writings were to inspire James Hilton's 1933 novel *Lost Horizon*, which depicted Shangri-La, the mythical land of peace and harmony in the Himalayas.

In 1927, after becoming intrigued by Eastern thought, Ruth enrolled on a two-year course in Indian Philosophy and Sanskrit at Chicago University and three years later, in 1930, became a member of the American Oriental Society.

The same year, the family travelled for three months to Japan, Korea and China, to pursue her interests. In Japan, through an introduction by the American adventurer William Montgomery McGovern (1897–1964)[2], they met DT Suzuki, who taught Ruth basic Zazen sitting, and his wife, Beatrice Lane (see this volume), who was also an American.

In 1930, Ruth and Edward published *Far East for 90 Days*, which documented their visit to Japan.

In 1932, at the age of 40, Ruth returned to Japan to deepen her practice, and took up Zen practice under Nanshinken Roshi (Kono Mukai), master of the Rinzai Zen monastery in Kyoto at Nanzen-ji established 1291, which she continued from 1 April until the end of July. On her return to New York, in April 1933, she met the Japanese Rinzai monk, Sokei-an Roshi (Sasaki Shigetsu 1882–1945), for the first time.

Sokei-an was the son of a Shinto priest and a sculptor. Sokei-an (1870–1954) who first came to America in 1906. He had trained in Rinzai Zen under Sokatsu Shaku. Sokatsu Shaku was a student of Shaku Soen (1860–1919), DT Suzuki's teacher and incumbent of Engaku-ji. Shaku Soen had spoken at the World Parliament of Religions, which was dubbed the first meeting of the World Interfaith Movement, in Chicago in 1893, and had taken DT Suzuki with him. Sokei-an was given *Inka* by Sokatsu in 1928. He founded The Buddhist Society of America in 1930 and wrote books on Zen and Buddhism.

Ruth then returned to Kyoto with Eleanor for further study and was later joined by Edward in 1934. In 1935, Edward retired from his law firm due to failing health. In the same year, Ruth's teacher, Nanshinken Roshi (Kono Mukai), also died.

In 1936, Ruth travelled to London at the invitation of Christmas Humphreys to give a talk at the (The Buddhist Lodge) Buddhist Society on her experiences of training in Nanzen-ji and for Eleanor to study piano with George Woodhouse. While in London, they both meet the Zen Buddhist Alan Watts, who Eleanor went on to marry in 1938.

Eleanor married author and Zen Buddhist Alan Watts in 1938, a former editor of *The Middle Way*, and student of Zen Buddhism since his schoolboy days in England, at Kings School Canterbury, and friend of Christmas Humphreys. Watts was a seminal figure in the transmission of 'Eastern thought' to the west and much loved by the counterculture of the 1960s, having studied and practiced Zen Buddhism and attended a seminary to train as a Christian priest. Watts, together with Gainsborough and Chaudhuri, founded the American Academy of Asian Studies in 1951, which later morphed into the California Institute of Integral Studies.

Edward's health continued to decline and in 1938, he was moved to a sanatorium in Hartford, Connecticut. In the same year, Ruth took up *koan* study with Sokei-an, who gave Ruth the Buddhist name Eryu, meaning Dragon Wisdom and Ruth began editing Sokei-an's publication, *Cat's Yawn* (1947).

In 1940, Edward died, and in the following year, Ruth bought a brownstone at 124 East 65th Street on the Upper East Side of New York, where she intended to rehouse The Buddhist Society of America, Sokei-an, her mother, herself and a Zendo in different apartments. Her mother however, died at the age of 78 before she was able to move in. The house opened on 6th December 1941, the day before the attack on Pearl Harbor in Honolulu, Hawaii, and was later renamed The First Zen Institute of America.

In 1944, following his release from Rikers Island where he was interned, Ruth and Sokei-an married, however he died shortly after, in 1945.

Ruth then returned to Kyoto in Japan where she had previously had her first training experiences in Zen.

Ruth built up a sub-temple of Daitoku-ji, Ryosen-an, as a place where Westerners could come and train. Ruth established it as the First Zen Institute of Japan in 1957. She devoted the rest of her life to Zen practice, study and the translation of important Zen teachings.

She was joined by Walter Nowick 1950 to study with Goto Roshi and later Irmgard Schloegl in 1960, who both went on to start training temples in the West.

Her literary works included *The Record of Linji*, a collection of sayings of Linji, the founder of the Rinzai sect of Zen Buddhism, who died in 861, which she translated with a commentary. The publication was edited by a prominent team of scholars and translators around her in Kyoto including Iriya Yoshitaka, Kanaseki Hisao, Yokoi Seizan and four Europeans, Phillip Yampolsky, Burton

Watson, Gary Snyder and later Walter Nowick, who were all distinguished in their own way. The work remained unfinished for many years after her death until the Zen scholar, Thomas Kirchner, took up the unfinished manuscript. It was published as *The Record of Linji* by the University of Hawaii Press in 2008.

Her other publications include *The Zen Koan: Its History and Use in Rinzai Zen* (1965) with Isshu Miura and *The Recorded Sayings of Layman P'Ang: a Ninth-Century Zen Classic* (1971).

At the age of 66, she was ordained as Abbot of Ryosen-an, the first woman and Westerner to be given this title. Never without her pearl earrings and martinis, Ruth was an extraordinary woman and led the way for Westerners to train in Zen Buddhism in Japan as well as in the US and Europe. She died in Kyoto in 1967 from a heart attack brought on by exhaustion.

Notes

1. Pierre Arnold Bernard, (1975–1955) established at Clarkeston Country Club one of the largest Sanskrit libraries in the United States. He was a student of Yogi Sylvais Hamati who befriended him when he was thirteen years old and named Perry Baker in Lincoln Nebraska. *The Great Oom: The Improbable Birth of Yoga in America*, Swami Satyananda.

2. William Montgomery McGovern.

Ruth Fuller Everett Sasaki

A Zen Student's Experience and Advice

Ruth Everett, 1933

I n 1930, I made a trip to Japan and China with my husband and daughter, and while in Kyoto, through an introduction from my friend, Dr William M McGovern, I met Professor and Mrs Suzuki. I had studied primitive Buddhism to a considerable extent, and had begun further studies in the Mahayana. On telling Dr Suzuki that I was eager to study meditation, he told me that I ought to arrange to stay in Kyoto for some time, and study in a Zen temple. This I was later able to do. I revisited Kyoto last March, and through the kindness of Dr and Mrs Suzuki, was able to take a Japanese house with Japanese servants, and to take up the study of Zen at Nanzenji, one of the large Zen temples in Kyoto. For three and a half months I lived alone, except for my servants and my interpreter-secretary, spending from six to twelve hours a day in meditation, for six days a week.

My Roshi gave me the use of his private house (he himself lived in the Roshi's house of the monastery), just outside one of the gates of a temple. There I went every morning and spent most of the day alone in meditation. After three weeks I was invited to go to the Zendo for the evening meditation with the monks, and thereafter went every night for the remainder of my stay in Kyoto. The one period of Sesshin (a week of concentrated meditation) which took place during my stay, I spent entirely at the temple. I went at three in the morning to the temple and remained all day, eating the same food as the monks and living nearly as possible the same regime of meditation, sutra-chanting and relaxation as the monks did. I cannot convey to you the happiness and reality of these three months of my life.

I had prepared myself for my studies by the practise of concentration, acting on the advice and instruction given me by Dr Suzuki on the occasion of my first visit, and I will now explain the system and methods I followed.

Dr Suzuki taught me this method, and my Roshi gave me permission to teach it to others. It is very simple, but you will find as you study Zen that everything in Zen is reduced to its most simple form.

You seat yourself on your cushion in a comfortable posture. Then you begin to breathe slowly and deeply, the lips being closed, both inhalation and exhalation being taken through the nostrils. As you INHALE you will distend and raise the chest, pull the abdomen in, and in so doing raise the diaphragm. When you EXHALE you will depress the chest, distend the abdomen, and push the diaphragm down. This way of breathing is exactly the opposite from the natural way and from most systems of breathing. If, when you are inhaling, you will think of pulling up as far as possible the wall of the diaphragm, and when you are exhaling, you will think of pushing it down and out against the solar plexus, I think you will find the mental picture a help to you. What happens as a result of this breathing is that an enormous amount of activity is amassed in the area of the solar plexus. As you continue, and do not have to concentrate so much on the muscular control of breathing, you will find that you can appear to press the diaphragm down still further until the final pressure seems to come just below the navel.

Now as you sit breathing, begin to count the breaths, one, two, three, and up to ten. Then begin over again at one and continue up to ten, counting in this way indefinitely as long as you are practising the exercise.

You will keep your mind on the breath count and on that alone.

When other thoughts come in, do not try to get rid of them, but just keep on counting and push them out of the way. A determined (wilful) attempt to keep away other thoughts seems only to make for more disturbance. Just keep patiently coming back to the counting. At first I found this exercise of keeping the mind concentrated on the numbered breaths very difficult, I was advised to begin with ten minutes' practice, then 15, and to increase gradually until I could sit without moving for an indefinite time. Three hundred counts, that is, ten counted 30 times, is considered the goal to aim for. But these 300 counts must be made without another thought of any kind intruding during the entire course of the practice. And when one breathes sufficiently slowly, to count 300 will take close upon three hours.

I practised this method sitting in a chair, and I eventually succeeded in sitting still for an hour and a half, but I did not succeed in keeping out vagrant thoughts during the whole time.

One important thing to remember is, that it is to the exhaled breath that one directs most attention. The exhaled breath should be considerably slower than the inhaled breath. The exhaled breath and the downward pressure should continue so long that in reality the inhalation is a reflex action from the exhalation. Also remember that you must keep absolutely relaxed during all this practice, the correct position maintained, but with no nervous tension.

If you will study the posture of the meditating Buddha rupas of the Japanese schools, the Buddha of Kamakura for example, you will see that the abdomen is distended and the shoulders just a little drooping. This is quite different from Indian or Burmese meditating Buddhas. My own Buddha rupa is a Tibetan, but of the Indian type. He sits with raised chest and shoulders and contracted abdomen. I think no better picture for one's own meditation posture can be found, one to keep in the mind's eye, than the Kamakura Buddha. As you continue our meditation in accordance with the Zen methods, you will gradually become conscious of the depressing fold coming in your own abdomen above the navel, and the distension below the navel.

This exercise is, as you can see, quite different from the usual methods taught. There is no concentration upon a problem or an idea or a verse or a diagram or an image, or upon the tip at one's nose. This method seems to me quite consistent with the attempt of Zen to always get rid of form.

If you will refer to Dr Suzuki's translation of Asvaghosha's *Awakening of Faith* at pages 132–134, you will find instructions for the practice of sensation of the mind, which also says that one should not let the mind dwell on this or that or the other.

***

Comments from the editor: *Readers should remember that the foregoing is instruction in the preparatory part of Zen meditation. Mrs Everett practised this at her own home in America before going to Japan to take up her study of Zen methods at a Zen temple. Anyone contemplating the study of Zen methods should, therefore, start with the above preparation.*

The next point to consider is the question of the most suitable posture when practising meditation. Mrs Everett was kind enough to send some excellent explanatory photographs, which I regret I cannot reproduce, but I trust that the following description will be understandable.

***

Japanese people, particularly of the old school, sit on the floor, and use no chairs. Meditation posture in a Zen temple is of two kinds, one for men and one for women. The men sit in full 'lotus posture,' that is, with the right foot on the left thigh, and the left foot on the right thigh, just as we see the Buddha depicted. Or they may sit in 'half lotus posture,' that is with the right foot on the left thigh and the left leg stretched out at a right-angle to the other, or the reverse of this, namely, left foot on right thigh with right leg stretched out in front. The monks call this the 'bodhisattva posture.' During long periods of meditation they will change occasionally from one of these postures to the other, in order to relieve the muscular and nervous tension.

They sit usually upon two cushions, called a *zabuton*, one about 30 inches square moderately well padded, which is used as the actual seat, and the other, which is about the same size, being doubled in half and placed under the back half of the other. This gives a sloping surface, of course, there being three layers of cushion at the back and one layer in the front. This slope throws the body slightly forward, and helps to keep the body in the correct posture without tiring the spine.

Japanese women who do Zen meditation usually sit just as Japanese people sit at all times, with the lower leg and the foot doubled back under the thighs, and the buttocks on the upturned heels. Many, however, sit on cushions, but arrange them differently: they use similar cushions, but the thicker is placed on the floor and the thinner one is folded in two and is used as the actual seat, the legs being bent and placed one on each side of the folded cushion that is being used as the seat.

In both these cases the arrangement of the cushions tends to throw the abdomen slightly forward, which relieves the strain somewhat.

Even the Japanese people who are accustomed from childhood to sit in postures very similar to those described above, find the muscular strain of Zen meditation very painful at first. For foreigners it is much more so. But my experience leads me to believe that such methods of sitting as I have described are absolutely necessary for any great progress in meditation. The centre of gravity of the body differs according to posture, and the correct posture is best attained and retained by using the cushions described. When one has conquered the physical obstacles, meditation thus practised becomes much easier, and also when studying at a Zen monastery if one is able to sit as monks do, the sense of difference of nationality and background is much less pronounced. I was told that if I found any real difficulty in using the cushions as seats I might meditate in a chair, and I believe that with few exceptions foreign people have meditated in chairs, but after trying the chair for the first ten days and being unable to 'find my seat,' as they express it, I decided to try the cushion, and have thereafter always used the cushion method, and I still do so.

I would advise any prospective student to begin at once using the cushions as his seat. He (or she) will get accustomed to it, and should he go to Japan he will not have the trouble of getting his muscles accustomed to the strain after he gets there. Let him get a low table, about 15 inches from the floor level, and use that as his desk or writing table. Practice sitting at this table whilst he is doing his main reading or writing, for as many hours a day as he can. This will be exceedingly painful if one sits long at first, but a start should be made with short periods and they should be gradually lengthened until one can sit for at least three hours without moving from one's seat.

Men should use the 'bodhisattva posture' at first, and they may, of course, shift the leg posture from time to time, as above explained. The women will sit on the folded cushion, described, and will not change their posture.

***

Comments from the editor: *In answer to questions about the size and filling of the cushions, Mrs Everett replied thus: A 'hassock' would not be suitable, as it would be too firm and you would find that the buttocks would 'go to sleep.' I had two cushions specially made, each about ten inches square, and stuffed moderately hard with cotton filling: these I put one on top of the other on a larger loosely filled cushion. I sit on the two smaller ones, with my legs doubled, one on each side of the cushions used as the seat, and resting, of course, on the larger cushion. I find this quite satisfactory, and more easily arranged than the folded Japanese zabuton. The large cushion should be about three inches in thickness and two smaller ones, stuffed rather harder than the large one, should be at least six inches in height, when placed one on top of the other. They sink considerably when sat on, of course.*

***

The question of the study and solution of the koan is a long one and a most interesting one, but I do not feel that I have done enough work to be able to say much about it. As hereafter explained, I did not quite complete the solution to the first koan. However, this much I can say, the 'answers' which one takes to one's Roshi are not, really, from an intellectual standpoint, *answers to the koan* at all. They are the putting into words, or the attempt to do so, of a continuous series of inner experiences. At first, my 'answer' would take several sentences, but each time the words necessary became fewer and fewer. My last 'answer' consisted of four words only. The final 'answer' must be made without words, but as to whether this is made by a sign, or simple silence, that is a problem I am still working on.

I speak from my own experience only, it must be understood, since no one talks over with another his koan answers.

I was able to make considerable progress in solution of the koan given me; in fact, one night the solution was so near that it seemed as if only the thinnest veil of gauze separated it from me. But I had worked very hard for days, and when this moment came, I was exhausted and could go no further, there was no more strength left in my body. Later my Roshi told me that he had hoped to have me realise the solution that night. I tell you this, not as a matter of accomplishment, for the solution of first koan, while it is a definite step, is such a small one: one knows how there is much, much further to go. But I tell you this because I want you to know that I was able to make what one might call definite and formal progress in Zen. Few foreign people have as yet studied Zen, and I would like those who are really interested to know that it is possible for a foreigner to accomplish something so formal and tangible as the solution of a koan.

As one progresses further, meditation on one's own koan continues through all of one's waking hours, and even, I think, during one's sleep. The most advanced monks are given practically no time at all during the day for formal sitting and yet they must go as many times for 'koan interview' as the young monks who spend the larger part of their waking hours in formal meditation; and yet I am told that the older monks solve their koans faster than the young monks. Meditation becomes a habit of mind, and again the formal side is discarded as much as possible.

***

We now come to what may appear a minor point, but to those who contemplate going to Japan to study Zen at first hand, a very important one, namely, the problem of language. It is impossible and I say that unequivocally, to get a satisfactory interpreter for koan interviews. Interpreters seem to be divided into two classes: those who know nothing at all of Zen and those who know a little. Both have their limitations. The former are inclined, not understanding Zen themselves, to feel the need of understanding each sentence the Roshi speaks before they can interpret it to you. This means that by the time they have understood and got ready to translate the original words, these have been lost; the psychological moment has gone: and that moment is of the utmost importance. The second type are apt to use their own judgement (unconsciously no doubt) in telling to the Roshi just that part of what they want to say that they themselves deem important: and in translating to you the words of the Roshi they again delete or colour with their own interpretation the Roshi's words.

And those words, just as they come at the particular moment at which they come, must be seized. I cannot stress this too strongly.

Now, foreigners will always be liable to labour under this handicap of language, but I hasten to add that even a slight acquaintance with Japanese is very helpful. I found that my knowledge of Japanese, slight as it was, was of the most profound importance to me: and I stress the word *profound*. Any serious student of Zen, or prospective student of Zen, should set himself earnestly to the study of the Japanese language at *home*, before he goes to Japan. This much I may say in explanation: as one's real experiences in meditation continue, the words necessary for the expression of them become fewer and simpler, and the instruction which is given by the Roshi becomes more simple and still more simple. That is how I, with my inadequate knowledge of Japanese, could go to koan interview alone.

Simple and few as the words may be, one should earnestly endeavour to acquire the ability to express them oneself, and one should likewise earnestly endeavour to grasp the words and the meaning of the words in which he replies. Study them over with a dictionary later, as you are bound to do, but get them just as they come from his lips, and somehow just what he means to convey to you, you will be able to get.

Please do not misunderstand what I have said by thinking that there is no one to help with interpretation. There are many people who can help a little, and a few who know English fairly well, who are most earnest and sincere and willing and generous in their desire to help. I am under the greatest obligation to many friends in Kyoto, and I gladly acknowledge my debt to them. But sincere as the desire may be, there are certain things which one cannot do for another, and while the Japanese are eager to learn English and to help English students, we English-speaking students must not put the entire burden upon their shoulders, but should be willing to meet them at least half-way. I am sure any serious student who takes this advice will never regret the time thus spent.

Dr Suzuki makes the ideal Zen interpreter, but he stands alone, for there is no one else who has a thorough knowledge of both Zen and English. He is more than generous with his time and his ability in helping, but one cannot ask such a sacrifice of time from him. He has more important work to do.

***

Some teachers stress the importance of crossing the legs during meditation in order to keep the magnetic currents freely circulating through the body, whereas Zen practitioners appear to place no importance on this, Mrs. Everett replied: I spoke several times to my Roshi about the question of closing the 'magnetic currents,' but he did not seem to think the matter of any importance. He seemed willing to let me sit in a chair, and did not suggest that I should sit otherwise, and I changed to the cushion seat of my own accord; but although he did not seem to lay stress on this matter, I found out later that his really serious acceptance of me as a student began when I changed over to the accepted posture.

I have recently received news from Japan of the formal opening of the Foreign Hospice at the temple of Empukuji, near Kyoto. The Abbot and Roshi of this temple, Rev. Tesshu Kozuki, I grew to know quite well. He is a man of the finest calibre, energetic, sincere and of deep understanding. He is very desirous of having foreign students at Empukuji and has made the most excellent arrangements for their care. The Hospice was finished and furnished before I left, though the grounds were not in order, so can speak as one who has seen. The rooms are small but adequate; the beds are foreign or Japanese style as preferred; so also are the chairs or mats. The sanitary arrangements are the most modern. There is a small kitchen with electric stove and other equally modern equipment for them who prefer to cook their food to taking that of the monks. The Hostel is situated in the beautiful pine forest about five minutes' walk from the monastery itself. The nearest village, Yawata, is about three miles away, and from it Kyoto can be reached by electric train in 30 minutes.

It was the contention of some people, that a mistake had been made in building the Hospice at a place so remote from the general interests of life as Yawata, but if one goes to Japan to study Zen one must be prepared to *really* study it. One must give up all idea of art exhibits, of language study, of Noh plays, and of sightseeing. When one is devoting long hours to Zen meditation, one is trying, as the Roshi explained to me, to rid the mind of discriminative ideas, to leave the world of form for the world of non-form. One should devote oneself to meditation upon one's koan 24 hours a day, not just at formal meditation periods. It is true that one needs some relaxation and some change, and that a little sightseeing can be thrown in, but such must be very superficial and occasional. For the serious student, all thought of any other study than that of Zen meditation should be put aside during the time one gives definitely to this work. That is why I consider the location of the Foreign Hospice at Empukuji so ideal: there are no worldly distractions. Work and meditation and the companionship of nature are the regime for the student of Zen if he really wants to make progress.

Infinite patience, persistence, moral and physical courage are all required, and when one has exhausted all he has of these qualities he begins to realise that he has only begun to make demands upon them. But he will be received with the greatest kindness, and everything possible will be done to assist him in his struggle on the Path. And all the struggle, no matter how hard, and no matter how short the distance one goes, is repaid in infinite measure. But patience above all things, for one is not learning, one is 'becoming,' and any such growth must of necessity be very slow.

Originally published in *Buddhism in England*, May–June 1933.

LOUISE JANIN

1893–1997

An artist involved in the Parisian avant-garde and a Buddhist who used her insights to break down barriers between different artistic genres.

Louise was born on 29 August 1893 in Durham in New Hampshire in the United States to well off parents. The year after the first public library was founded there in 1892, the population at that time was about 900 souls. Significantly, her father was an art collector who largely collected Asian art. He had come from France to New Orleans, where he made his fortune from mining.

The marriage did not last and her mother remarried, and she and Louise moved to San Francisco where in 1906 they lived through the earthquake and the subsequent fire that engulfed the city. Louise attended the California School of Fine Arts from 1911 to 1914 and William Meritt Chase's last summer school in Carmel-by-the-Sea, that ran from July until December 1914. Chase was a leading American artist who had travelled widely in Europe, an impressionist who founded the Chase School which later became Parsons School of design. Louise then travelled to Asia in 1915 with her parents where she was inspired by Buddhism, as well as eastern spirituality and culture in general, in particular Daoism and Hinduism. On her return she worked and exhibited in San Francisco works mainly of an eastern theme, before moving to New York in 1921, where she exhibited in Chicago and St Louis. She then embarked on a European tour, visiting London Italy and Paris.

In 1923 she moved permanently to Paris where her painting was promoted by Édouard Schuré, a writer, Wagnerian musicologist and a leading figure in the Theosophical Movement. His book *The Great Initiates; a Study of the Secret History of Religions* (1889) influenced Louise and others of the *belle époque*. She exhibited at the Bernheim Jeune gallery in 1924. She participated in the 1920s in the Salon des Orientalistes, in the Union of Women Painters

Louise Janin, *Gravure Composition Musicalisme*, 1940.
@ ADAGP, Paris and DACS, London, 2021.

and Sculptors Fair, in the International Exhibition of Modern Decorative and Industrial Arts in 1925, in the Paris Colonial Exposition in 1931, and in the Salon des Tuileries. Personal exhibitions took place in 1924 at the Galerie Bernheim-Jeune, then four years later at the Galerie Georges Petit. In 1924 the National Museum of Franco-American Cooperation at Château de Blérancourt acquired the canvas entitled Le dragon. It is at that time that her figurative paintings began to acquire abstract decorative motifs.

Louise attended the International Exhibition of Modern Decorative and Industrial Arts, which was held in Paris in 1925 to celebrate Modernism, following the World Fair of Paris in 1900 postponed to 1915 and again until 1925 consisting of national pavilions including the Soviet Union, whose pavilion was designed by Konstantin Melnikov and Alexander Rodchenko. Louise describes the exhibition as a 'A milestone in the development of the visual arts, helped to break down the barrier erected by officialdom to separate the fine arts from the applied arts'. La Studium de Louvre used a design of Louis's to make a tapestry 'L'apres Midi d'un Faune' for their pavilion for which she was honoured with an award. The exhibition led to the split between modernism led by Corbousier who argued that art must follow function and those who sought not an either or but a harmonious union of function and beauty as we see in nature that became Art Deco; the Corinthian capital in classical architecture, expresses that spirit, the New York skyscrapers such as the Chrysler building, and music and perfume as essential aspects of life. Louise would have considered Modernism both unnecessary and deplorable.

In 1932 Louise joined the Paris 'musicalist movement', the depiction of music in art, with her friends Henri Valensi, and František Kupka with whom she attended group events. 'Musicalism' was studied by the painter Kandinsky (who it is said had the condition called synaesthesia where by colour and shape is often perceived musically and heard sound is perceived as sound and colour) and led by the idea in Plato's Republic: 'Painting is regulated by the same laws as musical rhythm.' Later this was taken up by the animation of Walt Disney in Fantasia. Louise called some of her paintings Cosmogrammes or Osmotic Painting and used marbling techniques of the ancient Persians.

She was influenced by Japanese scroll painting with textile mounts to improve composition, the mounts the become an intergral aspect of the work itself, which can be clearly seen in some of her paintings of the period that show the Japanese influence. She says of this period 'I had been attracted to the Japanese method of mounting scroll paintings with strips of contrasting brocades which gives tasteful attention to their different widths....From this example I was led to designing picture frames decorated with symbolic motifs, or with oriental fabrics laid between carefully selected mouldings. Some pictures I reasoned might have their composition better integrated and enlarged in this way'.

Louise moved from figurative work to the creation of cosmogrammes (osmotic paintings) derived from her study and interest in Persian marbling techniques. She was particularly interested in work that occurred without the intervention of the intentional will, or when the intervention of intention is supended, taken up later by *avant-garde* artists and composers such as John Cage, a student of Zen Buddhism. Something she doubtless also learnt from her own studies of Buddhism. She explored, as well, the way that immiscible materials come together, in her cosmogrammes. The way that material opposites opposites relate to each other, another Buddhist theme.

Having more or less abandoned literalism she continued to experiment with various techniques and modes of production., wrote poetry and contributed to the *ABC of Art*, *Rhythm*, a journal published in Calcutta and *Leonardo* a journal published by Pergamon Press. It is from *Leonardo* that these quotes are taken.

Following her internment from Corsica where she was living, to a camp in Italy, during the Second World War, she continued to exhibit her work at the Salon of Sacred Art, the Salon of Women Painters and Sculptors, the Salon d'Automne and at the Salon des Indépendants, presenting works that incorporated symbolism, musicality and spirituality that combined figurative material as well as abstraction.

She died on 26 July 1997 at 12, Rue Marthe Edouard Meudon 92190, Île-de-France at the age of 105 and left an artistic legacy that helped dissolve the meaningless barriers that exist between the Fine Arts and the Applied Arts. She was an eager and eternal student much influenced by the spirit of Buddhist philosophy and others which she explored and much of which she expressed in her work. Louise was often commissioned by *The Middle Way*, to contribute her work for the frontispieces.

The texts below accompanied the publication of Louise Janin's artworks, which appeared as frontispieces to *The Middle Way* in the 1930s.

Our Frontispiece January 1930

The picture is a reproduction in black and white of one of the most beautiful paintings of that accomplished Buddhist artist, Miss Louise Janin of Paris, and we are sincerely grateful to her for permission to publish it and for the gift of the copies themselves. The original is in the possession of the French Theosophical Society.

'Mandara', the artist tells us, is a generic name for 'assembly pictures', that is, groups of Buddhist divinities or symbols of the same. Its nearest equivalent in Western theological terminology is the 'Communion of Saints'.

While no detail of the paintings is copied from ancient sources, and from the decorative point of view it is wholly of the artist's imagination, it is all in the mystic tradition of India and archaeologically correct.

Our Frontispiece May 1931

Buddhism is often regarded as a passive, not to say placid form of religion, but an examination of Miss Janin's picture will remove this illusion. Achala, known in Japan as Fudo, is the personification of control. In one hand he holds the cord wherewith to bind the lower passions and in the other the sword wherewith to slay desire.

Unscathed in the midst of the fires of Dosa, Lobha and Moha, he dominates the prostrate figure of the lower self with awe-inspiring calm.

Our Frontispiece June 1930

Our frontispiece this month is a black -and-white reproduction of another of Miss Janin's Buddhist paintings, the subject being the Great Renunciation.

Our Frontispiece May–June 1932

The illustration this month is from the brush of our distinguished contributor, Miss Louise Janin, who thus describes the painting of which this is a photograph: 'The inspiration for this figure, which is over life size, was due to a Japanese drawing in my possession representing Hsuan Wu (Mysterious–Unfathomable) ... Of a similar attitude and an equal (as I hope intensity of facial expression), this painting brings to a Zen conception some entirely personal ideas expressed in the surroundings and in the intense blue of the twilight sky.'

ISALINE BLEW HORNER
MA PhD OBE

(1896–1981)

Gifted Pali Scholar, President of the Pali Text Society and contributor to the understanding and transmission of Buddhism to the west.

Isaline Blew Horner was born in Walthamstow, Essex on 30 March 1896. In 1908, at a garden party in Cambridge, she met Professor TW Rhys Davids, the great Pali scholar, translator and founder of the Pali Text Society; she was 12 and he 65. Impressed by her natural curiosity and intelligence, he suggested that she take up the study of Pali and Sanskrit.

In 1917, she received a BA from Newnham College, Cambridge in Moral Sciences. From 1921, Horner travelled to Sri Lanka (known then as Ceylon), India and Burma, where she was introduced to Buddhism, its literature and related languages. In 1923, she returned to England, where she accepted a Fellowship at Newnham College and in 1928 became the first Sarah Smithson Research Fellow in Pali Studies. In 1930, she published *Women Under Primitive Buddhism*, a work derived from Canonical literature, and the Commentaries, the *Jatakas* and the *Milindapanha*, the *Vinayapitaka* (especially the Bhikkhuni Khandhaka and the Bhikkhuni-Vibhanga), the *Therigatha* as well as scattered references throughout Pali literature. The study reveals the spiritual experiences of some of the lay and almswomen living during and shortly after the lifetime of Buddha and describes the various social conditions that prevailed during this period.

In 1933, Horner edited her first volume for the Pali Text Society, the third volume of the *Papancasudani* (Majjhima Nikaya commentary). In 1934, Cambridge awarded her an MA and from 1939 to 1949 she served on Cambridge University's Governing Body. From 1926 to 1959, Horner lived and travelled with her companion Dr. Eliza Marian Butler (1885–1959), known as 'Elsie', who was Schroeder Professor of German at Newnham and author of numerous books, including the influential *Tyranny of Greece over Germany* (1935) that argued Germany's weakness to ideological thinking had its roots in the study of ancient Greek literature.

Horner received a PhD for Pali language from Ceylon University in 1964, a PhD from Nava Nalanda Mahavihara in Sri Lanka in 1977 and an OBE for Lifelong Contribution to Buddhist Literature in 1980 from HM Queen Elizabeth II.

She was a frequent contributor to *The Middle Way*, a member of The Buddhist Society and Honorary Secretary of The Pali Text Society from 1942, which she became the President and Treasurer of in 1959. It is understood that she spent almost her entire inheritance as sole beneficiary of the family money, on The Pali Text Society, thus enabling it to continue its invaluable work. Ven. Ajahn Amaro, Abbott of Amaravati Monastery in Hertfordshire is her second cousin. She died on 25 April 1981.

The Foundations of Theravada

IB Horner, 1949

Buddhism is a comparatively recent name given in the first place by Westerners to the vast synthetic and syncretic totality of teachings attributed to Gotama, the Buddha, the Sage of the Sakyan clan, and believed to have been uttered by him during his life time, which was one of intensive teaching, in Northern India in the sixth century before Christ.

The sayings and utterances attributed to him were not written down however until as much as about 400 years after his attainment of Nibbana. This totality of teachings, each one of which is so closely interwoven with others that to speak of any one of them is not easy unless there is some knowledge of them all, is usually known as Theravada, or the doctrines and utterances of the Elders – those elder monks who were Gotama's companions and fellow-workers, striving for the same goal and by and large furthering their Master's doctrine, his Dhamma and his teaching *Sasana*. The Sayings were carried in the memory of the disciples and of their disciples – in a succession or various successions of teachers and pupils, until at last, having been sorted out, and 'edited' at various Councils, they were committed to writing and survive now in the Pali canon. The teachings contained in this mass of 'literature' are still followed with more or less exactitude by the peoples in three countries in South East Asia: Ceylon, Burma and Siam. For owing to a variety of causes Buddhism no longer exists in India, where Gotama taught, with the exception of Nepal. But in about 250 BC the great Buddhist Emperor Asoka sent a Buddhist mission from India to Ceylon, and this met with immediate and overwhelming success, many people adopting Buddhism as their way of life as seeming to them preferable to any teaching they had hitherto known. And they, like the peoples of India, had known a great many, and were ripe in their judgments on fundamentally important subjects.

The Councils had been necessary, in face of various splits and disagreements, to decide what should go forth as the most authoritative compilation of the Master's teachings. Never had there been anything sacrosanct about the word of the Buddha – Buddha being a title meaning 'awakened,' awakened to the truth as it really is of things as they really are, *yathabhutam.* Never had Gotama said that his teachings were to be believed in whole as he gave them; he always advocated testing them for yourself. And never had he said that they must be repeated verbatim or else there would be failure, such as was incurred by the contemporary Brahman priests if they made a mistake in repeating their mantras.

Further it was not only not possible to remember all his teachings precisely as he gave them, they were besides not always completely comprehensible – the inner meaning of things said by one who had access to Reality has sometimes escaped the lesser men who have come after him. For what he is said to have said often appears to have an inner meaning in addition to its more obvious meaning; or a meaning that can only be more fully comprehended by knowing its affinities with other parts of the teaching and what exactly it refers to, what else he had in mind at the time. The situation is further complicated for us today because we do not in all cases know what the words meant to the people who used them in the ancient world of India.

So the Buddhism of the Buddha, as it is sometimes called, with its subtleties, its hints, its clear pointing to something more than was actually said in so many words, offered a vast field for exploration, deduction and creativeness. And the field was no barren soil. Buddhism spread to other lands and in the course of time was adopted by them, such as China, Japan and Tibet. Those thinkers in these countries who realised its profundity took various words, points, ideas and lines of teaching they found in Theravada, and, with these as a basis, erected a vast architectonic, devotional, metaphysical, philosophical, often highly intellectual and sometimes unprovable, which they called Mahayana, or the Greater Vehicle for going Beyond. For this, in the Indian idiom, is man's final aim – to go beyond the temporal river of death, Mara's stream, to the timelessness, deathlessness, and consequent security and stability of the Further Shore.

This is the aim, simply and fundamentally, of Theravada: 'to have opened the door to deathlessness.' 'I sound the drum of deathlessness,' are among the first statements that Gotama made after he had won enlightenment. To achieve deathlessness is a great aim. It is not peculiarly Buddhist. It is that of all religion and all folklore, and the catchwords of folklore turned into the signs and symbols of the Perennial Philosophy, to which Buddhism contributes no less than do the other great religions and the great poetry of the world. Under Buddhism, Man's goal may have many names: arahantship, bodhisattvahood, deathlessness, Nibbana, enlightenment or awakening, to become Brahma, freedom or deliverance, or the Highest good, the subtlest reality, *paramattha*. Although Buddhism gives the goal these many names, and there are others besides, and although some of these names, but not all, are peculiar to Buddhism, it is important to realise that the aim itself is not only Buddhist, not only Indian, but universal. Moreover, if we think of Buddhism as a teaching which suddenly blossomed forth owing no derivation to the profoundly experienced and sublime thought which for centuries had preceded it in India, we shall miss a great deal of its wisdom, misunderstand and perhaps misapply it, and the misapprehensions concerning Buddhism – and these have been and still are numerous in the West – will be as great and as lamentable as are the misapprehensions under which the West views Hinduism.

Whatever name is given to the goal in Buddhism, fundamentally freedom, *vimutti*, is implied: 'Just as the mighty ocean has but one taste, that of salt, so does Dhamma have but one flavour, that of freedom.' Freedom, that is, from what is, metaphysically speaking, unreal, and therefore mutable and destructible; and freedom into what is, metaphysically speaking, real, and therefore immutable and indestructible. Always these two spheres are in opposition, but always opposites must be resolved. For this there is the Middle Way, the mean between two extremes. On the one hand there is man as we know him, and in Early Buddhism interest centres on man, not on God, not on the animal kingdom, or on those realms which, although populated by beings, *yakkhas*, *petas*, *devas*, *devatas*, etc., which are not human, and yet in close touch with the world of human beings. On the other hand there is That which man may become, by his own efforts if he follows the Way for going beyond that which is pointed out to him. The Way, middle and causal, is the mean between this pair of opposites: man as he is in the world of empirical consciousness, and man as he may really come to be.

Man is an aggregate of the five *khandhas* or groups of ignorant grasping: after material shape, feelings or emotions, reflex or habitual tendencies, perceptions, and consciousness or mental awareness of sense impressions. These *khandhas* are impermanent, unsatisfactory and not-self. The firs, material shape, *rupa*, may, as body, *kaya*, last for about 100 years; the last, cognition or awareness, changes from moment to moment, as restless as the monkey in the jungle. The very nature of the *khandhas* is their mutability: however pleasant and alluring they may be, they cannot stand firm like the eternal. As Mahayana would say, they have no self-substance. As they fade and pass away, pain is experienced. What is impermanent and therefore painful is not-self. Therefore a wise man, who wants to nuke Self his refuge, stops grasping after the *khandhas*, the groups whence attachments and longing arise. But to come to the stopping place is a long process and can only be fulfilled gradually, *anupubbema*. 'I do not say that the attainment of profound knowledge comes straightaway, but it comes by a gradual practice, a gradual working out of cause, a gradual training.' A man, simply because he is a man, that is while he is in body at all and that is while he is still subject to birth, grasps after all the *khandhas* as not only here and now in this life itself, but also in 'life' as understood by Buddhism. This consists of a series of lives, of recurrent birth and recurrent death, until finally all the residuum for a new life has been cut off and rooted out, and the *khandhas* have no longer any fuel or nutriment, and are hence burnt out or completely cooled and can no longer come into existence. Becoming is now stopped, and the stopping of becoming is one of the 'definitions' of Nibbana. 'Liberating knowledge has taken the place of the ignorance which, since an incalculably distant beginning, has fettered the being in his long, long faring on in which he is chained to the wheel of Samsara. As a means for man to break away from the shackles of this wheel or from the hobble of death (as it is called in the *Rig Veda*), there is the other and opposing Wheel of Dhamma, the Dhamma-cakka. If a man adheres to this rolling wheel, if he plunges into the stream of dhamma and has vision of Nibbana, not only is he a *sotapanna*, one who has entered the stream of dhamma which is a river of Life, but, because he is 'bound for enlightenment,' he can make the plunge into Nibbana itself, *nibbanogadha*. By now he has walked the Walk to Brahman, the *brahmacariya*, which 'is lived for immergence in Nibbana, for going beyond to Nibbana, for culmination in Nibbana.' He has come to the end of the Way, and has no further need for it. It is to be left behind like the raft that has been used for crossing over from the hither to the Further Shore.

Nibbana, besides being a synonym for the Further Shore, is also called the state that changes not. To win it, which may be possible here and now and not merely on the dissolution of the body after dying, demands the destruction of the desire for the impermanent, the (essentially) unsatisfactory, and for those factors which are not-self, rather than the attempt to destroy the *khandhas* themselves. If desire for them is stopped, they will stop; and there will follow birthlessness, the Void or Emptiness of Mahayana and which does not belong to the domain of our relative consciousness.

All this can be done by man himself. His activities, his discipline and training, his true asceticism are to be directed to attaining the Further Shore, the freedom and unshakeability of mind that guarantee for him immunity to all the pleasures and delights, and they are in the long run fraught with pain, by which Mara, the Evil One, has tried to lure him to stay on this Hither Shore, in the tails of the world which here means the world of the senses which are in a man's own fathom-length body. Mara was at Gotama's side all through his life, trying to tempt him to lead a life of ease and pleasure. But Gotama broke through all snares, human and non-human, by his complete comprehension of Truth. He taught the Way of dhamma to others, so that they too might win freedom from pain and death, possible only by self-reliance and self-control. First there are the silos or moral habits to be observed rigorously and constantly for purifying all bodily actions; then there is *samadhi* or contemplation or concentration, for purifying thought; and then there is *panna*, the intuitive wisdom that gives direct access to Reality, to things as they really are.

Originally published in *The Middle Way*, vol. 4, winter 1949.

PRINCESS POON
PISMAL DISKUL
1896–1990

Granddaughter of the King of Siam, who was immortalised in the film The King and I. *A highly educated writer who realised the value of the Thai Buddhist heritage, a moderniser with the 'common touch' who worked for the acceptance of Buddhism throughout the world and supported efforts towards women's understanding of the inner values of the dharma, and true independence of mind.*

Princess Poonpismai Diskul – the granddaughter of Mongkut Rama, King of Siam and the daughter of Prince Damrong – was born on 17 February 1895. Her grandfather, who lived from 1804 to 1868, was best known as King Rama IV, the king that the 1956 musical film *The King and I* is based on.

Princess Poonpismai was educated in the Grand Palace in Bangkok where she grew up, and was taught English, French, History, Geography, Religion and Literature among other subjects. Her best teacher was her own father, Prince Damrong (Prince Damrong Rajanubhab, 1862–1943). She was very close to her father and accompanied him on his travels in Thailand, and later in Europe, and then into exile in Penang following the 1932 revolution. He was a most respected Thai scholar, who was known as 'The father of Thai History', and who founded the National Library of Thailand as well as Thailand's National Museum.

Princess Poonpismai was greatly interested in Buddhist teachings and studied the subject deeply; the dharma being established in her heart. In 1950, she was invited to lecture at San Francisco University for a year. Later, she became a consultant in the Faculty of Buddhism in Chulalongkorn University and Thammasat University, both in Bangkok. She also gave many lectures to institutions all over Thailand.

She was a member of the Standing Committee on Women of The World

Fellowship of Buddhists (WFB), which had branches in many countries, including Australia and Nepal. She was a contributor to *The Middle Way*, the journal of The Buddhist Society and an honoured guest of the Society.

The Thai Royal family continued their visits to The Buddhist Society and donated a shrine room to the Society's headquarters in Eccleston Square, London, which remains unchanged. She was Vice President of the Buddhist Society in Thailand and a member of the Thai delegation to the World Fellowship of Buddhists meeting in Colombo, Sri Lanka in 1953, where she became Vice President. In December 1964 she attended the World Buddhist meeting in Sarnath, India, on the occasion of Buddhist Jayanti – 2500 years since the passing of Buddha – which was also attended by Christmas Humphreys, the King of Sikkim and Princess Poonpismai's niece, Princess Noy Svasti, who is still a member of the Society.

H.S.H. Princess Poonpismai Diskul, was unanimously elected as the first Thai President from B.E. 2506 (1963) and the Headquarters was consequently shifted to Bangkok, Thailand, until 1984, when she was succeeded by H.E. Professor Sanya Dharmasakti.

In B.E. 2512 (1969), at the Ninth General Conference of the World Fellowship of Buddhists, the meeting resolved to make Bangkok the permanent venue of the Headquarters of the WFB. She also founded a library and museum on History and Literature. She published many books on Buddhism, one, written especially for children, *Buddhism for The Young* (1929), which received a prize, as well as the title *Thai Traditions and Customs* (1975) published by Khasem Bannakit. Princess Poon also wrote books on her travels to London, Paris, Soviet Russia, India and America where she travelled for various meetings and seminars. She wrote a Hollywood film script in the 1950s. Her diaries are much read by most educated Thai people. She also wrote several books including *The Relevance of Buddhism in The Modern World* published by the Buddhist Publication Society, Candy, Sri Lanka, in 1969.

In 1984 she became Honorary President of the World Buddhist Federation until her death on August 1990 at the age of 95.

Publications

Buddhism for the Young (1929) Prachandra Press.

Thai Traditions and Customs (1975) Bodhi Leaves No. B 43.

The Three Worlds of Existence

Princess Poon, 1947

The three popularly accepted worlds or planes of existence are Hell, Heaven and Earth. Practically all the religions of mankind lend countenance to such crude belief. Heaven, for example, is pictured as the abode of bliss and is believed to be the place where the good and the just are resting and enjoying the fitting reward of their good lives. Hell, on the other hand, is thought to be that place of torment where sinful souls are placed to expiate their past peccabilities. Frescoes and mural paintings in temples and churches, East and West alike, give ample proofs of the existence of these popular beliefs.

The revolting sight of these gruesome tortures filled me with a sense of disgust, and yet their intended meanings were quite clear to me, notwithstanding the wide gulf between East and West, and I need not wait to be told of the nature of the sins whose punishment was meted out so graphically that I had to admit that, in the vulgar minds the world over, there was no difference in the ideas of punishment at all.[1] Conversely, Heaven was made to appear peopled with hordes of smiling and contented angels ethereally and gracefully floating about and flitting from place to place to the tune of music from the spheres, their cherubic expressions entirely devoid of any sign of toils and moils usually associated with this vale of tears of our world. One cannot help gathering that those who held on to such belief of celestial bliss must have suffered so.

What is to be regarded as the purpose of this world of ours? One would not be far in the wrong to answer that ours is a place of probation, the threshold of those other two worlds, although many are still suffering under the delusion that ours is a place of bliss and are labouring feverishly towards the gratification of their senses. If one were bold enough to look facts squarely in the face one would readily come to the conclusion that it was our past Karma which consigned us to where we are now, to make up for our sins of commission and omission. Then, and then only, will our mind cease from making so many unreasonable demands as to mar its state of serenity. No desire is an end in itself but is always the forerunner of future desires. Hence we are taught to put a curb on our mind, to train ourselves to suffer meekly, to atone for our past misdeeds so that ultimately we will be free. By purging ourselves from all drosses of sins we put an end to the debit side of our nature and destroy further bondage. When we succeed in so doing, we shall pass on to that world of spiritual freedom –call it Nirvana, if you like. There supreme peace reigns, there is no ill-will, hatred, lust of vengeance and no evil karma to cause us to wander aimlessly again in that ocean of Samsara!

All of us are moving towards our destination according to our desert. As long as we continue to burden ourselves with pride, with desires for vengeance, for retrieving lost fortune and for getting even with those who injured us in the past, we shall merely bind ourselves to the three worlds with no chance of escape. In order to gain our spiritual emancipation, to reach the calm shore of Nirvana, we shall have to strive strenuously and shall not merely content ourselves with procrastination and lip-service. The least that we have to do will be, firstly, to avoid all wrong doing, at least by keeping the five precepts of Lord Buddha; secondly, to perform meritorious deeds, to do good ourselves and to help others toward their goals, and lastly, to cleanse our mind of all unbecoming thoughts. In so doing we may look forward with confidence to that for which our souls yearn – the peace of Nirvana. May the Triple Gems of our Refuge inspire us, one and all, to advance further in our effort for doing good.

Translated by Professor Sugit Nimanhaeminde

Notes

1. In our traditionally cosmological Siamese book it was stated those guilty of the sin of unchastity would be compelled to pass aeons of time in climbing up the thorny trunks of the counterpart of the Silk-Cotton tree (*Bombax malabaricum*) in the region under the rule of Yama, the Hindu Pluto, too!

Reprinted from *The Middle Way*, 1947.

DHARMA-MOTHER EKAI

(1899–1999)

***Shin Buddhist who played a vital role
in the formation of the Shogyoji Sangha***

Miyo Nonaka was given her Dharma-name Ekai by
her master, Venerable Daigyo-in Reion Takehara,
and followers of Shogyoji Temple would respect-
fully call her Dharma-mother Ekai. She was
awakened to pure faith under the guidance of
her master at the age of 26 and helped her master
to lead people to the Shin Buddhist faith as his
spiritual interpreter. They cooperated in the creation of the Shogyoji sangha
with pure faith in their hearts.

After the death of her master Dharma-mother Ekai became the effective
leader of Shogyoji Temple for some 40 years, whilst remaining a lay person.
In actual fact she was instrumental in making young people such as my
present master, Venerable Chimyo Takehara and me become Shin Buddhist
priests. Acutely aware of the reality of this world, she gave spiritual advice
and suggestions not only to those who live alongside her in the temple but
also to those who visited the temple, seeking to solve problems in their own
lives. Amongst those followers there appeared social leaders who attained
pure faith, including university professors and managing directors of major
Japanese companies.

Being aware of the importance of international harmony, she was
very happy to see young followers going abroad to work or study. It
was in this context that she sent me to DT Suzuki so that I could learn
Buddhism under his tutelage. As a result, at the request of Venerable
Chimyo Takehara, I have been in London for over 26 years, enjoying wonderful encounters with good friends both British and Japanese.

Text by Kemmyo Taira Sato, Japanese Shin Buddhist Priest, Abbot of Three Wheels Temple, Acton,
London, instrumental in the Reconcilliation of war veterans. Author of *Living in Nenbutsu* and *Living
with Thanks*, *The Haiku of Buson*, *The Haiku of Issa*, all published by The Buddhist Society Trust.

On the Way to the Land of Happiness

Dharma-Mother Ekai, 2020

I am supremely happy to have encountered Buddha's teaching, for it has enabled me to live freely and unobstructedly in this world of hardship known as the 'ocean of impassability.' I am extremely grateful for the chance to restart my life as a human being.

The seventh chapter of the *Tannisho* reads:

'The *nenbutsu* is the single path that knows no obstruction. This is because the gods of heaven and earth bow down in reverence before one who practises the *nenbutsu* with pure faith. No *maras* (demonic beings) or heretics (non-Buddhists) can obstruct such a person. No evil deed can bring upon him karmic retribution, nor can any form of good equal his *nenbutsu*. Therefore it is called the single that knows no obstruction.'

Now, in the light of Buddha's teaching, I know that the 'gods of heaven and earth,' '*maras*' (demonic beings) and 'heretics' (non-Buddhists) stand for all the blind passions that lie latent in my mind.

Ignorant being as I am, were it not for Buddha's teaching I would have ever remained confined to the darkness of those blind passions, a prisoner of my own deeds. Throughout my life I would have had to go on suffering the agony produced by the turmoil arising within me from the differences between myself and others. However, I was vouchsafed the wonderful experience of transcending this desperate predicament. What supreme happiness I have achieved!

As I humbly reflect on this, a thousand emotions crowd my mind, tears stream down my cheeks unceasingly and I have to lay down my pen for a while. Scene after scene from my past life passes before my eyes as on the reel of a film. What an incredible thing it is I have attained! I am the happiest person alive. Embraced in a vast and infinite compassion, I will forever remain on the single path that knows no obstruction. As I think of this, *nenbutsu*, imbued with a deep sense of gratitude, wells up within me; 'Namuamidabutsu, Namuamidabutsu.'

In fact it was all those around me that enabled me to reach this place. Whether good or bad, all of them came to me as gifts from Tathagata. Through all these transformed Buddhas I came to realise the great compassion of the true teacher or the principal Buddha himself.

When I was young my father's house was almost destroyed by some close relatives. In addition to this traumatic experience, I was seized with a terror of death every time I witnessed a funeral taking place at a Shingon temple, which happened to be located very near our home. Thus I lived a restless life, beset by darkness.

At the age of 27, however, there came to me the solution to the great and mysterious riddle of life and for the first time I experienced complete peace of mind. It was the evening of 5 April, in the middle of spring four years ago, in that unforgettable temple at Futsukaichi, Shogyoji, that this momentous event took place.

Our teacher has decided to publish a commemorative pamphlet about our movement's opposition to the 'Religious Organisation Bill' and has allowed me to contribute as a member of this religious community, a community that came into being quite spontaneously as a result of our attempts to try and solve the problems of life and death. Hence I would like, with the deepest gratitude, to describe the way of leaving this saha-world of illusion and suffering.

Ever since I could remember, my mind had known no unity, always divided against itself, and my life for the past 20 years or more had been nothing but a continuous train of private struggles against others. According to Buddhist teaching all this was because of my ignorance, dating back from time immemorial. As a young girl, despite my eagerness, I had not been able to enter secondary school. Furthermore, without a roof over my family's head I had been unable to experience the normal joys of childhood. Later on with my husband I had known none of the usual happiness of marriage. In my darkness I was blindly probing the mysteries of life. My sad and wretched existence in those days was like that of a wanderer lost in the vast wilderness of Siberia. There can be no justification for living like that.

On the other hand, as I rapidly became more and more introspective, I also became aware of my own past karma at work within me. Immersed in books in an effort to train my mind, visiting town-halls to attend lectures by prominent men of the time, I did my best to enlighten myself. However my efforts were all unavailing. I could not help but lament my mental weakness when, on being faced with a very real problem, my conceptually conditioned mind melted away like frost beneath the rising sun.

Later on in life, I damaged my stomach and bowels. Accompanied by my mother, I went to the Funagoya hot spring to recuperate and stayed at an inn called Gyokusenkan. Unexpectedly this spa became an unforgettable place for me and one where I took my first step towards the attainment of faith. While there I fell into conversation with a certain Mr Zenjo Arita, a student who had also come to the hot springs to recuperate and was staying in the room next to mine. Mr Arita told me, 'If you continue with this method of spiritual training of yours, you will have to spend the rest of your life seeking after truth and end up tracing only a very gradual path of self-improvement. You may not reach the summit where lies the mind of peaceful awareness.' I was astonished at this simple statement and the student took on for me an air of great nobility. This was the first time I had ever been given such an intimation. Ever after I aspired with all my heart to the acquisition of the 'peaceful awareness' of Shinran Shonin (親鸞聖人のご安心). Soon afterwards, my elder brother died from stomach-cancer at the age of 48. My longing for 'peaceful awareness' became more intense, compelling me to seek the truth without delay.

However, as I lacked the wisdom to choose a teacher to help me achieve emancipation (*vimoksa*), I was unable to determine how I should proceed. Thus, I once more returned to the realities of daily life and was engulfed in an even deeper sadness than before.

Around that time, too, my husband was transferred from the Fukuoka police school where he had been a teacher of *kendo* to Futsukaichi police station in accordance with the annual changeover amongst officials of the Fukuoka Prefecture police. It was because of his unfortunate demotion that I first came to encounter my true teacher, Takehara-sensei.

Takehara-sensei is the person who really saved me from the transmigration of birth and death. His sermons, always seemingly self-contradictory, were mysterious and way beyond my understanding; they all presented a powerful challenge to the way I had been thinking. This made me reflect deeply upon every word he said. Although the books and lectures I had read or attended up till then in my search for instruction had been comprehensible enough when one thought about them, nothing had ever moved me to my heart's core. What he taught was way beyond this world and wholly unattainable by whatever means one tried. It was only natural therefore that I, an ordinary ignorant human being, was unable to understand his discourse based as it was upon his own wonderful experience of the transcendental Dharma realm. Finally I began to lament out loud, saying 'Sensei, please help me enter your state of enlightenment.'

I felt that, if only I could solve the riddle of life set out in his sermons, it would be the moment of fulfilment of Amida Buddha's Original Vow within my own self. I believed that in this devout and pious priest, filled with adoration and overflowing with the joy of faith in a way I had never before witnessed in anyone, there was to be seen evidence of one who had attained the truth of life. I found I was desperately fighting to reach that goal myself. All his words, on the other hand, were diametrically opposed to my way of thinking. What is more, he would unexpectedly uncover my innermost mind. Though I would blush with shame, it never seemed to hold him back and it appeared at times as though he were pitying me. Sometimes crying, sometimes resentful, I could not help but go to hear his teaching. In this way I continued to go and listen to him morning and evening over a period of four months. When I recollect those days, I cannot hold back my tears. I feel so entirely indebted to this one teacher.

It was in order to solve in my mind the problem of transmigration through birth and death that I first started to listen to Buddhist teachings. I wanted to become a strong and resolute person. Thoroughly disgusted with my obscure and rootless frame of mind, which would brighten up or cloud over according to circumstances, I began to feel an earnest desire to become like Sensei, who with humble reverence practised day and night the three minds (三心) and the four ways of *nenbutsu* practice (四修). This ardent desire of mine lead to my forming a heroic resolution. I began to study Buddhist teaching very hard. The harder I studied, however, the more mystified I became. At times I would feel angry with my teacher, at other times with myself for my lack of intelligence, but I kept keeping myself awake night after night, thinking and thinking. This of course was not any sufficient reason to return to my previous spiritless way of life. Nevertheless, though I was learning the hard way and suffering a great deal, I could not gain the enlightenment of True Suchness. For about four months I went back and forth between home and temple, my mind in utter darkness. At the temple I was being taken to task for my apparent overconfidence, at home I was being admonished by my husband. Finding myself utterly unable to solve the problem of Rebirth in the Pure Land, I was almost on the verge of a nervous breakdown. My powers of comprehension seemed impossibly limited and I would moan over and over again, 'It is hopeless now. What can I do?' while the tears streamed down my cheeks. Nor did I even have the strength to wipe them away.

At long last, however, around three o'clock on the fifth of April 1925, a whole new spiritual dimension finally opened up to me. Although I had been told Shinran Shonin had indeed reached such a point, merely hearing such a thing about someone else without actually experiencing it at first hand would never have been enough for me.

On that day, in the room next to the one with the family Buddha shrine, Sensei addressed me and his wife saying, 'I know you have done your utmost to meet the Buddha. But what is the Buddha: a solid, a liquid, a gas?' All of a sudden my heart was in my mouth. The image of Amida Buddha, which I had revered since my earliest childhood, arose before my eyes and all at once its physical manifestation, which I had thought to be but an idol, started to move! So pleased was I with this that I blurted out, 'Now I can see that the Tathāgata does not dwell far from here, beyond many billions of Buddha-worlds. Illuminated by his great benevolent Light, the conceptions I held of law and morality have all vanished. I have come upon a vast world without limit.' But immediately Sensei snapped back at me, 'There is no such Buddha. Don't just make up any Buddha you please!' Scarcely had I time to feel a stab of anguish, then my mind like a magnet was drawn towards all those familiar faces, people I had loved as well as hated. Immediately, the difference between friend and foe simply melted away. I had had no time to answer Sensei before I discovered a world resplendent.

It was the experience of a single moment. All those distinguishing lines I had so carefully drawn were gone. Unceasingly, in gratitude, *nenbutsu* poured from my mouth. Tears filling his eyes, Sensei too was very happy. Just then a traveller came in and asked Sensei's sister to give him money for the train fare to Hakata. Suddenly Sensei stood up and went out to see the man himself. Afterwards Sensei's wife said to me, 'To have acted like that Sensei must have been really and truly overjoyed. I am very surprised to see him actually speaking to the traveller himself.' Having witnessed my attainment of faith, Sensei's wife then felt able to draw close and confide in me saying, 'I still don't quite understand. That ultimate instant of time (decisive moment of spiritual awakening) Shinran Shonin speaks of, it was that moment when *nenbutsu* burst out of you, wasn't it?' 'No,' I answered emphatically. 'It was that final moment of our talk when Sensei was reproaching me.' Tears of gratitude welled up in my eyes. Namuamidabutsu.

It was in this way that I attained faith, guided and tempered by Sensei's exquisite and perfect faith in Other Power. However, on the harsh stage of real life, my faith comes very close at times to being overcome by the karma I once thought I had rid myself of for ever. At such times there awakens in me the urge to take refuge in the infinite compassion of Amida. Alone, I return to the abode of the Inconceivable Honoured One, calling Namuamidabutsu, Namuamidabutsu.

> Boundless is the ocean of suffering
> of birth and death
> Where since time immemorial
> we have been submerged;
> Only the vessel of Universal Vow
> assures our safe passage.

Originally published in *The Middle Way*, vol. 95, no. 1, May 2020

LI GOTAMI

(1906–1988)

An unconventional trailblazer, artist photographer, traveller, convert to Tibetan Buddhism, and wife of Lama Anagarika Govinda.

Li Gotami was born Rati Petit in Bombay in 1906 to a wealthy aristocratic Parsi family who owned a hospital. She was strong willed and showed an aptitude for art early on. Privileged and educated in England she attended school in Harrow on the Hill and then the Slade School of Art in 1924. She travelled extensively across Europe, before returning to India in the 1930s, where she was a co-founder of the Camera Pictorialists of Bombay, an international movement that sought to make photographs more than representational records and for photography to be recognised as an art.

After a short marriage with the art collector and critic Karl Khandalavala she went to Shantiniketan, Rabindranath Tagore's famous Vishwa Bharati University in Bengal, against her parents' wishes. For 12 years, Rati studied the art of Bengal painting with Nandalal Bose and Abanindranath Tagore, who was so impressed by Rati's paintings that he became her mentor.

Rati also began to learn Manipuri dance, earned diplomas in arts and music and was a student of Lama Anagarika Govinda, a Bolivian-German Professor who also taught the future Prime Minister of India, Indira Ghandi (nee Nehru, daughter of Jawalal Nehru).

Rati and Anagarika Govinda were married in 1947 when she converted to Mahayana Buddhism and adopted the name Li Gotami, which was a shock for her orthodox Parsi family, who relinquished their support of her for many years. Li and Govinda travelled to remote places in Tibet and to Mount Kailash and she underwent enormous hardships in the cold Tibetan winter when taking unique photos in the dark temples of Tsaparang, the ancient capital of Guge Empire, with her little Kodak box camera, and copying the fresco tracings, which had never before been allowed in Tibet. These images of frescoes, published in the book, *Tibet in Pictures* (1979), which she co-authored with Govinda, are the last documentary evidence of the Golden Age of Tibetan Buddhism from the eleventh century prior to the mindless destruction of Tibet's cultural heritage by the cultural revolution following the occupation of Tibet by Chinese forces in 1950. Li also wrote poems, which she published in *Tibetan Fantasies: Paintings, Poems and Music* (1979).

Their travels then led them to Ajo Repa Rinpoche, one of Govinda's teachers and they were initiated in the Kagyu tradition of Tibetan Buddhism. Rinpoche predicted that Li would become a famous artist if she devoted her life to the Dharma. In 1949, Li returned to India with Govinda to live in the home of Walter Evans-Wentz, the great scholar of Tibetan Buddhism.

Li and Govinda subsequently founded Kasar Devi Ashram near Almora in the Kumaon Hills of Northern India, which had 40 acres of land. Li grew beautiful flowers there and powerfully protected the trees in this small paradise, which was endangered by the local people who tried to cut down the trees within the estate for wood. The ashram became so popular with the Beat Generation that they had to close their doors and open it only for a few hours in the afternoon for public talks and teachings. Some of the visitors reported that Li was like a dharma protector and chased everybody away to make sure that Lama Govinda could write his books undisturbed. She later said that, despite living with no electricity or running water and in spite of the leopard who visited when she wanted to fetch water from the spring nearby, their years there had been the happiest of her life.

Li and Govinda were great friends with Christmas Humphreys, the prolific author and founder of The Buddhist Society in London and were entertained at his beautiful home in St John's Wood and at The Buddhist Society in Eccleston Square, where Govinda gave teachings and contributed to *The Middle Way*. After Li developed Parkinson's and Govinda suffered a series of strokes, they emigrated to California and were looked after by Alan Watts and the San Francisco Zen Centre. In 1985, Govinda died laughing, of a heart attack. Li returned to India and spent her final three years with her wonderful and caring nieces until her death in 1988.

Painting by Li Gotami

Li Gotami and her husband Anagarika Govinda with a Tibetan Lama

Li Gotami and Anagarika Govinda

Freda Bedi: A Spiritual Odyssey

1911–1977

Norma Levine, 2018

This text is an edited version of a talk by Norma Levine commissioned
by the Buddhist Society and published in *The Middle Way*.

Ordained Buddhist Nun, international diplomat, instrumental in bringing Tibetan Buddhist lamas to the west.

The spiritual odyssey of Freda Bedi is a story that spans cultures, dimensions and consciousness. Freda's life was an epic journey set against the background of the greatest movements of the twentieth century: Marxism, the Great Depression, the rise of Fascism, the Second World War, Gandhi's anti colonialism, Indian Independence and Partition, the Tibetan diaspora, and the explosion of the 1960s counterculture.

'I met Freda Bedi not in her life but in her death.' So begins The Odyssey of Freda Bedi. My first experience of Freda was at Sherabling in 1980 when I was building a retreat house on a hillside and Ani Pema Zangmo, Freda's attendant, was building a nunnery. Zangmo walked fast and talked fast, mostly about Mummy-la whom she revered. What she talked about was Mummy's passing, it seemed, into nirvana. Yes, Mummy was sitting upright in meditation, there were rainbows, and her body didn't decay. Of course, I listened and asked a few questions. Was she doing *phowa* [one of the six yogas of Naropa][1], did she do a lot of retreats, where did it happen, did any of the lamas confirm it? I did get a few answers, but no one seemed to know much about that event and that made me feel a bit suspicious. I knew Tibetans 'saw' things that we didn't. Then Zangmo disappeared. She jumped the invisible wall during the Karmapa controversy and disappeared over the other side. There was no more communication. I tucked away this information in my mind and left it there.

Decades later when I was collecting stories about the sixteenth Karmapa, I went to see Freda's eldest son Ranga in Bangalore. He said he didn't have much to say about the sixteenth Karmapa but he had his mother's archives. The visit was intense and light-filled; intense because he talked for many hours about Freda or Mummy and he showed me her archives and the family shrine where her ashes were kept along with her Tibetan texts. The room was the guardian of the whole house and though dark, it was also light. It had an incredible lightness of being.

I asked him about his mother's death. His reply confirmed some, not all, of Zangmo's story and it became central to my thoughts about her again. Before I left he said, 'The ball is in your court if you want to write a book about Mummy.'

I soon became fascinated by her story. She was born in Derby in 1911 into a working-class family, in what's known as the north of England – the imaginary line that divides England into north and south and its inhabitants by class and geography. The north is mostly industrial, votes labour and is working class. The south is conservative, has most of the public schools for the privately educated elite, and is where the wealth, power and privilege lies.

I had imagined her as a memsahib, a British upper-class woman, a vestige of the Raj. But she came from what Harold Evans dubbed the respectable working class. Her father was a watchmaker but he hardly had a chance to ply his trade before he was called up to serve in the First World War and died at the Battle of the Marne when Freda was seven. So not even middle-class prosperity and stability in her formative years, but BOOM! as German zeppelins bombed the town and young men went away never to return. The only prosperity in the family came from her grandfather who was a coal contractor in the Peak District. The family embodied the values of the upwardly mobile working class, conventional norms of which Margaret Thatcher would have been proud. Although she was born into a typical non-religious Christian family, what set her apart was her interest as a child in the mystical side of Christianity. Every day before going to school she would sit in the local Chapel and meditate for an hour.

Later Freda, who was bookish, made it into the best secondary school, Parkfield Cedars, and became head prefect. Her family's status climbed a few notches into the safety net of the middle class.

Not privileged by class, income nor geography. Even her accent, which must have been regional at some point in her early years, marked her out as coming from the wrong side of the tracks. How did she make it into that bastion of male privilege – Oxford?

And how did she look so much the memsahib?

A twist of fate made her take the entrance exams to Oxford and she was admitted to St Hugh's, one of four women's colleges. She won a small bursary, enough to keep her, and there she awakened to the best of twentieth-century philosophy, politics and science: Albert Einstein, Mohandas Gandhi, Harold Laski, Rabindranath Tagore …

It was there at Oxford that she met her soulmate, BPL Bedi, a Sikh descendent in the lineage of Guru Nanak. He was a Marxist. She showed him a drawing she had made as a child and he identified it as a Buddha. Their pre-marital sexual relationship followed by an interracial marriage broke all the conventions of race and sex at the time. It caused a furore at Oxford and although her mother went to the ceremony at the drab registry office in Oxford, she actually didn't approve it either.

Although she graduated with only a third-class degree, Oxford was the re-making of her. The thoroughly English country girl learned to stand alone, to act on her ideals and to break the mould. She made the kind of friends, like Barbara Castle, and Olive Shapley, originator of BBC Radio 4's *Women's Hour*, who would be in positions of power. Her accent softened and became clear as cut glass and she eventually attained that combination of serenity and sheer nerve that marks the upper class.

Freda and BPL left for Berlin where their first child, Ranga, was born just before Hitler came to power in Germany. Leaving behind the Great Depression of the 1930's and the rise of Fascism that led to World War Two, their journey continued to India where they became political activists in Gandhi's Quit India movement and Bedi, though not violent, became a saboteur. They both spent time in prison, Freda only three months as a satyagraha, and Bedi six years in total.

They never had much money because they lived out their ideals. They moved from a fine villa with servants to rent free thatched huts in agricultural fields on the border of Model Town in Lahore. Their hut became a gathering place for artists, poets and leftist revolutionaries. A second child was born when they lived in Lahore. Tilak Zaheer (named after two revolutionaries) died in infancy due to preventable causes while Freda was occupied with fomenting dissent among Punjabi peasants. She was so accustomed to the suffering of the human condition by then that she could dismiss it. 'All in a day's work,' she wrote in a letter to Olive.

India's independence was born in the blood of partition; Gandhi was assassinated, and their next child, Kabir, was born. They then moved to Kashmir to help in the refugee crisis following partition, when terrorists from Pakistan invaded Kashmir to protest the Kashmiri decision to align with India. Freda was hands-on working in the camps. BPL was adviser to his political comrade, Sheikh Abdullah who became the first Prime Minister of Kashmir.

After the refugee crisis was over, there was a lull in Freda's life. She felt lost with nothing to do and began to study religions. First Hinduism, then Islam, practising each for one year. But nothing clicked.

After a few years in Kashmir the two comrades, Sheikh Abdullah and BPL fell out over political policy and the family moved to Delhi where Freda worked for the Government of India Social Welfare Board. She went into villages working together with the local people. It was this work that earned her an award on International Women's Day from Indira Gandhi.

In 1953 a new door opened in her life. She became part of a three member UN mission to re-organise social services in Burma and entered Swadgam Pagoda in Rangoon. It was there that she encountered the great master Sayadaw U Tittila. After a few weeks of vipassana meditation, the locked door of the mind opened. She had a profound experience of sunyata and fell to the ground, unconscious. That was her entry into Buddhism.

At this stage both Freda and her husband BPL no longer looked to politics to solve the world's problems. They had breakdowns or spiritual breakthroughs, though not at the same time. They both became non-communicative for a month or more; eating nothing, saying nothing, staring into space. And both made a natural slow return without medication, or psychiatric help. BPL became a healer in Italy where he lived the remainder of his life. They led separate lives but were symbiotic, entwined first as comrades and then as spiritual souls. And Freda – that's the best and most extraordinary part of the story. Through the Tibetan refugee camps in Assam where she became known as Mummy-la, the Young Lamas Home School which she founded to train incarnate lamas to teach in the West, and ultimately in a most extraordinary intimate relationship with the sixteenth Karmapa, she found not only the right place for her activity but also the truth she had been seeking all her life. She was the driving force behind the sixteenth Karmapa's tour to the West in 1974, his emissary and adviser. Many of the photos from that period show the relationship between them, somehow indescribable in words.

In 1968 Olive Shapley, one of her best friends from Oxford, visited Rumtek monastery to see Freda who had recently taken ordination as a nun. She brought her son Nick Salt with her and an Uber tape recorder to interview Freda. When she died she left a stack of tapes to her son Nick who kept them uncatalogued in his farmhouse in Wales until one day he realised he had some valuable archival material. When I heard about this I drove down many narrow winding roads to his farmhouse and listened to the recordings. Olive Shapley greeted her friend, transformed from the Mona Lisa – as she had been known at Oxford – into a plump nun with a shaved head in shapeless maroon robes living in a primitive Tibetan monastery in Sikkim – with the standard courteous opening line, 'You haven't changed a bit!' And then asked her about how she came to be there. So here is Freda in her own words talking about her spiritual odyssey.

An Interview with Freda Bedi conducted by Olive Shapley

Olive Shapley: By what road have you come to this? Here you are in this monastery in Sikkim, a very remote part of the world; what has brought you here?

Freda Bedi: You mean, what is my life story? I was born in Derbyshire, in Derby; funnily enough in a place called Monk Street. After that I lived in the countryside near Derby – of course, now it must be a suburb of Derby – a place called Littleover. And I had a very pleasant country childhood. I went to a secondary school in Derby and then to Oxford. While I was at Oxford I broke away from what one could call my Christian background.

Of course, what brings you to a life of meditation, life as a Buddhist nun, life in a monastery, is a deep thing. It's something that goes on for years and years and years; it doesn't come quickly. It was rather like a subterranean stream that went on underground all the while I was leading a very active life which finally emerged. At that point, I realised that was the mainstream.

OS: Just to go back for a moment, how strong was your Christian background as a girl?

FB: My father was a deeply religious man. He was killed in the First World War when I was quite a child. I was sent to church and Sunday school as a child. I don't think my mother had any strong religion herself, but she had a feeling that she should bring up her children in a good Christian way and sent us to church.

I was always interested, especially in the Old Testament. And when I was about 14 I was confirmed in the Church of England. I took great interest in the mystical side of the Christian religion. I don't like the word 'mystic' very much, I mean the deeper side of the Christian religion. I think my first interest in meditation began there. I read the lives of the founders of the Anglo-Catholic movement, Cardinal Newman and other Catholic saints; the two St Teresas. I felt that this was something that I must find out more about.

This busy life of a girl going to school and doing all kinds of school work and studying for examination, it used to trouble me a lot and I felt I needed peace. I used to go to church in the early morning everyday – before going to school – for about an hour and sit there quietly, which I suppose is not a usual thing to do. I never told anyone I was doing it, either.

When I got to Oxford, suddenly a lot of doors opened and I understood something about different religions and ways of thought; a country girl, going to Oxford. At that time, I didn't really know what to do, but one thing I was sure about was that the Christian religion was not the final answer as far as I was concerned. I'd nothing against the Christian religion – I still haven't, in fact, I think all religions are good – but I felt it wasn't the final answer for me, and I must have the freedom of finding out for myself. At that time, I stopped going to church.

Then I lead the ordinary life of a university student. While I was at Oxford I met an Indian student. I felt very interested in and connected with India. This was a natural interest; of course, as a Buddhist I think it may be something to do with my samskaras as we called them, or the thought formations coming from former lives. That's how we explain these inclinations.

I got married shortly after taking my degree and came to India about a year later. That was in 1934. When I reached India, although I should have felt strange being in a strange country, I felt very much at home. I love India, from the moment I put my foot on Indian soil. It's been a real home to me. Not that I didn't love England, I did love England, and I still have feeling for England, land of my birth. But there was something very, very deep in my love for India although I couldn't really speak the language or communicate.

In the beginning, we lived in the Punjab, which is my husband's home. It was a time of great stress in India; it was the time of the freedom movement.

Both of us were full of idealism about the Independence of India and took part in the movement, but that's a long story I needn't go into. Anyway, it was a very busy life: I was bringing up a family, my first child was born in 1934; I was a lecturer in one of the first colleges for women in the Punjab, in Lahore; I used to write and move about a lot in the villages (mostly on this work connected with the Independence movement). It was a very, very full life, but still that feeling persisted; that I must find out the meaning of life, the meaning of suffering. Why and what and how – all the things one asks.

In about 1937 I met a very interesting English woman (I don't know if she's still living). She used to be a big pianist at one time, she later became a Hindu Swami. She said to me, 'If you're interested in these deeper things, why don't you meditate?' She told me one or two things about meditation and from that – it was just an ordinary conversation, it wasn't really a lesson – I started meditating on my own and found it so absorbing; so revealing and satisfying. I used to try to keep on doing it and I meditate also before writing; it helped me a lot, it helps the creative side of life. When I went into the Himalayas in summer (it's very hot in the plains in India) then I used to have periods of meditation.

Nobody knew about it really, except my own family, of course, all my family knew.

I used to take interest in practically all the Eastern religions. I didn't choose between any of them, I didn't get converted to any of them. I used to read Sri Ramakrishna and the life of Guru Nanak, my husband comes from the family of Guru Nanak –

OS: That's the Sikh leader?

FB: Yes, the founder of the Sikh religion. My husband comes from the descendants of Guru Nanak. I also used to read the *Quran Sharif*, which is the Muslim's holy book; *The Bhagavad Gita*, which is the main book of most Hindus; some mystic poems from different religions, and the Bible still. I used to keep the books on my table and just pick them up and think about them and meditate. The meditation was not on anything. It was an attempt to reach beyond the mind.

To cut a long story short, I had a very busy life. After Independence we naturally remained in India. We were living in Kashmir and in Delhi. I was working as a social worker and a writer most of the time; bringing up my family (I had three children by then). Still this interest was very deep in my mind.

In 1953, I got the opportunity to go to Burma for six months with the United Nations' Social Services Planning Commission. It was very interesting. Because I had to go for six months, I had to leave my family behind for that short period so I had more time to meditate. While I was there, I met a most remarkable Buddhist teacher, a very remarkable monk, who had been in England for 14 years through the last war, had been in ARP [Air Raid Precautions] and through other things, who really understood England and was a very saintly person. He taught me meditation on my request. It was then, after about eight weeks, I got my first flash of understanding, or call it more than that. It changed my whole life. I felt that, really, this meditation had shown me what I was trying to find. Something of it at least I understood and I got great, great happiness; feeling as though I'd found the path.

Although I really didn't know much about Buddhism at that time, I felt the Buddha had been 'the leader supreme,' or 'the guide supreme,' and therefore that I should take the Buddhist faith. I told my family about this, everybody was very understanding and I became a Buddhist.

That was in 1953, then in 1956 His Holiness the Dalai Lama came to Delhi with a lot of Buddhists from all over the world for the 2500 anniversary celebrations for Lord Buddha and I got his blessing then.[2] In the meantime, I was studying meditation with another very wonderful Burmese guru, Venerable Mahasi Sayadaw, to whom I'm always grateful. I went to Burma two or three times, carrying on a full life as a mother and doing a government job as a social worker; I was editing a social worker magazine.

This went on until 1959 when the Tibetans refugees came into India and at that time I felt a great wish to help them. I felt with my particular background, both as a Buddhist and as a mother and social worker, perhaps I could help in the refugee camps. The upshot of that was I was sent, on my own request, to one of the transit camps near the frontier. I worked with the Tibetan refugees for about six months helping the mothers and babies and doing all things women can do, and also getting to know the lamas and understanding their problems.

There were many lamas, I think the percentage must have been about a quarter of the total refugees. Nobody quite knew what to do with them; they couldn't understand why they couldn't do the ordinary sort of work. They thought they were shy of work which wasn't true because they worked terribly hard even in their monasteries. But they have to have the right sort of work because, after all, they've given up everything to be a lama. Everything that all human beings want: a home, family, comfort, the freedom of moving around and so on. Why have they given up it all? There's some reason for it and they're not going to give it up without a wrench. Of course, there are the few who come into contact with modern life and naturally give up their robes and decide to take to a lay life, but that's different. Those who are really dedicated, we have to find out really what they want to do and how to help them keep the tradition alive because it's very deep and very beautiful.

We say of the teaching of the Buddha, that it's beautiful in the beginning, beautiful in the middle and beautiful at the end. It is the way across the ocean of suffering in the world. When you once realise the suffering of the world then you've realised there is a way across it. That is the time when you take the renunciation and you feel the only thing really worth doing is not the physical, actual work of the world, but helping the minds of people. Helping them to overcome the suffering that every human being has.

Norma Levine's talk conclusion

When Freda took Olive to meet the Dalai Lama he asked, 'What do you call Khechog Palmo?' Olive answered, 'I call her Freda.' The Dalai Lama promptly replied, 'I call her Mummy.'

This is the story of a woman who was far ahead of her time, an early feminist and spiritual seeker, a working mother of three (the actor Kabir Bedi is one of them), an activist and the first woman to receive full ordination as a Buddhist nun.

Her contemporary, Didi Contractor, had this to say about her:

From the beginning Freda was a romantic looking for a noble cause. At the same time if she wanted something, it happened. There was always about her the epitome of the English schoolgirl. She was a practical earthy woman with her mind in the sky. She kept moving as people do when they are on a journey.

As Ayang Rinpoche says, 'Freda Bedi was first a worldly lady, finally she became a great spiritual lady. She was very great, not an ordinary lady. She was definitely a tulku or emanation. I believe she was a dakini.'

She remained in meditation at death, with all the signs of enlightenment, the first Westerner to attain that exalted state.

Notes

1. Transference of consciousness at the time of death.

2. Buddha Jayanti.

Norma Levine also known as Naomi Levine is an author, businesswoman, speaker and Buddhist practitioner. She started Windhorse, importing Buddhist meditation artefacts. Her books include *Stepping Stones: Crossing the River of Samsara, A Quest for the Hidden Lands, Kailash: Precious Snow Jewel, Chronicles of Love and Death: My Years with the Lost Spiritual King of Bhutan* and *The Miraculous 16th Karmapa.*

Reprinted from *The Middle Way* Vol. 93 no.2 August 2018

Chogyam Trungpa Rinpoche, Freda Bedi, Choje Akong Tulka Rinpoche

Freda Bedi with (on her right) Trungpa Rinpoche, Ringu Tulku and Akong Rinpoche

The Collected Letters of Alan Watts

(1915-1973)

Joan and Anne Watts, 2019

Daughters of Alan Watts and granddaughters of Ruth Fuller Everett Sasaki, editors of The Collected Letters of Alan Watts and international speakers.

This text is an edited version of a talk given by Joan and Anne Watts on the occasion of the launch of *The Collected Letters of Alan Watts* at The Buddhist Society, 20 July 2019.

Joan Watts: I will read a little bit of history, some of which you may or may not know, which was in the foreword of my book. It was an interesting experience for the two of us putting this together, because we play a role in his letters; we are mentioned, and it is a microcosm of us growing up as well.

Alan Watts. It is amazing to us what mentioning this name at a social gathering will often evoke. Overwhelmingly, the reaction is, 'You've got to be kidding, he's your father? His books changed my life.' Other reactions have included statements such as, 'May I kiss your feet?' 'Can I touch you?' or, 'You seem too normal to be his daughter!'

Alan Watts, philosopher and interpreter of Eastern philosophy and religions and Christian doctrine, had for years answered the big questions – 'Why are we here?' and 'What is the meaning of our existence?' His explanations resonated with people of all walks of life and beliefs. It has been over 40 years since his death, and yet his writings and lectures are more popular than ever worldwide. Glance through YouTube to view him lecturing, or Google his name, and you will find many sites with information about him. Wikipedia has a long synopsis of his philosophical beliefs, personal life, accomplishments, and bibliography, as do many other sites. His books are published in more than 27 countries and in many languages including Chinese, Korean and Japanese. There are at least five Facebook pages dedicated to discussions about his life and writings. Amazingly, there are murals that bear his portrait on public buildings in at least three countries.

We are the first- and second-born daughters of Alan's seven children. I was born in 1938, the year Alan married his first wife, Eleanor Everett, and the year he immigrated to America to avoid the oncoming event of World War Two in Europe. Anne was born in 1942, the year he entered seminary to become an Anglican priest in Evanston, Illinois. By his second wife, Dorothy DeWitt, he fathered five more children: Marcia (Tia), Mark, Richard, Lila and Diane. One could say that we've had the longest relationship with him except for his father, Laurence, who died at the age of 93, a year after Alan.

We often wonder how, in the magnificent plan of this universe, we came to be the children of a world-famous thinker, writer, philosopher and authority on Christian and Asian religions. After all, we could have been the children of a parent involved in any sort of occupation, but the universe thought we should be daughters of Alan Watts.

A precocious child, born to an English couple of modest means in a suburb of London, Chislehurst, Kent. Alan, our father, born in 1915 in World War One, was the only surviving child of Laurence and Emily Watts. Alan was absolutely cherished by his parents who doted on him, encouraging his intellect and interests at every turn. Alan was equally devoted to his parents and as the reader will see, stayed in constant contact with them through his life of letters, addressed to 'Dear Mummy and Daddy.'

Although he grew up in a modest home, his mother was very creative. She taught gymnasium and needlework to the daughters of missionary families, who often presented her with items from the Orient: embroidered silks, china, figurines, and other art objects graced the walls, cupboards and mantelpiece of their home. These art objects stirred Alan's imagination, as did the many books his father read to him, especially *Just So* stories, *The Jungle Book* and *Kim*, all by Rudyard Kipling. His father worked for the Michelin Tyre Company and eventually for the government, in the capacity of director of the Lord Mayor's Hospital Sunday Fund, a non-profit organisation for the benefit of London hospitals.

We both had the opportunity to live in his birthplace with his parents, Joan for one year and Anne for five. We loved Rowan Tree Cottage, as the home was named, and the exquisite garden our grandparents had created. They had the equivalent of an acre and a half, artfully designed with flowerbeds, grassy paths, extended by beautifully trimmed shrubs named after Queen

Mary and Queen Elizabeth, rose trees, fruit trees of all kinds, a vegetable patch and hen house. It was just the way we would imagine the garden in *Alice in Wonderland* to look, with nooks and crannies, rabbit holes and trees where one might hide. This is the environment in which Alan grew up.

Eventually, his parents realised they should send him to a school where he might get a better education than at the local school he had been attending. So, at seven, he was sent off to St Hugh's School, a boarding school near Chislehurst and then eventually at age 13, to King's School, Canterbury in 1928. He discusses his experience at an all-boys boarding school at length in his autobiography, *In My Own Way*, in which he writes about his education as considerably more than book learning.

When Alan was 14 the family of a schoolmate at St Hugh's took him to Paris and introduced him to the European lifestyle, which he found to be more stimulating than the rigid environment of King's School in Britain itself. Alan began to picture himself as an adult. During his years at King's School he discovered Zen Buddhism. Eventually he became involved with the Buddhist Lodge in London, after he had submitted a pamphlet entitled *Zen* and was invited to speak to the members, who were shocked to learn that Alan Watts was a mere lad of 15.

This was also his introduction to his mentor, Christmas Humphreys, and others involved in Buddhism. Alan's father accompanied him to Lodge meetings and eventually became the institution's treasurer. As his parents did not have the means to send him to university, he set about learning more on his own, voraciously reading the works of DT Suzuki, Friedrich Nietzsche, Laozi (Lao Tzu, Lao-Tze), HP Blavatsky, Robert Graves and CJ Jung, to mention a few. All of this material had been screened out of the general school curriculum.

At this point he was 17 and he was also being influenced by many people he met in philosophical circles. It was during this time that he met DT Suzuki. He was quite active at the World Congress of Faiths held in London in 1936. By the time Alan reached 20, his first book, *The Spirit of Zen*, was published. He and others had discovered that he had the gift to word craft: the ability to describe the meaning of what he was writing in a such a way that it is easy to grasp, almost as if he were painting a picture with words. Through all this, he learned that he wanted to experience life on his own terms, not necessarily according to the societal or ideological morays of the time.

Now Anne will proceed from what she wrote.

Anne Watts: I just want to say, I for one am not a student of Alan Watts. I'm not a student of Zen. I know what it is to be the daughter of Alan Watts, that's what I can tell you. I had tried to read his books, but I found them so dense, but I loved listening to him. I grew up listening to him. I was always carted off to his lectures and I would be in the background and it just imbued into me. As most people, I just loved the sound of his voice. So, when we started working on these letters, it was fascinating to me the level of brilliance at such a young age. I would be reading a letter, and I would say, 'How old was he when he wrote this? 20? 21?' It was just extraordinary. We'll read some of these to you and tell you his age as we go along. When I wrote this preface, I wrote from a sense of my overall experience.

'These collected letters give the most complete and vibrant perspective into Alan's very full, rich life ever published. They enable us to follow the development of his mind, philosophies and personality. We get to witness his brilliance, his kindness, and his foibles. I remember as a child having the thought, 'The greater the person, the greater their faults.' It seems to be a part of our human condition to put people on pedestals and expect them to be perfect. Of course, no one lives up to these expectations, not Gandhi, not Martin Luther King Jr., not even saints! The sad thing about putting someone on a pedestal is that there is only one way to go – off. Once their 'imperfections' are discovered, they are often discounted as completely no good. This is a great shame. In Alan's case, given the huge number of individuals worldwide and over the years whose lives have been positively affected by his work, it is my hope that the readers will keep that which is illuminating and valuable to them and leave the rest.

Alan tried valiantly not to be put on a pedestal, called himself an entertainer, a trickster/coyote, and other such names. My hope is that the readers of this book will be nourished by his brilliance and have compassion for his human failings, as he so clearly had for others. I once had a conversation with Ram Das (Richard Alpert), who knew him well, in which he said of Alan, 'He knew IT, and he wasn't IT.' That made sense to me.

This is a treasure trove of writings through which my sister and I have had a deep, emotional, and bonding journey.'

AW: So, this is a letter he wrote when he was 13, from King's School Canterbury.

21 June, 1928.

Dear Daddy,

When this letter reaches you it will be your birthday, and I am sending it to you to wish you many happy returns. [...]

I don't think it's fair you shouldn't have a birthday procession.

I have no chance to get you anything for your birthday yet, but I will get something as soon as possible.

With much love and best wishes from,

Alan

JW: And in the book, he has done a drawing of a procession of rabbits. It's just such a lovely drawing. I felt so fortunate that we could get some of his drawings in the book, because they are so dear.

He was actually quite a good artist and he thought that he would be an artist and not a writer. We have a few of his paintings and artworks that have gone onto our children. I'm going to read a letter that was written in December of 1928. This is one of his more memorable letters as it involved the enthronement of a new Archbishop of Canterbury on 5 December 1928. Alan was selected to be one of His Eminence's two train bearers for the event, which was reported on the front page of the London *Daily Express* with the headline, 'New Primate Enthroned in St Augustine's Chair in the Presence of Nearly 5000 People.' That just tickled me, that the Primate was enthroned.

Dear Mummy and Daddy,

Thank you for your last letter. I have got crowds of news for you this time! I shall see the enthronement of the Archbishop all right, another boy and myself have GOT TO CARRY HIS TRAIN!!! We have got to dress up in all sorts of complicated affairs, we have got to wear ruffs! And red cassocks! I have been to several rehearsals of the service and it is going to be a very pompous affair. The Premier and the Lord Chancellor are going to be there and the Lord Mayor of London. We have got to go to the Arch B's Palace and wait in the Hall until he comes, then pick up his train and follow him!

This next bit was taken out of his autobiography. He had this wonderful mentor Francis Croshaw, but later on as his autobiography tells us, 'his place was taken by Christmas Humphreys and his wife Aileen who ran the Buddhist Lodge from their flat in one of the long residential streets of Pimlico in southwest London, a dreary street of high houses pressed together.'

So, that's at the very beginning.

According to Alan's biography *In My Own Way*, it appears he went to France in the summer of 1929. In the next section of letters written from school we start interestingly with a letter written to Sokei-an Sasaki. Little did he know at the time that this Zen priest would eventually become his stepfather-in-law. Sokei-an Sasaki was of the Rinzai Zen lineage and was sent by his master to teach Zen in America. Sokei-an's father was a Shinto priest and his mother a concubine taken by his father because his mother was unable to bear children. Sokei-an was sent to art schools where he learned wood carving as a young man prior to studying Zen. When he arrived in America he travelled extensively through the Pacific Northwest and in San Francisco. He was briefly a student at the San Francisco Art Institute. Eventually, after several trips back to Japan, at the age of 48 he was ordained a Zen master and went to New York City in 1928. There he started teaching Zen to a handful of followers and in May 1931 Sokei-an and others signed the incorporation papers to the Buddhist Society of America, which eventually became the first Zen Institute of America.

He met our grandmother Ruth Fuller Everett in 1933 and they became friends. She became a formal student of his in 1938. He was interned during World War Two but was released in 1944 because of ill health. Ruth and Sokei-an were married shortly after that but the marriage was brief. He died in 1945. I'm not sure how Alan initially came to communicate with Sokei-an Sasaki, perhaps the Buddhist Lodge in London had published Sasaki's writings. His communications in 1932 with Alan, then aged 17, showed respect for his interest in Zen. In answer to Alan's letter below, he cautioned that it is very hard to judge the ultimate attainment of Zen without observing the daily life and establishing close contact between teacher and disciple in order to make certain whether attainment is one of mere conception or that of really standing in its centre.

He wrote this letter to Sokei-an at age 17.

Dear Mr Sokei-an Sasaki,

Many thanks for your most interesting letter of the 1st. From what you say there and from what I have read elsewhere, the essence of Zen is to regard Existence universally or impersonally, or so I understand.

Instead of thinking 'I walk,' you think, 'There is a walking,' until you begin to see yourself as a part of the Universe not separate from other parts while the 'I' is as the whole. I have tried this and the result is that there comes a feeling calm, of indifference to circumstance.

In the Sutra of Wei-Lang (Hui-neng) sixth Patriarch, I read that one should get rid of the pairs of opposites – good and evil, joy and pain, life and death. Surely it is by the personal attitude to Existence that these opposites arise; by thinking 'I do,' instead of 'There is a doing.' By regarding oneself objectively in this manner one becomes detached and an idea of 'oneness' prevails. Is this what you mean when you say, 'The master regulates his cognisance of the body of relativity (i.e. the pairs of opposites?) Ceasing to follow its movement (ceasing to think 'I like' or 'I do' or 'I hate'?), he realises serenity.' Surely this is seeing Existence from the standpoint of Tathata, which is the very basis of Existence and yet is undisturbed by it? It is really rather hard to explain! But I somehow feel that as soon as I start looking at things impersonally, the 'I' which thinks about the opposites vanishes, while a sort of calm 'universal' feeling takes its place. Am I on the right track?

Yours Sincerely,

AW Watts

And in the book, *Zen Odyssey*, which is the story of Sokei-an and Ruth Fuller Sasaki, our grandmother through our mother, there is the response from Sokei-an to Alan's letter.

1 April 1932

Dear Mr Watts,

It seems to me that you are on the track that all Zen students have passed along. But it is very difficult to judge through correspondence whether you are surely on the main track of Zen or not. Conceiving the general idea of Zen and realising the samadhi of universal life is not sufficient. It is very hard to judge the ultimate attainment of Zen without observing daily life. Unless close contact is established between teacher and disciple in order to make certain whether attainment is one of mere conception or that of really standing in its centre. From my standpoint life must be Zen itself and we do not care much about the conception of it. I am quite sure you are on the way of Zen and I hope someday in the future we will meet each other.

So that is Sokei-an's response to Alan's letter. And so these two books are very interwoven, the story of our grandmother and the story of Alan. I just think her story is really extraordinary as a woman and American who was the first woman and foreigner accepted into the Zen priesthood in Japan. It was pretty extraordinary because the Japanese at the time held the view that a woman couldn't do that kind of thing. Of course in her very determined way she proved them quite wrong. And then I'd just like to share in the spring of 1937, Ruth took Eleanor to London. Again leaving Warren, her husband, in the hands of her sister. For Eleanor it was an opportunity to study piano with George Woodhouse, a renowned performer and teacher who had arrived at insights about musical practice with parallels to Zen. Ruth, at the invitation of her friend Christmas Humphreys at the Buddhist Lodge, gave a talk about her experience at Nanzenji. Eleanor was present, as was Alan Watts. It seemed inevitable that they would meet. Christmas Humphreys thought they should and introduced them. They quickly found that they had much in common, much to talk about and vivid curiosity towards each other.

JW: I'm thinking about the time when he had been here, and my parents got married and they went to the United States. I have some commentary here.

The years 1936 and 1937 were an expansion of Alan's self-imposed university. He pursued his work with the Buddhist Lodge as a protege of Christmas Humphreys, editing and writing for *The Middle Way* which was apparently not called *The Middle Way* at that point, and eventually becoming the Lodge secretary. During this time Alan became somewhat of a 'man about town', enjoying social activities with theatre, symphonies and opera, visits to art exhibitions and museums and dating young women. He relished hanging about in bookstores, finding more books on Eastern philosophies and art. He wrote *The Spirit of Zen* in 1936 in an attempt to bring together Buddhism, Vedanta, Daoism, Jungian psychology and Christian Mysticism. He wrote *The Legacy of Asia and Western Man* which was published in 1937 which he later characterised as a somewhat immature book. In the summer of 1937[1] he again attended the World Congress of Faiths, this time held in Oxford, and found the conversations with many illustrious scholars formative and stimulating. He met Krishnamurti from Benares, India; adopted son of Annie Besant. She was the leader of the Theosophical Society who promoted Krishnamurti as the vehicle of the coming world-teacher. Krishnamurti disavowed such a notion along with allegiance to any particular religion, but became a speaker and philosophical writer that Alan greatly admired all his life.

JW: One of the things I thought people might be interested in is what happened when Alan decided to go from his interest in Zen to becoming an Anglican priest and chaplain at Northwestern University. There was a letter that he wrote to his parents in March of 1941. He and my mother were living in New York City. In the letter to his parents he said, 'Now the main thing I want to tell you about is that I am planning a peculiar but important affair which may not after all surprise you. At present it's somewhat in the air but everyone here thinks it's a magnificent idea. My work is taking a very logical course and has brought me more and more in contact with church people who turned out to be most responsive, much more so than anyone else. I've been wondering for a long time how to extend that work and make it really effective and it seems to me that the obvious way is to cooperate with those forces in the churches, which are feeling out along these lines. For this purpose it would be of enormous value to be a minister and I have found that everything I want to say can be said in Christian language. In working up this last series of lectures I have delved fairly deeply into Christian theology and found that given a certain point of view, the whole scheme has admirable good sense, providing that you emphasise its psychological symbolism and do not tie yourself slavishly to merely historical or metaphysical interpretation.'

Then he says later on in the letter, 'Please don't talk to Toby about this just yet, I will write to him in due course when things are more definite, but I feel strongly that in these times when our institutions are threatened, there is no purpose in dividing our efforts into thousands of little sects and groups. I feel I am cut out for this work by inheritance and education and that I would be wasting my talents elsewhere. I believe it was at one time your own idea for me.'

AW: In this book there is also a letter that Alan wrote to Carl Jung at age 21 in which he's giving him some information that he thinks Carl Jung didn't know. He writes to a man 40 years his senior just as if they are equals. It's extraordinary to me. They did eventually become friends and Alan went frequently to speak at Jung's place in Switzerland. Then, there's a letter he wrote to Toby, his mentor, at the age of 26, where he is reviewing the book of poetry that Toby has written and again it's not like this man is his senior, it's like they are equals, completely in his tone. I think it's quite extraordinary, all the people he met, it was all equal to equal, it didn't matter who they were.

Adapted from a talk given by Joan and Anne Watts on the occasion of the launch of *The Collected Letters of Alan Watts* at The Buddhist Society, 20 July 2019. It was first published in *The Middle Way*, vol.94, February 2020.

Notes

1.   [1936 Conference of the World Congres of Faiths was held in London. The 'follow-on meeting' was held at Balliol College and Somerville College from 23–27 July. Sir Francis Younghusband, the founder, was in the Chair. The proceedings were 'The World's Need of Religion'.]

Alan Watts, D.T. Suzuki, Ven. Myokyo-ni
© The Buddhist Society

Joan Watts studied Japanese ink painting in Japan and won awards for her art. She has worked as a fundraiser in the non-profit world and recently had a solo exhibtion, 'bodhi'. She is also editor of *The Collected Letters of Alan Watts*.

Anne Watts is a hypnotherapist, educator, facilitator and counselor. She practices in Santa Rosa, California, and co-edited *The Collected Letters of Alan Watts*.

FREDA NEWTH WINT

(1917–2015)

Lay pioneer of Theravada Buddhism in England, a Director of The English Sangha Trust and a follower of Maha Boowa of the Forest tradition of North Thailand helped in bringing the Thai Forest Tradition and Venerable Sumedho to England. She wrote under the pseudonym 'John Frederick'.

Freda Newth Wint was born on July 25 1917 in India to Alfred and Mildred Mettam, who had spent their lives there. Her mother was a Marathi speaker (SOAS) with a considerable knowledge of Sanskrit, who started the first women's teacher training college in Baroda, Gujarat.

Mildred returned to England with the express purpose of educating her children and enrolled Freda from the age of seven at Bedford High School for Girls, a school run on Christian lines, where hymn singing and deportment were of great importance. Freda went on to win a scholarship to Somerville College, Cambridge, to read English.

In 1939, while working for the British Council in Istanbul, Freda returned to England to work at the Ministry of Information, later transferring to Delhi to work in broadcasting. Freda first encountered Buddhism in 1956, the year that the English Sangha Trust (EST) was established by Venerable Kapilavaddho Bhikkhu (William August Purfurst, who was known later as Richard Randall) and assisted by Maurice Walshe and others. Freda was a lay disciple of Buddhism in the Theravada Tradition and in 1965 visited the monastery of Ajahn Maha Boowa (Ajahn Maha Bua of the Forest Tradition) in his monastery Wat Pa Ban Tat in Thailand, for meditation instruction, which was considered novel, unusual, and even dangerous to some at the time.

Maha Boowa's central teaching was on the indestructible nature of the heart/mind (*citta*) that becomes entangled with defilements or human passions (*kilesas*), and experiences itself as suffering, impermanent and 'I'-bound. These 'teachings' were later developed and published by Freda in *The Middle Way* in a series of four articles entitled, 'The Luminous Mind', under the pseudonym John Frederick.

In 1974, during a period of closure for the Hampstead Vihara (which had been set up by the EST), while the EST's objectives were reviewed, Freda, led its Chairman, George Sharp to make contact with Ajahn Pannavaddho, to seek his advice on how the Sangha (Buddhist Community) in England could be best established. Through her introductory letters and existing friendships, Freda smoothed the way for George Sharp's visit to Thailand, where he met Ajahn Maha Boowa and Ajahn Chah. This in turn, led to Ajahn Maha Boowa (Bua), Ajahn Pannavadho and Bhikkhu Cherry visiting England in 1975.

In 1979, Freda Wint joined the EST as a Director. Later, in 1979, Venerable Sumedho, a disciple of Ajahn Chah was invited to England, which led to the founding of *Cittaviveka*, Chithurst Forest Monastery in West Sussex, and subsequently to the founding of Amaravati Buddhist Monastery in Hemel Hempstead.

Freda was very supportive of the EST, which she attended without missing a single meeting until 1992 and was a good friend to The Buddhist Society until the end, and an example of the contribution a lay devotee can make. She died in 2015 at the age of 98.

The Luminous Mind

Freda Wint, 1988

itta (mind or heart) is a key word in the Pali suttas. One of the difficulties in trying to understand the teachings of the early Buddhist scriptures, however, is that we have no precise concept of the *citta*, and no word for it in modern western languages. (The Middle Ages were richer in this respect.) One way of tackling this problem is to look at significant passages in the suttas in which the word *citta* appears and try to unravel from them its essential meaning.

'Mind' and 'heart' have both been used for *citta* in English translations of the Pali texts, and both words are needed, although, even taken together they do not convey its full sense. 'Heart' connotes the depth, the centrality and the integrating function of the *citta* within the human organism. 'Mind'[1] expresses its cognitive activity. (It has to be remembered that the *citta* can be cognitively wrong, or to put it in another way, it can 'know things wrongly'. It is one of the objects of the dhamma-training to cure this.) 'Thought' and 'thoughts', which are even thinner and much more misleading usages in this context, occasionally appear as translations of *citta* in the English versions of the suttas.[2] They have one contribution to make to our understanding of the word, however, and that a valuable one – the term 'thoughts' conveys the notion of a process. This is appropriate for the *citta* which is presented in the suttas as an ever-changing flow, a stream, not a static entity or substance. This is an important idea in Buddhism:

'Just as a monkey, faring through the woods, through the great forest catches hold of a bough and letting it go seizes another, even so that which we call *citta*[3] arises as one thing, ceases as another, both by night and by day.' (S.II.95).

It is necessary to emphasise at the outset that the *citta* is not a 'self'. Modern Theravada orthodoxy has felt apprehensive that if it allowed a 'heart' into its exposition of the Buddhist teaching, this might be mistaken for a 'self', an *atman*. As a result, it has tended to play down the importance of the *citta*, and this has had the curious outcome that the early Buddhist system of dhamma training has often been presented to the West with a hole knocked into its core. 'There is a path' cautious commentarial voices have said, 'but nothing to walk along it; a training, but nothing to be trained; a goal of freedom, but nothing to become free.'[4] In fact, we read in the suttas that it is the *citta* which does all these things, and there are words that describe it in these different roles: *cittabhavana*, the training or development of the heart, *vimutta-citta* or *celo-vimutti*, the freed heart. The idea of *anatta*, not-self, is essential to Buddhism, but at first it seems so strange to people who come to it from other ways of thinking that, from the earliest times, Buddhists have felt somewhat embattled in this area. It is really not necessary, however, to sink the *citta* in the smoke of this encounter with other philosophies. It is not difficult for us to understand, at least superficially, that along with all other phenomena in the universe, the *citta* is not myself, not me, not mine; that I do not own it any more than, for instance, I own my foot. The individual himself is not responsible for the rules by which any of the components of his being are governed, and as the human foot has a function to perform, so has the human heart. What that function of the *citta* is, from the Buddhist point of view, the dhamma-teaching gradually reveals.

There is, moreover, an extremely important principle involved here. The notion of training for enlightenment has often struck people who meet Buddhism for the first time as 'selfish', since it seems to differ from the proposition of service to a higher power which is the basis of most theistic religions. This is where the doctrine of *anatta* (not-self) reveals its crucial significance in the Buddhist model. Since the *citta* (mind/heart) of an individual cannot be regarded as 'himself', to think of it as 'mine' (which of course initially we all do) is a seriously wrong view. To train the *citta*, therefore, and thereby, among other things, to overcome this wrong view is not a selfish act. It is an undertaking which is required of us by 'the nature of things', the higher law, *dhammata*.

There is a radical statement about the *citta* in the *Anguttura Nikaya*:

'At *Savatthi* the Blessed One said: The heart (*citta*) O bhikkhus, is luminous (*pabhassara*), but it is defiled by adventitious defilements (*kilesa*) ... This the instructed noble disciple understands as it really is. Wherefore, for the instructed noble disciple there is training of the heart (*citta-bhiivanii*), I declare.'

(A.I.10).

We have to consider what brings about the darkened condition of the luminous mind or heart (*pabhassaram cittam*). The passage just quoted describes it as a prey to 'adventitious defilements' – adventitious here meaning that the defilements are not essentially part of its constitution, but that they invade it. The fundamental nature of the *citta* is clear and luminous, but it has within it two potentials, one for development, the other for receiving corruption in its unregenerate state. The Pali word for latent corruption within the *citta* is *anusaya*. The aim of the training is to purify and strengthen the *citta* so that, at the final stage, corruption can no longer enter it.[5] The *citta* of the Arahant is described as luminous likewise,[6] but it is a stable condition.

We are told in the texts that human life is exceedingly precious because it is a state which is propitious for this training in dhamma. So, if human life is favourable for the spiritual quest, what goes wrong? How is it that we allow our opportunity to turn into our downfall? One of the propositions in the Buddhist scriptures is that the *citta*, as we normally experience it, has a wrong attitude to things; it is particularly deficient in discernment. This condition is called primal ignorance – *avijja*[7] which does not refer to quality of intellect: spiritual dullness which is an attribute of *citta* can be accompanied by high intellectual capacity. The situation in which we find ourselves when we firstopen our eyes upon the world is that we are connected, or, more accurately, the *citta* is connected with a set of tools for living, the body, the senses and the mental functions, i.e. the whole of the psycho-physical make-up of body/mind. This is called in Buddhism the *khandha*-system.

The system of the five *khandha* is older than Buddhism, but it provided the Buddha with a convenient formula for the body/mind, and one which his audiences would recognise. The *khandhas* are listed as 'body, sensations, perception, karma-formations (*sankhara*) and consciousness'. Their mild complexities can easily be looked up in books and dictionaries of Buddhism. They are all, with one exception,[8] said to be subject to dissolution at the death of the body. The *citta* is never mentioned in the same passage as the *khandhas* when those are broken down into their constituent parts. Yet, ironically, *mano* (which is the *khandha*-factor of 'mind') and *citta* have become hopelessly entangled by modern translators and commentators. Both have indiscriminately been called 'mind', and this constitutes a severe obstacle for people who are using the English translations in trying to understand the specific nature of the *citta*. *Mano*, or 'mind', which is listed under 'consciousness' in the traditional list of *khandha* categories, is primarily presented in the Pali texts as the central recipient of sense-impressions, which include – in Buddhism – ideas. This is done in order to be consistent with the simple *khandha*-framework. But this is too restrictive for the thought of the suttas, and there *mano* also has an active function. It is the thinking, reasoning, logical mind, the intellect. The *citta* is not presented as 'thinking'. It knows; it is aware; it is capable of profound intuitions (when it has been trained to use this faculty). But thinking about the phenomena which constitute life in the world (*samsara*) is the function of *mano*.

The *khandhas* are looked at in the texts from two angles. In the first instance they are simply the *khandhas*, for example in the *Samyutta Nikaya* (S.III.47):

'And what, bhikkhus, are the five *khandha*?'

The answer follows: they are the body, sensations, perceptions, karma formations and consciousness. Then follows the significant question:

'And what, bhikkhus, are the five *khandha* connected with grasping (the five *upadana-khandha*)?'

The same five *khandha*-factors follow (body, sensations etc.) but in this case the *citta*'s relationship with them is *upadana* (grasping, clinging) accompanied by the *asavas*, the deep obsessions.

It is not the *khandhas* themselves which cause the problem, but the fact that the *citta* becomes obsessively involved with obtaining satisfaction through them, forgetting its high potential. The major error of judgement into which it falls, as a result of grasping and obsession, is the conception that it owns the *khandhas*, that they are 'itself'. Even 'an innocent baby boy', so runs a text, has the latent conviction (*anusaya*) that his body belongs to him, and this and other errors of the *citta* become for the infant, and later for the adult, 'fetters binding him to the lower shore.' (M.I.433).

The *citta* is described in the Canon as having two basic moral/immoral dispositions. There are three fires within the heart: greed, hate and delusion (D.III.217). These are balanced by three propensities of the opposite kind: unselfishness (*caga*, a word which means both generosity and the willingness to let go), kindness and wisdom. The three fires are aroused by the passions and false attitudes that overwhelm the *citta* in its partnership with the *khandhas*. The three nobler tendencies, always more or less present in human life, though largely as possibilities, are held to become fully operative and constant only after prolonged exposure to teaching from a higher source (which for Buddhists is the dhamma). Practice of this teaching brings about what Buddhaghosa described as 'the awakening from the sleep of the continuum of the lower nature' (*kilesa-santana-niddaya-utthahati*). (DhsA 217).

In considering the relation of the *citta* with the *khandhas* we must avoid the pitfall of dualism. In Buddhist teaching there is no suggestion of a higher principle entering into and being sucked down by an evil element called 'matter' and having to disentangle itself. The *citta* and the *khandhas* together comprise the individual. This is how he or she is. In the early Buddhist model there is no unchanging essence, no inhabitant with a superior nature lurking within the conglomeration. The whole bundle operates together, and within one lifetime constitutes the *satta*, 'being', or *puggala*, 'person'. Here again we are in trouble with modern Theravada orthodoxy which has been carried away by the notion that neither the 'being' nor the 'person' exists.[9] This is a scholastic problem which is studied elsewhere. Here it is enough to say that 'person' or 'being' are terms which are used in the suttas to designate an individual during the course of a single life. In reply to a rhetorical question: 'And who, brethren, is the person (*puggala*) who has understood?' the Buddha replies:

'Such and such a venerable one, of such a name, of such a clan. This one, brethren, is the person who has understood.'

(S.III.159).

We are reminded many times that the 'person' or 'being' is composite (*sankhata*) and that among the factors which influence it are the results of past kamma (Skrt. *karma*) and the world-conditions prevalent during his/her lifetime; likewise it is ever-changing (*anicca*); subject to misfortune (*dukkha*); and that it is not a 'self', or something which belongs to the ego.

Good and evil tendencies arise within the heart (*citta*): the *khandhas* are morally neutral. Nevertheless, so closely do *citta* and *khandhas* interpenetrate each other that a strong reciprocity is set up between them. For instance, the discursive abilities of *mano* (the *khandha*-factor of mind) can be occupied with thoughts of a base or trivial nature to such an extent that they become habitual, and the *citta* loses its orientation. There is an example in the verses at *Udana* 37:

'Ignorant of the thoughts of mana, he runs with bewildered *citta* from life to life.'

Mano, however, is comparatively easy to re-direct, and when the instrument (*mano*) is under control it has its proper uses:

'One should not restrain *mano* from everything ... but whatever is evil. One should restrain *mano* from that.'

(S.I.14).

The body (*kaya*, another *khandha*-factor) can also be affected by the *citta* with wholesome or unwholesome properties – and conversely can influence the *citta* because of habits that have been developed within the body. An example of a moral effect arising from a bodily habit is given in the *Majjhima Nikaya* (M.I.239) where it is said that a longing for an unwholesome pleasurable sensation (*sukhasaragi*) will not persist in one who has 'developed" that is to say practised restraint in the body (*bhavita-kaya*). Another example of mind-body interpenetration is the description of the meditator who has 'suffused his body with a *citta* that is utterly pure and utterly clean, so that there is no part of his body that is not so suffused."[10] (M.I.277).

We find in reading the suttas that a certain dramatic ambiguity seems to exist between the 'person' and the *citta*. If we deny, as in Buddhism we do, the existence of a 'self' within the system, what are we to make of the grammatical subject/object 'I, me, you, he, him' which seems to engage in argument or fights with the heart? For instance, it is said to be the Venerable Sariputta's special teaching that –

'The bhikkhu whirls the *citta* around according to his wish: he does not whirl around according to the *citta's* wish. (A.IV.34).

And in the *Theragata* a disciple called Talaputta reproaches his *citta*, saying that for a long time it has urged him to follow a better way of life, but as soon as he takes up its suggestions what happens?

'Now you go back to all your former loves,
Craving and ignorance and lusts and hates.'
(Ta.1124).

This looseness of syntax is not resolved in the suttas in a fashion that satisfies our logical instincts. It is, however, natural, and true to our experience. We all recognise the inner dialogue. We experience it as one side of the heart arguing with another side. The *Dhammapada*, for example, presents in its poetic way the *citta's* mobility and wantonness:

'The *citta* is very hard to perceive, extremely subtle, it flits wherever it lists ... faring far, wandering alone, lying in a cave is the *citta* ... let the wise man guard it.'
(Dh.36, 37).

'The wise man' in this case is the wise heart, the *citta*, not some other entity. The *Majjhima Nikaya* makes this clear: 'He should cultivate, restrain, curb and dominate the *citta* by the *citta*.' (M.I.l20). Likewise he should 'exert, gladden and take care of the *citta*' (AIII.435) for 'so tamed it brings happiness.' (Dh.35).

Another problem with language is that by giving it a name – the heart, the *citta* – we mistakenly apprehend the *citta* as a fixed entity. If we pause from naming it, and look inside, we immediately perceive it as a series of events: notions, feelings, wishes, decisions, indecisions, judgments and so forth. This is its natural mode in the phenomenal world. It is capable of other modes, and fleeting suspicions of these are wonderful to it and intermittently draw it in that direction. Before looking at this side of sutta teaching, however, we need to consider another aspect of the operations of the *citta* in *samsara*.[11] As it is presented in the Canon, the *citta* is a continuum which survives the death of the body. We examine the textual evidence for this in Part II.

Published in *The Middle Way*, vol. 62, no. 4, 1988.

Notes

1   Mind: the customary word for what we understand as 'mind' is *mano* in Pali. *Mano* is a *khandha*-factor (the *khandhas* will he explained later). *Mano* operates closely with but is distinct from *citta*.

2   Thought, thoughts: the customary words in Pali are *vittaka. vittaka*.

3   In this simile of the monkey, *citta* is coupled with *mano* (mind) and with *vinnana* (consciousness) which are both *khandha*-factors (the *khandhas* are analysed later). This is because all three functions share the quality of mutability. Unfortunately, the fact that *citta*, *mano* and *vinnana* appeared together in this passage has led abhidhammists and commentators to suppose that these three very different words had the same meaning. In the suttas, *citta* is never included among the factors of the *khandha* system.

4   This is not to suggest that commentators in the Theravada had lighted upon the Mahayana concept of 'emptiness'. In the Theravada *dhammas* exist. (This word *dhamma*, when used in the plural, means the factors which underlie composite phenomena.) In the Mahayana all dhammas have been swept away, they do not exist, they are all 'empty', and this includes the *citta*, the Path, and even the transcendental, *nirvana*. The Theravada approach is equally consistent, in its own fashion, except for the commentarial (not the scriptural) tendency to suppress the heart, or agent in the spiritual quest, by suggesting that the *citta* is part of the *khandha* system, and therefore subject to death. This accounts, to some extent, for the unconscious annihilationist bias which has overtaken modern Theravada orthodoxy.

5   D.III.235.

6   S.V.92, A.I.257, A.III. 16.

7   S.II.171. The Pali expression for the condition from which the enlightened heart cannot fall back into corruption is *akuppa ceto-vimutti*.

8   The exception is an aspect of consciousness *(vinnana)* which has a momentary part to play among the impulsions which lead to a new birth. This is a complex subject which belongs to another study. References are D.III.105 *vinnana-sota* and M.II.262 *samvattanika-vinnana*.

9   See footnote 4. The question is discussed at greater length in Jayatilleke's *Early Buddhist Theory of Knowledge*, paragraph 618.

10 This is a temporary effect of certain meditational practices. Before Arahantship no such effect is lasting. This is not to suggest that the body, even of the Arahant, becomes immune from disease or accident. The mental relationship with the body can, however, be transformed.

11 *Samsara*: the worlds of re-birth. The word literally means 'faring on'.

VENERABLE MYOKYO-NI

(1921–2007)

A Rinzai Zen Buddhist nun, head of the Zen Centre in London, an inspiring Zen teacher and author who established two Rinzai training centres in the UK and is now formally known as Daiyu Myokyo Zenji.

Venerable Myokyo-ni (Irmgard Schloegl) master Daiu was born Irmgard Schloegl in 1921 and raised in Austria. She obtained a PhD in natural sciences from Graz University before joining the Zen group at The Buddhist Society in London under Christmas Humphreys in 1950 while pursuing post-doctoral research and teaching at the The Royal School of Mines at Imperial College London.

In 1960, she began traditional Japanese Zen training at Daitoku-ji monastery in Kyoto under Oda Sesso Rōshi, here she met many of the small international community of Zen Students including Ruth Fuller Sazaki, Walter Nowick and others.

After returning to England after Sesso Roshi's death in 1966 for nine months, she started a small Zazen group at The Buddhist Society. She then returned to Japan to continue her training in Daitoku-ji under Oda Sesso Roshi's successor Kannun Roshi before returning permanently to England in 1972.

In 1979, together with Dr Desmond Biddulph and James Whelan, she helped to formally establish the Zen Centre as a charity.

During this period, from 1979 until his death in 1983, when he bequeathed his house to the Zen Centre, she lived at the home of Christmas Humphreys, whom she affectionately referred to as 'Father' (who died on 13 April 1983).

On 22 July 1984 she was ordained as a Zen nun by Soko Morinaga Roshi, who had been head monk at Daitoku-ji when she first went to Japan, as Myokyo-ni (Mirror of the Subtle). The house was consecrated as *Shobo-an*

(Hermitage of the True Dharma) and become the main administrative location and training temple of the Zen Centre. Fairlight, a second training monastery, which became her home, was opened in Luton in 1996.

Myokyo-ni continued teaching at The Buddhist Society where she remained a Council member and Vice President until health prevented her from doing so. She spent most of the remaining years of her life at Fairlight where she received visitors and continued to teach until the very end.

She was an inspiring Zen teacher who touched many hearts and was much loved and respected by her numerous students in the UK and around the world. She was also the author of many books on Zen and Buddhism including *The Zen Way* (1987), as well as the translator of *The Teaching of Rinzai* (1976). Her many publications includes *Towards Wholeness* (2018), *Gentling the Bull* (2011) and *Look and See* (2017).

Shobo-an and Fairlight continue to function for Zen training, following the traditional ways, with facilities for laypeople to practice as well as resident Western monks and nuns, and lay students who are able to come and visit and stay for varying lengths of time.

Until Myokyo-ni's return from Japan in 1966, Buddhism had been a largely intellectual practice, spearheaded by such pioneering luminary Scholars as Edward Conze, DT Suzuki and Christmas Humphreys, and by the excellent translations of the Pali Canon by TW Rhys Davids. The period of her teaching life coincided with the arrival in the UK of Venerable Sumedho of the Forest Tradition of Thailand as well as the influx of Tibetan monastic teachers who together with Zen heralded the true beginnings of Mahayana teaching in the UK.

Theravada Buddhism had been established in England since 1926 by Anagarika Dhammapala and the Chiswick Vihara. The ordained western members of the Forest tradition were of enormous influence and established the Southern tradition here in the UK.

From the late 1960s onwards Buddhism, whether of Theravada or Mahayana, began to be seen as a transformative practice engaging both mind and body, which was something very new at the time.

Myokyo-ni's teaching style was very direct, unencumbered by technical terms, though her friendly manner and warm engagement did not reveal the steely presence that she reserved for her students in the interview room.

Myokyo-ni, who was a close and lasting friend of Christmas Humphreys, wrote many books and articles, took part fully in the life of The Buddhist Society and was for a time almost synonymous with it.

She died in 2007 in Fairlight surrounded by her disciples.

Reflections on the Direct Teaching
of the Buddha

Venerable Myokyo-ni, 2006

The Buddha diagnosed our human ailment as attachment, and prescribed as a way of life or training that would, if correctly undertaken, with right dosage and at right times, effect a cure.We, however, due to our basic delusion (*Avidya*) easily misunderstand his instructions and either stick to the surface meaning of the words – like reading the label on the medicine bottle and expecting this to be sufficient; or proudly displaying the bottle on the shelf for all to see that I have it, telling others to also get it and what it can do, but as to myself drinking it? All such are only further feats of attachment and crusades that, undertaken in this spirit, will be productive of disillusion at best. We know what happened with our medieval crusades! Better refrain and set the own heart at rest before meddling with what I cannot encompass. There are various warning stories in the teachings to just that effect. As Westerners we are particularly prone to such antics as our history shows, past and present!

However, if the Buddha's course of treatment is truly taken up and followed, then each step of actual and genuine practice enables to see a tiny bit deeper under the surface of what seems, and so we begin to have an inkling of the actual causes that stir us – and with that also why Bodhidharma enjoined us not to stick to the surface meaning of words and letters.

In the Diamond Sutra, the Buddha warns not to depend on or abide in any situation and not to indulge in any discriminations, because only then is it possible to clearly see the vastness of Reality and to realise that all worlds and all things are equal and non-dual. Reading such a teaching, I naturally, to begin with, cannot see that such an insight presupposes a voiding of all thought of I, in effect the absence of I as expounded in the Buddha's deathless teaching of No-I (*Anatman*). I may thus be tempted to experiment with 'not depending on or abiding in' anything, in short not to let the heart run off searching, not to think erroneously, not to get involved in things – without realising that my very trying is just giving rise to all these three! I cannot help doing so, for the heart urges and insists, as the Buddha stated in the first teaching he gave, 'The house is on fire, burns with the fires of delusion, ill-will and desire – there is no staying in such a house!'

Do we understand that correctly? Yes, of course and that is what I want to be, untouched by things and 'beyond' the hubbub of daily life and so beyond any usual suffering. No more feeling hurt, upset, worried – just not feeling at all! But that would rather make me a monster, would it not? And the Buddha's Way is not productive of such! It rather is productive of strength or power not to be swayed or carried away by the passions, rather to see clearly the pictures they paint but without denying them and without discrimination, willingly responding to the demands of the situation. What, without discrimination? Not possible. I rear up again, right/wrong, good/bad, life/death, Buddha /Mara – the very teachings exhort us to be clear about them. Yes, quite, but how DO WE distinguish? We take sides – good, great, right, light – yes! And at that moment already the other side is constellated: down with the bad, small, wrong, dark – execute, kill, get rid of it! What travesty, for in our world of night and day, of dark and light, joy and sorrow: ease and terror, this is the way things are. We will never get rid of one side only, and into just the pity of these conditions the Buddha had insight. From this arose his immense compassion with our suffering from which he then taught the Way out. His Way leads toward that same insight. Coming to terms with the opposites, it brings peace to the heart, with compassion for all that lives. There is no 'going beyond' in the Buddha's teaching; water will always wet us, and fire will certainly burn as long as fuel lasts. Mountains are high and valleys lie low, there are good people and bad people, too. No longer deceived, but seeing clearly yet without judgements and evaluation will give rise to 'right action' in given situations. Day and night are. Why is it that out of all nature only we humans are contrary, light the night and are up until all hours, to then sleep long into the daylight?

So to mend our ways would rather entail to humbly hold to be harmless, simple, kindly, and warm-heartedly, and this even when it means endurance of the dark patches, which are as much part of life as night is of the 24 hours that we are pleased to call one day. Change is inevitable in due course, it depends on our karmic actions both past and present, individually and collectively. This concatenation is so deep and vast that it far exceeds the possibility of our human understanding. So the insight dawns that what cannot now be changed might at least be ameliorated, and the rest willingly endowed because endured it has to be, the attitude with which this is done is decisive. Why?

Because such endurance in willing awareness (the Christian rendering of the willing endurance of Christ in his passion is the ultimate example) is in harmony with the situation, in harmony with life and may perhaps prove to be a veritable blessing because it has the power to open wide the gates of perception that lead to the human heart.

The '10,000 things all go back to the One,' as the Third Patriarch told us. These 10,000 things are all pairs of opposites, and only become perceptible as such. White cannot be without black (or colour), and black is the foil for white; so with beautiful and ugly, good and bad, life and death. This is our existing relative world. In the signlessness of the Absolute they are faded away into *Sunyata* – Nothingness. And of this final prime pair, too, one cannot be without the other, and so they both, and simultaneously, are and are not!

This Way might be pondered, nurtured, cultivated, weeded and watered so that in due time it may take root and sprout into everyday life to be of benefit to many.

Originally published in *The Middle Way*, vol. 80, no. 4, February 2006.

Sōkō Moringa Roshi and Venerable Myokyo-Ni

AYYA KHEMA

(1923–1997)

A German refugee, Buddhist nun, founder of Buddhist monasteries and prolific author, who promoted and encouraged the ordination of women in the southern tradition.

Ayya Khema was born Ilse Kussel in Berlin in 1923 and became a Theravada Buddhist nun and author.

In her autobiography *I Give You My Life: The Autobiography of a Western Buddhist Nun* (1997), she wrote that her 'secure and privileged childhood' in Berlin was completely dashed by the time she was 15 in 1938, following the publication of the *Nuremberg Laws* in 1935, which stripped Jews of their German citizenship. By 1938, persecution had stepped up, the Kussel family was forced to leave Germany for Shanghai and Ilse was sent to Glasgow on a Kindertransport train.

During the Second World War, she travelled to Shanghai to join her family. Later however, they were confined to a ghetto where her father died, an event that she described as her 'first real death'.

She met her first husband in Shanghai and they married when she was 22. Events forced them to flee to San Francisco and then on to San Diego where they had two children. Her dissatisfaction with domestic life and her interest in spiritual matters, however, led her to divorce.

Through her interest and study of the Essenes, a Jewish sect that flourished in Palestine from the second century BCE to the first century CE, she was led towards Buddhism and met her second husband Gerd while studying the Essenes in Mexico. They travelled through South America, Asia, Pakistan, New Zealand and Australia, until they settled in New South Wales.

After studying with Venerable Khantipalo, a Buddhist monk in the southern Theravada tradition, who was born Laurence Mills in London in 1932 and re-ordained in 2010 under the name Minh An, Khema travelled to the US. To further her studies, she visited two *Soto* Zen Centres, the San Francisco Zen Center where she studied Zen and the Tassajara Zen Mountain Center where she worked for three months. Khema then spent three weeks in Burma where she studied meditation with students of Sayagyi U Ba Khin, the world-renowned meditation teacher and civil servant, who was said to be a fully realised Arahant, and whose disciple Goenka has spread *Vipassana* meditation all over the world.

In 1978 Khema founded the Wat Buddha Dhamma forest monastery in New South Wales and installed Venerable Khantipalo as abbot. In Thailand she studied with Tan Ajahn Singtong for three months. She then visited Sri Lanka, where she met Nyanaponika Thera who introduced her to Narada Maha Thera, who gave her the name 'Ayya Khema'. She ordained in Sri Lanka in 1979 as 'Khema' when she was 58 years old, named after a nun in Buddha's time, who was known for great wisdom. She was very eager to re-establish the ordination of women in the southern tradition, as the custom of women being ordained in this tradition had died out. To this end, she founded Parappuduwa Nun's Island. She was also one of the organisers of the first International Conference on Buddhist Women in 1987, which led to the foundation of the Sakyadhita International Association of Buddhist Women.

She was only able to obtain full ordination through Hsi Lai Temple, a Chinese Mahayana temple under the Fo Guang Shan Buddhist Order in 1988, as Bhikkhunī ordination had died out in Sri Lanka and, as the succession had been lost, ordination for women was no longer possible, but was still extant within the Mahayana tradition in China and elsewhere.

In 1983, a return trip to Sri Lanka led Khema to meet her teacher, Ven. Matara Sri Ñānarāma of Nissarana Vanaya, who inspired her to teach *jhana* meditation. She then established monasteries and Buddhist centres in Australia, Sri Lanka and Germany, and became a prolific writer. *Being Nobody, Going Nowhere* (1987) won the Christmas Humphreys Memorial Award. Her books include *When The Iron Eagle Flies, Buddhism for The West* (2000), *Know Where You're Going* (2014), *Be An Island: The Buddhist Practice of Inner Peace* (1999) and *Come and See for Yourself: The Buddhist Path to Happiness* (2002). She gave Dhamma talks at The Buddhist Society and attended its residential summer school. In 1989, she founded Buddha Haus in Germany.

Ayya Khema had a warm and straightforward teaching manner that was down to earth and demystifying. She showed through her life how it is possible for an average woman to emerge onto a new level of consciousness and find spiritual peace. She died peacefully at Buddha Haus in the rural village of Uttenbuhl, Germany, at the age of 74, from breast cancer.

Unhappiness is a Defilement

Ayya Khema, 1992

There is only one place where enlightenment is possible, namely in the mind, and all of us have the seed of enlightenment within. If that were not so, there would be no point in leading a spiritual life. But since the potential is in all of us, it is wise to cultivate that seed. If we have seeds for our garden and cultivate them, we have the chance of a harvest. We will water the garden, pull out the weeds and watch that the insects do not attack our plants. We keep an eye on the garden to see that everything is in good order. If there were no seeds it would be foolish to cultivate the plot. However hard we work, we would never see results. But since there are seeds, there is a chance of getting fruits. The same is true of our minds, yet we also have all the necessary weeds within to continue living in the world of duality, in the realm of birth and death. The weeds are our wrong thinking, based on the premise of our personal likes and dislikes. We approach people, experiences, situations with the view of gaining from them in some form. But how can we always expect to be given what we want?

Neither people nor situations nor experiences can be looked at in this way. They just are. Whether they are of benefit to ourselves or not, whether they enhance our egos or not, what difference can it make? Our mind with its luxurious growth of 'craving to exist' approaches everything from the standpoint of 'what's in it for me?' This creates constant disappointment until we change our attitude.

We have a mind in which Samsara and Nibbana can be found just as both happiness and unhappiness are present. It's almost like going to a department store and picking out what one wants. Why not pick out that which is beneficial? If we go to a shop and buy everything we cannot use, that's rather foolish isn't it? And at the same time, in the same place they are selling everything we need, so why not get that? Everything we need for our own and others' happiness is to be found in our own mind. Although all is available, people again and again pick that which has no benefit, for the simple reason that most people have neither heard about nor trained themselves to make mental and emotional choices. If we couldn't learn to make choices there would be no point in meditating. If everything was predestined, frozen into a pattern long before it happens, that would be fatalism. The Buddha described that as wrong view. If it were true, one could find no reason for being a truthful, decent person. One would not even find a reason for getting up in the morning, but could just as well stay in bed. We do have choices however. We can get up in the morning or stay in bed. We can tell ourselves that early morning is a good time for meditation, or we can say to ourselves, how silly it is to get up early and prefer to stay in bed. We can convince ourselves either way. That's a choice isn't it? We can see that we have choices under all circumstances.

There may be powerful situations arising, where someone is abusive, stealing, threatening to kill or to defame. One believes oneself to be justi-fied in feeling despondent about that. Why? One can choose and need not be forced to feel unhappy. We can recognise our potential to change our mind. The more often we choose a wholesome reaction, such as equanimity or loving-kindness, the more habitually the mind will be happy. The more wrong choices we make, the more often the mind will revert to unhappiness. The more anger we allow ourselves, the more geared towards anger our mind becomes. It's really quite simple, just a matter of creating the proper habit patterns in our mind. This then facilitates meditation which opens the door to break through the ego delusion.

Although we know about our ego delusion this understanding may not really have taken a hold yet. There is a great difference between knowledge and experience. As long as one is still trying to find a foothold somewhere in the world, whether it be wealth, fame, friendship, knowledge, understanding or anything else, one will be threatened by adversity. What is it that every-body is looking for? Only one thing – happiness. We want beautiful sights and sounds, pleasant tastes and comforts. But can these really continuously be experienced, or can there be a kind of happiness which does not rely on our senses? An inner voice may whisper that happiness is actually based on purity and that unhappiness is a defilement. When one has a first inkling of that, there is amazement and often rejection. Most people find themselves unhappy quite often and don't want to admit to such a large measure of defilement. But how could being unhappy be a virtue? If we feel unhappy about others' suffering there is only one way to deal with that, namely to help alleviate the suffering if we can. Otherwise such unhappiness results in emotionalism which clouds clear thinking.

When the Venerable Ananda was standing at the deathbed of the Buddha and crying, the Buddha reprimanded him. It was a sign that the Venerable Ananda was not yet enlightened, had not yet relinquished craving. The Buddha said to Venerable Ananda: 'Come Ananda, what are you crying about? Are you crying because this old body is finally breaking up?'

Venerable Ananda replied: 'I am crying because my teacher is leaving me.' Unhappiness arises because there is resistance and rejection, which is craving to get rid of things as they are. Resistance and rejection are part of anger because nothing will ever be exactly as we wish. If we are still looking for satisfaction in worldly matters, we haven't seen Dhamma (the Truth) yet. That doesn't mean, however, that we have to find dissatisfaction. Actually, there is neither one nor the other. There is eating, drinking, sleeping, and digesting, talking, being silent, looking, hearing, tasting, smelling, touching and thinking. What else is there? Where can we find satisfaction or dissatisfaction? There is nothing to be found, everything just is.

Being born and dying doesn't just mean our birth and death anniversaries, but rather that our thoughts and feelings are born and die from moment to moment. That's all we can find in this human realm. If we look for total irrevocable satisfaction, we won't find it, but to be dissatisfied is just as unskilful. What we have to look for is underlying absolute reality, paramattha dhamma, that which shows itself as having no personality, no identity.

How will we find that? If we get concentrated in meditation we may, at one point, know only awareness. At that moment we can experience that there is nothing in this world that can be added onto us, nor is there anything that can be taken away. The only reason we know about this is because there is awareness which can be placed wherever we like. We can, at this moment, put our awareness into our home, and think: 'I'd like to be there. All my friends are there.' Wherever our awareness goes, that's where our thoughts will go.

So why not put our awareness on the fact that this world is empty of anything that has significance? We need not put our awareness on: 'I am going to find something that will make me totally happy,' because all of us have tried that without success. We are all intelligent people, yet nobody has found ultimate worldly happiness, always believing to have made some sort of mistake. But if we put our awareness on the underlying reality that there is nothing in this world which contains anything of substance, we may actually find ultimate happiness.

Within the constant movement of birth and death, of arising and ceasing, there is no solid point which one can hang onto. There is also the realisation that fulfilment cannot come from outside but has to originate within, so that one doesn't look for anything worth knowing, owning or possessing. That can be experienced for a moment in one's meditation when one becomes aware of a pause between the breaths or between the thoughts; an awareness arises that there is nothing, only awareness.

Nothing. Why not put the attention on that? The mind will say: 'Nothing? Maybe I can yet find something. I am still looking and don't want to come back empty-handed.' The stars, moon, sun, clouds, dogs, cats, birds, fish, lotus flowers, what will it be? People, children, grown-ups? Uncles, mothers, fathers? Whom can we select to bring us perfection? We can start from that premise and search, rather than assuming; if we tackled it correctly, we would find the ultimate in worldly conditions.

Dukkha (unsatisfactoriness) goes away when one doesn't want anything, when there is nothing to be found that's worth having. When dukkha goes away, no choice needs to be made because then our inner department store is selling only one kind of goods, namely happiness and peacefulness. But when there are still happiness and unhappiness available, we must realise that the latter is due to resistance; either not getting what we want or getting what we don't want; not having things in the world in accordance with our own ideas or still hanging our happiness on a star out there. Sometimes we think happiness may be embedded in some mysterious person we haven't met yet. How can any other person experiencing dukkha, lacking core substance, ever bring us happiness? Just as everything in nature arises, gets born and dies, such as trees, birds, cats and flowers, we are exactly the same. Although we can talk about it, there is absolutely no difference between us and them. It is our inflated sense of ego which proclaims that we are the cream of the crop, the apex of creation.

Because we can reason, we believe we are different. But if we could really reason properly, why would we be unhappy, even for a moment? That's not very reasonable, is it? We have to come to that understanding through the meditative process, which will show us that the mind does not have to carry this ballast around. As long as the mind is burdened by likes and dislikes it will experience dukkha.

It is like a porter carrying a lot of luggage which is really heavy. As we are used to that, we think that's the way it has to be. In meditation we can experience moments of utter lightness, no burdens at all. Why then carry that baggage in daily living? It is not necessary to have it along, since it doesn't contain anything of value. More little suitcases filled with bricks. If it were of any value, then it would be a great pity that we are constantly losing all our thoughts and can hardly ever recapture them.

If we experience one single moment of lightness in our meditation where none of this mental baggage is burdening us, surely that gives enough impetus to continue. Feeling inner lightness and no projections into the future or clinging to the past will be our source of contentment then.

Ambhapali was a prostitute in the Buddha's time and Angulimala was a murderer; both became enlightened. If they had clung to the past they could never have achieved freedom. People cling fast to less weighty subjects. They cling to what somebody said, or what they replied, what they did or didn't do. The human theatre is absurd. Why do we do all this? There can be only one answer. If we have no happiness with which to support the ego then we must at least support it with unhappiness.

Without projecting into the future, or hanging onto the past, we can actually be without any mental burdens. When we drop all these thoughts for a moment we realise that we were engaged in a totally unnecessary, exhausting mental exercise.

If we have the choice of carrying 100 pound weights in each hand and walking around with them, day in and day out, or of putting them down, what would we do? We would choose to be without them, wouldn't we? We have that choice in the mind too. Meditation teaches us that choice. If we know that unhappiness is a defilement, then every time it arises we can say to ourselves: 'There is something wrong with my approach to this matter.' Check unhappiness out against craving and letting go of that, you will be one of the rarest people in the world: one who is always happy.

Originally published in *Little Dust in our Eyes*, 1988. Republished in *The Middle Way*, vol. 7, November 1992.

NINA COLTART

(1927–1997)

Medical doctor, Freudian analyst, author, speaker and Theravada Buddhist

Nina was born Elizabeth Cameron Coltart in Kent, England to parents of the Christian faith. Her father was a physician and both of her parents died when she was 13. Nina and her younger sister Gill were brought up by their maternal grandmother. Nina read English and Comparative Languages at Oxford. She received a medical degree at St Bartholemew's Hospital and worked as a psychiatrist then trained in psychoanalysis. She started private practice in 1961 and converted to Buddhism.

She was involved with the formation of The Chithurst Monastery in Sussex, and Amaravati Buddhist Monastery in Great Gaddesdon in Hertfordshire and chaired The Hampstead Buddhist Group. She also practiced Calligraphy and enjoyed living alone. Although a great deal is written about Buddhism and psychoanalysis, rarely do authors practice both and have enough knowledge and experience to write accurately. Nina was the exception and was experienced in both the practice of Buddhism and psychoanalysis. She contributed to *The Middle Way* and was admired by members of The Buddhist Society. She left a rich legacy of talks, articles and books including *Slouching Towards Bethlehem* (1992), *How to Survive as a Psychotherapist* (1993), and *The Baby and The Bathwater* (1996). She suffered from chronic pain and ended her own life in voluntary euthanasia in 1997 aged 70.

The Practice of Buddhism and Psychoanalysis a Freudian View

Nina Coltart, 1991

I have never, from the earliest days of my 22-year career, felt any sense of conflict about combining the practice of Buddhism with that of full-time psychoanalysis. Of course there are differences, and it is important to know what they are, and to maintain certain distinctions clearly in one's mind. But there are many more extensive and subtle ways in which they flow in and out of each other and are mutually strengthening.

Before considering differences, I should perhaps say that I am assuming that whatever opinions one may hold of some of Freud's theoretical ideas, one must acknowledge that his thinking over the period from 1895 to the mid-1930s provides the foundation for all the great burgeoning of psychological development in the twentieth century, and his phenomenal output over these years (the Standard Edition runs to 25 volumes) is still a rich source of thought-provoking concepts to many who have further developed different theoretical and technical paths. In the British Psychoanalytical Society we still use this huge output as the core of our training, though of course our tradition is now enriched by many who came after him – Klein, Ferenczi, Glover, Fairbairn, Bowlby, Winnicott, Balint, Kohut, Laing and Searles, to name but a few. To my mind, it is a waste of time to use it up by niggling away at criticism of ideas which, like them or not, have their place in our history, and which have often served as springboards for further thought and theorising. It misses a larger very relevant point: namely that anyone who is engaged in the great diverse field of psychotherapy, whatever their school or training, is essentially: (a) fascinated by human nature, and (b) keen to effect what reparation of ills they can with the tools available. By now we are more or less agreed on two enormous main factors: (1) that there is an area of the mind that is unconscious, and (2) that human behaviour has meaning, and that it can be understood psychologically and that this is in itself therapeutic.

Concerning differences. Dynamic psychotherapy is non-religious; it has evolved in the West from centuries of philosophical thought which goes back to the establishment of Cartesian rationalism. If there is one central question at the heart of the Western systems, out of which Freud himself grew, it is 'Who am I?' Christianity has, by its basic doctrines, helped to perpetuate the cult of the individual, and we are deeply conditioned in the West to the necessity of establishing a strong and stable ego-identity. Psychotherapy is geared to this end, and, though it may in effect have many other by-products, its aim is thus limited, unlike the Eastern spiritual traditions. Theoretically it can therefore be said to have goals and end points. The rooted assumption prevailing in the West is that a strong and resilient self can live in this world in a state of more or less happy adjustment.

Freud's great contribution was that an increase in self-knowledge, in the context of a faithful adherence to truth, can 'liberate the human spirit' – his own words from a wonderful late paper, 'Analysis Terminable and Interminable.' His famous dictum, 'Where Id was, there Ego shall be' expresses the goals; psychoanalysis is the means. In the Western view of psycho-structure, the ego is the mediator between the unruly passions and fantasies of man, and the external world – and the more self-knowledge leads to satisfactory adjustment between the two, the more successful the outcome of analytical psychotherapy is considered to be. I repeat, therefore, that psychotherapy is essentially a means to an end, and not an end in itself. Freud himself persistently maintained that he was not constructing a philosophy of life, that his investigations into the nature of the unconscious in relation to man's whole sense of self were not intended to be an ethical system, and that his intention was that much of man's suffering could be healed or diminished by the growth of self-awareness. Attempts to bend his theory into a long-term philosophy of living or world view – whether this is seen to be morally okay, or, as has so often been the case, amoral or even immoral – are a misinterpretation of his own thought on the matter. Psychotherapy in our tradition encourages deep reflection but knows nothing of meditation. By his phrase 'liberation of the spirit' Freud did not mean the same thing as is meant by 'liberation' as an Eastern religious goal; he meant freedom from neurotic symptoms, inhibitions and anxiety. He never in fact used the word 'identity' in the sense it has taken on in the post-Freudian era, but his intention was to strengthen our sense of individual identity.

I would like here to quote a succinct passage from an essay called 'Psychiatry and the Sacred' by Jacob Needleman. This essay appears in an excellent book, *Awakening the Heart* (ed. John Welwood. Boston: Shambhala. 1984), which contains contributions from people who know something of the practice of both sorts of discipline. Needleman says: 'In the great traditions [referring to the Eastern spiritual ones] the term self-knowledge has an extraordinary meaning. It is neither the acquisition of information about oneself, nor a deeply felt insight, nor moments of recognition against the ground of psychological theory. It is the principal means by which the evolving portion of mind can be nourished by an energy that is as real, or more so, as the energy delivered to the physical organism by the food we eat. Thus, it is not a question of acquiring strength, independence, self-esteem, and security, 'meaningful relationships', or any of the other goods upon which the Western social order is based and which have been identified as the components of psychological health. It is solely a matter of digesting deep impressions of myself as I actually am from moment to moment: a disconnected, helpless collection of impulses and reactions, a being of disharmonised mind, feelings and instinct.'

Before proceeding to similarities or overlap, I would like to say a bit here about what might be called 'meditation and muddles'. I refer to the ways in which the practice of meditation, the heart of Buddhist practice, can be misunderstood or misused by us in the West, and I refer most specifically to those of us who work in the field of therapy. Roughly speaking, however much we might disguise the stark nature of the fact from ourselves, I think it would be true to say that one starts on both these paths – therapy and meditation – with the wish for increased comfort and peace of mind. Muddles can occur however, when aims are lost sight of – and there is a particular danger peculiar to the West which I think cannot be over-emphasised. For a Westerner to proceed healthily on the spiritual path which may lead to self-transcendence and loss of 'the fortress I', there must already exist a stable, strong sense of personal identity – not necessarily a happy one. If this is lacking, then psychotherapeutic help may be needed to repair and stabilise the ego first. Eastern teachings either take for granted that a person already has a healthy structure, or they define this differently in a totally different culture. This kind of assumption is dangerous in the West. If a person has not developed the ability to make wholesome personal relationships, or is ignorant or unable to express his feelings, or is plagued by anxieties, then psychotherapy may well be necessary before embarking on meditation. Psychotherapy helps people to understand themselves in ways that are essentially pragmatic.

I quote from John Welwood in the same book: 'To attempt to skip over this area of our development in favour of some spiritual bliss beyond is asking for trouble.' And Robin Skynner, in his essay 'Psychotherapy and Spiritual Tradition' adds: 'Some people following sacred traditions do indeed change a lot, and problems which might have taken them to the psychotherapist fade away imperceptibly – but they may inadvertently take from the spiritual movement that which actually keeps the ego strong. Or some may, as a result of going into a spiritual system, become more closed, narrow and intolerant. This group is the most intractable of all, for the knowledge derived from a religious tradition has been put to the service of perceptual advances, of complacency, of narcissistic self-satisfaction, of comfort and security.' A note of clear warning is issued by many authors in this book, of which I again select John Welwood for one final quote: 'The psychologising of Eastern contemplative disciplines could rob those disciplines of their spiritual substance. It could pervert them into a Western mental health gimmick, and thereby prevent them from introducing the sharply alternative vision of life they are capable of bringing us.' To this I would only add that one sees too often that such a spiritual practice in the West may be used as an escape from growth; spiritual growth may for a while be commensurate with psychological growth, the latter here being the road to self-mastery through knowledge, towards a more flexible and healthier adjustment to the world in which we find ourselves living out our existence. Psychotherapy does not aim at self-transcendence, and there may be a sad confusion of concepts when, say, detachment lends to it a kind of neurotic spiritual inflation, or a certain depth of awareness leads to a mistaken and crudely omnipotent notion that one is nearing enlightenment or even 'has it'.

Psychological adjustment is not liberation. The path of spiritual growth cuts off at an angle to that of psychological growth, and to confuse the two may be to get stuck unawares, or with a sense of disillusionment. Why do so many people drop away from meditation practice? Either because they begin to break down under its influence, having misjudged its power, and really do then need psychological help. Or more commonly, because it genuinely does strengthen them, makes them more comfortable, reduces their anxiety, and then they are satisfied that they have reached a point which, properly speaking, is only a point on the road followed by the pragmatic secular psychotherapist, and is nothing to do with a spiritual search.

Now for the link-ups between psychoanalysis and Buddhism. Firstly, the Four Noble Truths. I think we who practise psychoanalysis would certainly be in agreement when I say that our work is about suffering. Indeed, the very word 'patient', (to which I notice some people have an aversion and prefer other words like 'client'), is an honourable old word, and comes from the Latin *patio*, 'I suffer'. We have to believe, to move on to the second and third Noble Truths: that mental suffering has a cause and that it is capable of being brought to cessation, or we would not do what we do. We therefore operate on the principle of Dependent Origination, and, without too much mind-bending, but with a simple attention to the inner meanings of the features of the Eightfold Noble Path, we can see that not only our own professional standards, but our hopes and aims for our patients are embedded in it. For example, another way of considering wrong view and wrong thought is that they present themselves to us as psychological symptoms: that a psychotic or neurotic view of life, of the self and of others, we believe to be capable of improvement, even full healing, by insight and change in the direction of what the Eightfold Path calls right view and right thought – that is, views and thoughts unclouded by fear, anxiety or delusion.

To move on to the last three features of the Path, we know that in our profession the patient has to do a great deal of the work involved; brilliantly accurate interpretation is no good if it falls on stony ground. Unless there is a growing openness on the part of both patient and therapist, each to the other, and a willingness by both to make efforts in an atmosphere of trust, no treatment occurs. Concentration on the matter in hand in every single session would be taken almost as a necessary given. Right speech, right action and right livelihood are not bald and static prescriptions; none of the parts of the Eightfold Noble Path is regarded as an absolute, except in the highest spiritual practice – for our purposes here, they are relative. People come to us with many variations of wrong speech, wrong action and wrong or inhibited ways of living. We see thought-block, excessive shyness, verbal inadequacy, much disturbed behaviour, often accompanied by aggression, guilt and shame. Feelings of powerlessness, meaninglessness and futility are energy-blocks and neurotic preoccupations which grossly interfere with effective action or peaceful life – and almost always, anxiety spoils any or all of the ingredients of the Eightfold Novel Path. Right wisdom may sound a tall order, even as a relative goal, but a moment's thought will enable us to translate the concept into something simpler, humbler, desirable, and often – as a result of therapy – attainable. It can hardly be said to be wise to be hampered by neurosis, especially if one earnestly and consciously longs for change; but change may not be attainable without the concentrated efforts of the therapeutic partnership in an atmosphere of mindful striving towards just 'getting better'.

Although the Eight Hindrances at first have a rather ominous biblical ring, as of the seven deadly sins, we can on reflection see that they are only names for the various kinds of psychological disease which turn people in our direction. A few examples will serve: destructive tendencies in whatever sphere; contamination of the potential for love by envy, pride or greed; the paralysing effect of doubt in such states as obsessional neurosis and, underlying them all, what is called 'ignorance', which for dynamic purposes I would most closely translate as the power of the unconscious. Our main efforts are always directed to loosening and reducing that power through psychological work and insight.

Finally, a few words about the use of meditation being central to the Buddhist practice and therefore, as I see it, to my life as an analyst, because really what the whole of this paper is about is a ludicrous falsity in any notion that for part of each day I am a sort of practising Buddhist, and for another part a sort of practising analyst, and for the bits in between a sort of nothing. Here it is relevant to say that I do love the inherent meaning of the very word 'practice'. It is all practice, and all the practice can only be today and here and now. Certainly the formal practice of sitting meditation, with concentration on the meditation object, is an important part of the day. In the Theravada tradition the object is either the breath (in Samatha), or the stream of arising and ceasing thoughts and feelings (which is Vipassana meditation.) One of its richest fruits, I think, has been a deepening of a quality which is essential for the good-enough practice of psychoanalysis. I refer to something for which there is no one exact word, but it has to do with patience, with waiting, with 'negative capability' which, inseparably linked with the continued exercise of bare attention, creates the deepest atmosphere in which the analysis takes place. I have slowly discovered that the more one just attends and the less one actually thinks during an analytical session, the more open one is learning to trust the intuition which arises from the less rational and cognitive parts of the self – and the more open one is to a full and direct apprehension of the patient and of what is actually going on. This is not to undervalue or dismiss the great and abiding importance of really knowing one's stuff, of being well-grounded in theory and technique, and capable of applying one's rational mind to problems thrown up by sessions in the intervals between them. Nor do I wish to encourage emotive, self-orientated and wild interventions which are unprofessional, and which can be frightening and burdensome to patients. The discipline of meditation practice enhances the disciplines of one's contribution to an analytical session, which sometimes is, in fact, almost indistinguishable from a form of meditation.

I do not teach my patients meditation. It has no role – except for me as analyst as described above – in the carrying out of what my patients expect from me, which is that I should use as flexibly as I can the tools of my own trade for their benefit. There are plenty of good meditation teachers around now, both inside and outside the Buddhist tradition, and if a patient should reach a point where he recognises in himself a real hunger to continue his search along that line, which is tangentially angled to ours, then he will begin to look further. Many patients do not reach that point and do not wish or need to, and it is not part of my job to push, encourage or urge them in that direction.

To end, I would like to quote the words of a wise and distinguished older Buddhist friend, which I think speak for the two inter-penetrating worlds of the practice of skilled analysis and of Buddhism. He said, 'I don't really know what enlightenment is or could possibly be. The only thing I hope for and work slowly towards is a process of gradual disendarkenment.'

This text is reprinted from *The Middle Way* vol. 2 August 1991

GELONGMA TSULTRIM ZANGMO

(1932–)

Tibetan Buddhist nun, author, devoted to Choje Akong Tulka Rinpoche and his family, resides at Purelands, Kagyu Samye Ling Scotland, having had historic encounters with many Buddhist and spiritual leaders of the last century.

Gelongma Tsultrim Zangmo was born Veronica Player in 1932; her father was a doctor whose parents died in Belsen. Her mother's parents were taken to Auschwitz. She was raised in London and married twice. She was greatly influenced by the work of Gurdjieff and the work of Krishnamurti. She set up her own design studio in London after marrying her second husband Michael Player. She met His Holiness the 16th Gyalwang Karmapa at the Friends Quaker House in London then later met Akong Rinpoche. This was her introduction to the Dharma and the beginning of her deep connection with the Tibetans. She arrived at Samye Ling in 1977 for the first time. She met many spiritual masters including Khenpo Tsultrim Gyatso, Chogyam Trunpa Rinpoche, Kalu Rinpoche, Tulku Urgen Rinpoche, Ven. Khenchen Thrangu Rinpoche, Goshir Gyaltsap Rinpoche, Sherab Palden Beru, Ani Pema Choskyi. She wrote her autobiography *Where The Bees Are There The Honey Is*, published by Dzalendara in 2014. She met the late Choje Akong Tulku Rinpoche in 1965 and many other leading figures of Buddhism including His Holiness the 17th Karmapa. She contributed to *The Middle Way*, journal of The Buddhist Society and her autobiography is available in its library.

Pilgrimages to India and Nepal

Gelongma Tsultrim Zangmo, 1999

The year 1998 was a year of opportunity to revisit places of interest to true pilgrims. Having just completed a retreat at the end of January, I travelled to Bodhgaya in India, where the Buddha attained enlightenment, in a party of Buddhist women led by Lama Yeshe Losal, Abbot of Samye Ling monastery in Scotland.

Although my legs were swollen from sitting the retreat, I was happy to be with the others and was looking forward to fulfilling a dream. Several of us had completed at least one if not two or three traditional retreats at Samye Ling of three or four years duration each. Nonetheless we were still technically considered to be 'novices' because there is no full ordination for women in the Tibetan Buddhist tradition. It does exist, however, in the traditions of Burma, China and Vietnam, among other countries. Therefore, it had been arranged and requested by Lama Yeshe Losal in consultation with the twelfth Tai Situpa and approved by His Holiness the Dalai Lama that we should be ordained at a ceremony to be performed by the Venerable Master Hsing Yun according to the Chinese tradition. Several of us had waited over ten years for this event, and about 150 nuns from many different lineages came to Bodhgaya to participate.

After a gruelling training programme which included relentless standing and kneeling on the marble floors of a beautiful Chinese temple, we were overjoyed to be allowed to go to the wonderful and inspiring Bodhgaya stupa early in the morning of the day before the ordination ceremony. We gathered around this most holy place and prayed according to our own tradition.

Then my friend Ani Chopel suggested that we all should join the other nuns from Ladakh and Bhutan who were a few paces closer to the Bodhi tree. As Ani Chopel placed her legs in the lotus posture, she fainted. She flopped forward and then to one side. I remember seeing her face and thinking how relaxed and very peaceful she looked. Chopel died under the Bodhi tree. She was the first person known to do so in the 2,500 years since the Lord Buddha's parinirvana. Many Buddhists pray all their lives to die there, and I remember her saying on a retreat that she would like to die under the Bodhi tree most

of all. It was with mixed feeling that we all attended the final ceremonies
without her. At the same time we thought it was a most wondrous event, and
she had actually got her wish.

After the ordinations, we all went with Lama Yeshe to Benares (Varanasi).
The other nuns went on a short pilgrimage to some of the holy places but as
I did not feel up to walking too much, I flew to Kathmandu in Nepal to join
Dr Akong Tulku Rinpoche, the founding president of Rokpa International.
Rokpa means 'help for those in need' in Tibetan, and he was visiting our
children's home established several years ago and helping to distribute food,
clothing and medicines to the poor and needy. Rokpa International also has
many projects in Tibet: clinics, schools and colleges and health and environ-
mental initiatives. Some colleges have been teaching Tibetan medicine so
that students can go back to their villages and help their own people. The
teaching of practical skills such as bicycle-repairing and carpet-making is
also being introduced.

Lama Yeshe and the others arrived a few days later. The party set out for
the famous Marateka Caves, where Guru Rinpoche (Padmasambhava), the
legendary hero of Tibet who was instrumental in establishing the Buddha-
Dharma there, is said to have attained eternal life. My legs were still swollen,
so I was grateful to be able to travel by helicopter with Lama Yeshe. The view
was simply magnificent as we glided through the valleys over remote villages
with terraced crops. Sometimes the mountains were dangerously close as we
entered the different ravines with ribbons of water passing through them.

The ceremonies and prayers took place in the lower cave, a wonderous
natural temple where, high on the rock inside, a footprint was left by Guru
Rinpoche as he flew out after his attainment. The candles and beautiful
surroundings were a great inspiration to our group and to the 15 Sherpas
who cooked and carried all the burdens, including tents and food. There is
a place at the entrance to the cave where, if you blow into a hole at shoulder
height in the rock, you can make a musical sound like that of a conch. This
is said to prolong one's life.

When we arrived, there were very few prayer flags but, with offerings
from us all, they were bought and strung everywhere – in front of the cave
and also on a nearby stupa. The view from this stupa towards the Everest
range is spectacular. I returned to Samye Ling with a full heart.

At the end of 1998 a generous friend offered me some air miles. I wished
very much to visit several monasteries in northern India that I had not seen
for many years. Arriving in Delhi on 15 December, I travelled up to Gangtok

in Sikkim and stayed at the new cliffside house of Ringu Tulku Rinpoche, one of my teachers, and his lovely family. He teaches meditation techniques, and there is a shrine room for some 200 persons.

My room gave a view of the snow-covered mountains and also of Rumtek monastery, the seat of His Holiness XVII Karmapa, Ogyen Trinley Dorje. In 1980 I had seen there the religious Lama dances and also the Lhamo dances, which depict the famous epic legends of Tibet. When our small party of European women arrived at Rumtek, we heard that Goshir Gyaltsap Rinpoche from Ralong monastery was visiting overnight. We were glad to be blessed by him there instead of driving three hours to his own monastery as we had planned. I was completely bowled over by this mighty lama with his piercing gaze.

I returned to Delhi and after delays owing to fog, I made the long journey to Sherab Ling monastery in Himachal Pradesh, arriving on Christmas Day. The landscape was littered with rounded smooth granite rocks, as if an unseen hand had strewn them in between the patches of rice paddies, which were beautiful shades of fresh green.

There was a very special atmosphere at the older of the two temples. I was deeply moved and wept in front of the shrine. In the new temple carvers were doing exquisite work on thick poles and figures in wood with great skill and speed. Artists were painting wondrously detailed murals on the main walls, and the ceiling was being decorated too. The temple certainly will be magnificent, but much remains to be done before it opens in some months' time. I also enjoyed spending the afternoon with the kind and wise nun who was leading the current retreat lasting the traditional three years. We listened to the powerful *Mahakala puja* (protector prayers) performed by seven nuns on retreat.

After journeying up to McLeod Ganj in Dharamsala to meet a scholar, I returned to Delhi – the skill of the bus driver in the fog amazed me. On the 28th I flew to Amsterdam, where I had a short rest with friends, before returning to Samye Ling. Visiting holy places and great masters, even for a short time, is such an inspiration.

Originally published in *The Middle Way*, vol. 4, August 1999.

FRANCESCA FREMANTLE

Author, translator, teacher, promoter of shared truths of philosophy, religion, and art.

Francesca Fremantle is a meditation teacher and writer on Buddhism, and a translator of Sanskrit and Tibetan texts. She read Sanskrit at the School of Oriental and African Studies, University of London, and received her PhD for her thesis on the Guhyasamaja Tantra. At a very young age she had developed an interest in Indian culture and philosophy and later travelled extensively in India. She practiced Hindu Tantra with Sochi Sen, an artist and devotee of Kali, in Kolkata.

Francesca became a student of Chögyam Trungpa Rinpoche, and collaborated with him on a translation of *The Tibetan Book of the Dead* published by Shambhala in 1975. In 2001 Shambhala published *Luminous Emptiness*, in which she explores the meaning of *The Tibetan Book of the Dead*, and which contains some revisions of the text. She is a teacher within the Longchen Foundation, established by Trungpa Rinpoche and Dilgo Khyentse Rinpoche and directed by Rigdzin Shikpo. She is a popular public lecturer at the Buddhist Society in London and contributes to its journal, *The Middle Way*. Her current interest lies primarily in showing the universality of the insights of meditation through discovering affinities in Western culture, whether in science, philosophy or the arts.

What is Tantra?

Francesca Fremantle, 2018

This subject, 'What is Tantra?' was suggested to me. I understand you've had quite a few talks lately about Tibetans and others about various tantras. There are so many different approaches to this question, one could answer it in any number of ways. I thought I'd take a different approach; not going into any details of the tantric systems, or the history of tantra, or anything like that, but speak in a more general way about the tantric view of life.

It is something that is much wider than simply the formal practice of tantra. The actual practice of tantra, of Vajrayana itself is very complicated. You have to have spent many years practicing meditation of various kinds and above all you have to have a very close relationship with a guru and a sangha of fellow practitioners with whom you work and who support each other. Without all of this background it's impossible to practice Vajrayana successfully. So that is something that is really quite hard to talk about.

In fact, we're not even supposed to talk about the actual practices of tantra, but tantra itself, as an approach to life, is something which is very much wider and which is not exclusive to India, or Tibet, or the Far East at all. My great interest nowadays is to try to find parallels in our Western culture and to show everyone how wonderful this approach to life is; how it's quite natural to all of us and how all artists and scientists as well, have expressed this in their work universally. So it's not a strange and esoteric approach at all.

You could express the particular attitude of tantra in several different ways, but I think one of the best ways of putting it is that tantra is known as vehicle of the result, or of the goal. That means it takes very, very literally the Buddha's original teaching that we are all Buddha. We all are Buddha right here and now, there is nothing in this whole universe that is not the Buddha nature. Because of our confusion (which means that we are living in samsara) we don't know we are Buddha. It is said the only difference between Buddhas and ordinary sentient beings is that sentient beings don't realise they are Buddha.

It's not that we have to become something different from what we are now; that we have to turn ourselves from ordinary people into Buddhas. We have to somehow clear away all dust from the mirror, is the Zen way of putting it. We have to cut through the confusion and let ourselves let go and rest in that essential Buddha nature which we all have and which we are all expressing all of the time. We are never wholly immersed in confusion; everything we do is a very strange mixture of absolutely natural, egoless, awakened expression in our actions of interest in other people, empathy, compassion. The way strangers rush to help someone who has an accident in the street; our appreciation of beauty; our sudden feeling of oneness with art, or with music, or with the street that you're walking down, or even in the London Underground – anywhere this awakening can take place.

This is present the whole time, but mixed in with this, because of the little twist of grasping that we have within us, there is confusion. This grasping, what in Buddhism we call ego (which is not the same as 'ego' in its psychoanalytical meaning, or in its everyday colloquial meaning), is simply the feeling, 'I am at the centre of all this, I own my body, my feelings, I am the creator of my thoughts, my emotions.' It's just like a spider sitting in the centre of a web and drawing everything into it, but really there's not a spider there at all. It's simply a feeling of grasping. It's a little twist of always putting this something at the centre of everything.

We know very well what it's like not to feel like that. We know very well when we are very close to another person. We know it when we are absorbed in something that we really love. We know it in all kinds of ways and we don't value the experience of our Buddha nature.

This picture is of Padmasambhava, who is always known to practitioners as Guru Rinpoche ('the precious guru'). It is a rather wonderful image that expresses this feeling of sudden awe and wonder – he's gazing up at the sky and making this gesture suggesting he is at one with the mind of enlightenment. This gesture (the Tarjani Mudra) also can be a threatening gesture because he is warding off, or pushing away Mara, who encapsulates all the confusion and the sense of grasping that assails us. What this sense of grasping does is jump on the bandwagon of what is already there and doesn't need it at all. It has nothing of its own, it's like a parasite on a tree, or on the back of an animal.

In order to practice tantra one leaps into this conviction that, yes, we truly are Buddha and everyone else around us truly is Buddha. Our practice is not to become Buddha, but to manifest Buddha nature through actions.

There's a lovely Zen story about two Zen masters. One was walking along the road and saw his friend meditating and he said, 'Why are you meditating? Do you meditate to achieve Buddha nature?' The one said, 'No, I meditate to express Buddha nature.' This is true from the very beginning, we meditate to express our Buddha nature. We couldn't achieve it however hard we tried. Our trying would in fact be totally destructive of achieving it.

Buddha nature is not an achievement, it is what we naturally are. You start from this in the practice of tantra and in order to do this we identify ourselves with what are called the tantric deities. It may seem very strange to speak of deities in Buddhism. They are not in the least what's meant by the deity in Christianity. They are not even what's meant by the Greek, or Norse, or Indian deities. They are simply different expressions of Buddha activity and Buddha qualities.

It would be very nice to just be able to rest straight away in our inde-finable, mysterious inexpressible Buddha nature, but we can't do that, our minds just don't work like that. We need to latch onto individual qualities and individual actions in order to arouse them and manifest them ourselves. This is why there are these countless forms of the Buddha, like Amitabha, Vairocana, Akshobhya, Avalokitesvara, Tara. They are not separate deities. They are manifestations of the Buddha nature in a way that our mind can relate to. Trungpa Rinpoche said they are not inventions of the mind, but expressions of the very nature of the universe.

In fact, they have no meaning apart from their expression. Avalokitesvara is a person who is expressing compassion. Tara is a mother looking after her child. The wrathful deities are people who with great energy and courage save others and maybe have to, apparently, cause some injury in order to do that. All the expressions of our natural human state can be used in an enlightened way instead of a confused way and it all depends on whether we are manifesting them with or without ego. Very often it is a mixture of both. Very often we do compassionate actions with some thing of self-inter-est as well. That's just the nature of samsara, we shouldn't beat ourselves up because of that. We should recognise the enlightened aspect in the actions of everyone around us.

They are manifest in the world outside us as well. We can see the energy which is represented as a Buddha by Amoghasiddhi; we can see that tremen-dous energy in natural phenomena like volcanoes, tornadoes, even just the wind blowing through the trees. We can recognise the warmth and compassion of Amitabha in the heat of the sun, in fire, in light. Once you get into looking at this tantric imagery it's so helpful and it's so skilful because it does connect with every single thing that we experience. Once we get used to this you can immediately link your mind with some aspect of Buddha nature and realise that the whole thing is an expression of this.

This way of looking at the world is called pure perception, or pure vision, or sacred vision and this is a tremendously important part of the practice of Vajrayana. This is what I find in so many aspects of universal human experience as well. This is what is expressed in music, and art, and poetry, and by philosophers. Anyone who deeply applies their whole being to the search for some kind of truth is following this path and is letting their ego step out of the way in order to immerse themselves in that work that they are doing. All forms of science and mathematics, as well, are equally like this. In fact, the great discoveries in science, just as much as the expressions of art, come from that place of non-ego and the awakened state where the true nature of reality arises spontaneously, and we don't have to do anything about it. It seems that these things don't come from ourselves, it often seems as though it's a gift from outside. The great mathematician, Ramanujan, used to say this about his mathematical discoveries; he used to say they were given to him by God.

Sacred vision, direct perception, obviously comes to us through the senses. The senses are what we have to work with and yet Trungpa Rinpoche said the senses are unnecessary complications of existence. He also said, the miracles of sight, sound and mind are the five wisdoms and the five Buddhas. So we have to imagine a different way of perceiving through our senses, including the mind. In Buddhism the mind is regarded as a sense. Thoughts are its object, just as sights are the object of the eyes, sounds are the object of hearing. Thoughts and emotions and whatever arises in the mind are the object of mind, a sensory organ. This is how it's seen in Buddhism.

Blake had a wonderful saying that we have to see through not with the eyes; and the eyes stood for all the senses. Just seeing with the eyes is just seeing in the ordinary way, seeing through the eyes is seeing, you could say, from our heart; that's probably the best way to express it. Seeing the true nature of what we are looking at. What we are looking at, we know from Buddhism, is impermanent, transient, a cause of suffering, it has now permanent existence of its own. When you see from the heart, or listen from the heart, or feel in one's skin from the heart, or taste the smell through the senses rather than with them, as Blake said, this is called direct perception in Buddhism.

This is how it is said the Buddhas perceive. It is said the Buddhas don't have senses, they don't even have minds; they have direct knowing, the Sanskrit term is *jnana*. We can't experience this direct knowing in the way the Buddhas do, but we can certainly intuit what it means. When you have an experience of any kind of perception where you feel completely at one with what you are seeing, or hearing, or touching; this is an example of direct perception. I think everyone knows that experience. We can't live in it the whole time, but we can certainly know what it means.

Blake said that he always saw with a double vision, meaning he saw both the apparent outward object and he saw, what he would have called, its spiritual essence. This is somewhat like the level of images in Buddhism, it's called the Sambhogakaya. Behind that, and what gives meaning to everything we perceive, is what in Buddhism is called *sunyata*, emptiness. It's not emptiness in a negative sense, it's emptiness in the sense of openness; the mysterious nature of everything. It means we can't know it with our mind. We can never grasp it, we can never pin it down.

Emptiness, is said on the Buddhist path, to be a medicine which you take at the beginning of the path because we are so severely bound up in our ordinary perception of everything, we are so attached to the objects of perception so we need to see their empty nature, and it seems like a negation for a while and then very quickly you realise, that actually it is a different kind of fullness. It is sometimes experienced as bliss, which is a very tantric expression; you can say bliss, instead of emptiness, or unknowableness or ungraspableness. It's this idea that the innermost nature of everything is totally mysterious to us and direction gives us a connection from the heart to that unknowable essence.

Trungpa Rinpoche said that the whole universe is always trying to tell us something, but we don't listen to it. It's as though everything is a symbol of itself; everything is pointing to its own inner meaning which is this infinite potentiality and mysteriousness. Many poets have expressed this. There's a little quotation from Philip Larkin, 'The trees are coming into leaf like something almost being said.' TS Eliot said, 'We had the experience, but we missed the meaning.' This, of course, is what we do all the time. We might recognise some significant experience, but we don't understand what the significance of it is. This is part of the training in learning to perceive the world in this way; to have sacred vision.

Here is one of Blake's lovely paragraphs from *The Marriage of Heaven and Hell*:

'The ancient Poets animated all sensible objects with Gods or Geniuses, calling them by the names and adorning them with the properties of woods, rivers, mountains, lakes, cities, nations, and whatever their enlarged and numerous senses could perceive.

And particularly they studied the Genius of each city and country, placing it under its Mental Deity; till a System was formed, which some took advantage of, and enslav'd the vulgar by attempting to realise or abstract the Mental Deities from their objects.'

So this is separating the ideal of a deity from our natural experience itself.

'– thus began Priesthood;
Choosing forms of worship from poetic tales.
And at length they pronounc'd that the Gods had order'd such things.
Thus men forgot that All Deities reside in the Human breast.'

That's the important line. This is the feeling that we all have this natural ability to perceive in this way, but because of the split that has been made over time and because religions developed into organisations which had to perpetuate themselves through laws and hierarchies, thus it became that people were really taught and persuaded that the deities are out there somewhere, whether it's a polytheistic system or a monotheistic system. They forgot that all deities reside in the human breast, which is exactly what Vajrayana tells us.

Blake also says 'in those days'; that means not those days long ago, but the potentiality that exists within us, but which we have forgotten and clouded over. He talks about the 'enlarged and numerous senses,' so our senses are actually capable of very much more; an entirely different scale of perception than what we are ordinarily used to. This is part of the sacred vision idea. Blake said that eventually everyone would attain this state of sacred vision through and increase in sensual enjoyment:

'The whole creation will be consumed, and appear infinite, and holy whereas it now appears finite and corrupt. This will come to pass by an improvement of sensual enjoyment ...

If the doors of perception were cleansed everything would appear to man as it is, infinite.

For man has closed himself up, till he sees all things thro' narrow chinks of his cavern.'

So this is how Blake saw it.

This is Blake's visionary painting, *Jacob's Ladder*. This is really how he perceived things in everyday life. He must have been in a state of samadhi the whole time because he would see people as angels and he would see the sun as a host of angels saying, 'Holy, holy, holy is the Lord God almighty!' He talked in terms of angels and fairies mostly. He would see plants and trees as having a spiritual essence, which would appear to him perhaps as a fairy. In one of his prophetic books he meets a fairy and asks is the material world is dead and the fairy answered, 'I'll sing you to this soft lute, and show you all alive, This world, where every particle of dust breathes forth its joy.' That's a very Vajrayana sentiment.

In connection with this painting of Blake's, which gives you the feeling of pure perception, there's a wonderful poem by Francis Thompson:

'O world invisible, we view thee,
O world intangible, we touch thee,
O world unknowable, we know thee,
Inapprehensible, we clutch thee!
Does the fish soar to find the ocean,
The eagle plunge to find the air –
That we ask of the stars in motion
If they have rumour of thee there?
Not where the wheeling systems darken,
And our benumbed conceiving soars! –
The drift of pinions, would we hearken,
Beats at our own clay-shuttered doors.
The angels keep their ancient places; –
Turn but a stone, and start a wing!
'Tis ye, 'tis your estrangèd faces,
That miss the many-splendoured thing.
But (when so sad thou canst not sadder)
Cry; – and upon thy so sore loss
Shall shine the traffic of Jacob's ladder
Pitched betwixt Heaven and Charing Cross.
Yea, in the night, my Soul, my daughter,

Cry, – clinging Heaven by the hems;
And lo, Christ walking on the water
Not of Gennesareth, but Thames!

So that is an example of a very Vajrayana approach to life, I think.

This is a picture, *Wanderer above the Sea of Fog*, by Caspar David Friedrich, which seems to sum up the whole Romantic movement in the arts which swept across Europe including this country in the 19th century.

A critic called Joseph Koerner said of his paintings – which very often have very desolate landscapes with maybe one human figure in them – that the way these figures are positioned in the landscape, 'the world appears to be an emanation from his gaze, or more precisely, from his heart.' Although we can't see his gaze or his heart you do get this feeling from this painting. I think what it expresses is, it's bringing back the importance of the human being and the importance of nature which are very much united. This is a great feature of the whole Romantic movement, in fact, and turning away from the idea of a completely external and separate god; bringing the importance of the feeling, the consciousness and the awareness of sentient beings into the centre of the whole thing.

Even though they didn't have the expression of being Buddha, or having Buddha nature in this painting and in many of the works of the whole Romantic movement. There's always a very close relationship with nature and seeing God in nature – they would have said God in those days certainly. Seeing the divine; seeing the idea of deity in nature itself and in human beings and respecting and valuing nature. In a sense, getting away from the split between reason and emotion which was something that concerned Blake very much. He said that reason and emotion must absolutely go together and that when they become separated then both of them, in their different ways, become destructive.

This brings us to a poem by Rainer Maria Rilke which he wrote after seeing this torso of Apollo.

Rilke is one of these great poets that express this very tantric approach to life and there are very many poems that could be quoted, we'll just have to have this one. What's really remarkable about it, I think, is what he sees in this statue and the final words of the poem; the effect that his way of seeing has on him, his intense identification with the sacredness that's expressed in this image:

'We cannot know his legendary head

with eyes like ripening fruit. And yet his torso
is still suffused with brilliance from within,
like a lamp, in which his gaze, now turned to low,
gleams in all its power. Otherwise
the curved breast could not dazzle you so, nor could
a smile run through the placid hips and thighs
to that dark centre where procreation flared.
Otherwise this stone would seem defaced
beneath the translucent cascade of the shoulders
and would not glisten like a wild beast's fur:
would not, from all the borders of itself,
burst like a star: for here there is no place
that does not see you. You must change your life.'

This is really what everything tells us when we see it with sacred vision. There is no place that does not see you. We look at anything, whether it's a work of art or a piece of rubbish in the street and the universe is looking back at us and seeing us. The whole universe is alive and responding to us just as we respond to it.

There's another poem of Rilke called 'Gong', and he says how the sound of the gong is no longer for the ears, but it's sound which completely envelopes us and which listens to us who think we are hearing, or something to that effect. It hears us, the apparent hearers. So when we listen to sound that sound is listening to us. When we taste something in our mouth the taste is tasting us. It's a thought that submerges us in the interconnectedness of everything and the oneness of everything. This is called one taste, or one essence in Vajrayana, and it's a fundamental principle that pervades the whole of our experience.

This is a painting by Jasper Johns which I believe is in Tate Modern, but it was exhibited at the Royal Academy last year [*Dancers on a Plane*].

He has a very interesting attitude to his work in which he says that painting is in order to revel something like the truth; as near to the truth as one can manage. Picasso said a nice thing, 'Art is the lie that shows us the truth.' He also suddenly became very interested in tantra, especially in Tibetan images. This painting is about dancers and is dedicated to Merce Cunningham, who was his friend. You can see that it's full of dancing. Just the impression; the whole thing is dancing, but it also has something in common with a Tibetan painting.

I believe he must have seen this painting in New York. There are all kinds of details of elements which he's put in *Dancers on a Plane*. There are tiny skulls, for instance. It's very difficult to point all of them out. The frame has cutlery embedded in it all the way round; knives, and spoons, and forks, and things which take the place of the weapons the deity, Samvara, is holding.

Why am I showing you this? It's the kind of feeling I want to give. In Tibet, or in India they made tremendous use of visual imagery, it's an extremely important part of tantric practice to use this imagery. But we don't have to restrict ourselves to this really rather weird cultural context. We can actually express this, and find it, and see it in cutlery, or anything. Anything we can see around us: sticks and stones, fire clouds, everything. So this is just one way. There are many, many examples in Western art, whether or not they've been influenced by Buddhist imagery, or Hindu imagery for that matter. They might not even have any interest in that, but they're expressing somehow the same kind of thing.

If you want to read an article about this painting it's available on the Royal Academy of Arts web page. On the Tate Britain web page they have a different explanation of its inspiration. They say it was inspired by a Hindu image of Shiva Nataraja, which means Shiva is Lord of the Dance in union with Shakti. Shiva Nataraja is not in union with Shakti so they are completely wrong there, but all the same, here is an image of Shiva Nataraja.

It is another very, very beautiful image which I think everyone can relate to as an expression of energy, an expression of the universe. It is the creative dance of the universe. He's holding a drum in his right hand which produces the vibrations from which everything arises. In his left hand, held up as a flame which will destroy everything in the end. It's a completely wonderful image. Going back to *Dancers on a Plane*, you can see the dancing element even though the image of Shiva Nataraja wasn't the one that inspired it.

The idea of dance is tremendously important in Vajrayana as well. It's often said that the whole of existence is a dance, or they can say a play, a drama. When we imagine ourselves as the deity, act as though really we are the Buddha, we are playing a role. In order to do that we have to realise we are actually playing a role right now. The most important thing before one can imagine oneself as a deity is to completely give up the idea of what we are right now. You have to give up the idea of being male, or female; give up the idea of your background; your age, absolutely everything that we cling to, that we think defines us. We become a being which is totally ungraspable, which has no attributes of colour, or shape, or solidity, it's a being of light.

The fallout of this practice is that one begins to understand that we are always playing a role. We have to do this; this is not to say this role is not important. Whenever we say something is like a dream or an illusion, or a role, or a part, a dance, it's never ever in a dismissive sense because this is what we are. Through the embodiment that we each have we manifest our Buddha qualities. It's totally wonderful that we are embodied beings, of whatever kind we are: short, or tall, fat, thin, clever, or not clever. Whatever we are, it doesn't matter in the least, we are using what we have incarnated as to express our Buddha nature.

Now a Buddhist expression of the dance. This is a Cambodian image.

These are just other examples of kind of similarities in Western art and Buddhist imagery. When you look at these kinds of paintings, when you just sit in the middle of Rothko's paintings and just gaze at them, yes, you do feel that they are gazing back at you and that they could tell you everything. If you looked at them long enough, you could actually find the answers to everything in them. So this is an example of this sort of Vajrayana approach to perception.

I did want to read a couple of quotations to express the feeling that one has and that Blake said of perceiving beyond the senses; through the senses. When the actual individual senses – the sight, hearing and so on – lose their importance there is a kind of essence of sensation and this also refers to what Trungpa Rinpoche is saying that the senses themselves are not essential. It is the direct perception that is essential, that is the thing that has significance for us.

Proust definitely had this feeling and he expressed if very beautifully in a famous passage. His book is to do with time, more than anything else, but to me even more interesting than what he found out about time was what he found out about the senses. He was plunged into his memories of the past through the taste of a little madeleine cake dipped in tea and that reminded him of his childhood and the whole three books unfold from that. But this is the passage that really I find more interesting from the point of view of Vajrayana. He describes what happened:

'No sooner had the warm liquid mixed with the crumbs touched my palate than a shudder ran through me and I stopped, intent upon the extraordinary thing that was happening to me. An exquisite pleasure had invaded my senses, something isolated, detached, with no suggestion of its origin. And at once the vicissitudes of life had become indifferent to me, its disasters innocuous, its brevity illusory – this new sensation having had on me the effect which love has of filling me with a precious essence; or rather this essence was not in me it was me. I had ceased now to feel mediocre, contingent, mortal. Whence could it have come to me, this all-powerful joy? I sensed that it was connected with the taste of the tea and the cake, but that it infinitely transcended those savours, could, no, indeed, be of the same nature.'

So he'd reached something absolutely beyond the sensation that had given rise to it.

Since we've had poetry and some art, I thought we ought to have a little bit of music as well. To introduce the prelude to Richard Wagner's *Lohengrin*, there's a quotation from a German poet Friedrich Schlegel which Schumann quoted at the top of his score for his Fantasie in C major for piano, which unfortunately is too long to play to you, but it is a most amazing work and if you can find it at home do please listen to it. At the top of that it says:

'Through all the tones
In earth's colourful dream
There sounds one soft low tone
Extended for the one who listens in secret.'

So for those who really listen, in this sense of direct perception, there is one tone which runs through the whole of existence.

There is an image of Samantabhadra which has the Tibetan letter 'ah' written at the top. The important thing is the sound 'ah', which of course, is like alpha in Western Christian and Alchemical tradition; the beginning of everything. It's also the sense of total letting go and it being the origin of everything dissolving into the primordial state of Buddhahood. So it's called the primordial 'ah.'

Reprinted from *The Middle Way*, vol. 93,no3, November 2018

ROSHI JOAN HALIFAX

(1942–)

Zen Buddhist teacher, Abbot of Upaya Zen Centre, founder of The Ojai Foundation and Being With Dying, author and anthropologist, student of Bernard Glassman, Thich Nhat Hahn and Seung Sahn.

Joan was born in 1942 in New Hampshire and attended Tulane University. She received a PhD in medical anthropology and was a research fellow at Harvard. She is Abbot of Upaya Zen Centre in Sante Fe, New Mexico and a director of many projects including the Upaya Prison Project, Being With Dying, and the Nomads Clinic in Nepal. She is an author of many books and contributes to Buddhist publications and The Mind Life Institute investigating the relationship between Science and Buddhism.

Mindfulness Practice

Roshi Joan Halifax, 2020

Mindfulness is the basis of everything that we do in being with dying. It is also the very basis of all meditation practices in the Buddhist tradition. Grounded in not-knowing, practicing mindfulness is a mental and physical commitment to bearing witness that comes from the desire to foster healing. It is based in the aspiration to free ourselves from suffering and to help others. This motivation is how we keep ourselves committed to practice. The desire to serve helps to give our practice energy and depth and makes our practice more tender and inclusive.

Trust and patience combined with openness and acceptance – qualities nurtured by mindfulness practice – enable us to sustain ourselves in being with dying. This helps us to develop the necessary relationship between compassion and equanimity and learn to respond from a place that is deeper than our personality and our conceptual mind. With equanimity and compassion as inseparable companions in our work we are also to be less judgmental and less attached to outcomes.

Mindfulness practice consists of intention, posture, diaphragmatic breathing, and awareness of the breath (or some other object of mind that is present for us.) Most often I use the breath as the object of concentration, because this very life depends on it.

Intention

As we sit down to practice mindfulness meditation, it's important to touch in with our intention. Why are we meditating? Is it only for self-gratification? Remembering interconnectedness – that if others are suffering, we cannot be fully happy – helps us see the futility of self-centredness. Recall someone to whom you feel especially close, whom you deeply wish to be free of suffering. Let your wish for this one help strengthen your aspiration to help others. As you experience fully how this feels, breathe deeply into your belly.

Posture

You can sit in a chair or on a meditation cushion. After sitting down, be aware of your breath and your body. Let your body soften. If you are sitting on a chair, relax your legs and put both feet flat on the floor. If you are sitting on a cushion, cross your legs loosely in front of you and be present to a sense of connectedness with the earth – gravity. Invite the stability and groundedness of the earth into your body and mind. Let your whole body experience the strength of your stable connection with the earth. Bring your attention to your feet and legs and breathe into them. Relax into the firmness of this stability.

Now bring your awareness into your spine. Breathe into your spine. Appreciate how vertical, strong, flexible, and conductive it is. Rock gently from side to side as you settle your posture. The strength of your spine allows you to uphold yourself in the midst of any condition. You can remind yourself of this strength by silently saying, 'Strong back.' Your mind and your back are connected. Feel the sense of uprightness and flexibility in your mind.

Now let your awareness go to your belly. Breathe into your belly. Let your breath be deep and strong as your belly rises and falls. Feel your natural courage and openness as you breathe deeply into your belly.

Shifting your awareness to your chest, touch in with the tender, open feeling of this space. Let yourself be present to your own suffering and to the fact that just like you, others also suffer. Imagine being free of suffering and helping others be free of suffering too. Feel the strength of your resolve rising up from your belly. Let your heart be open and permeable. Release any tightness you feel as you allow your breath to pass through your heart. Remind yourself of your own tenderness by saying, 'Soft front.'

Now bring your awareness to your lungs. With your spine straight, let your breath fully enter your lungs. Fill your lungs softly with air. With gratitude, remember that your life is hanging on each breath.

At this point the whole front of your body feels open, receptive, and permeable. Through your open body, you can feel the world, which lets you feel compassion. Through your strong spine, you can be with suffering, which lends you equanimity. Your open heart allows you to be with your strength of mind. Let all these qualities – equanimity, compassion, and strength – intermingle. Let them inform one another. Let them give you genuine presence. Strong back, soft front. This is the essence of our work in being with dying.

Bringing awareness to your shoulders, let them soften and relax. Then shift focus to your hands. Experiment with the following two hand positions and see how they inform your state of mind. One is to rest your hands on your knees, leaving the front of your body open. This is a way to enter into shared awareness as you subtly welcome everything into your consciousness. Alternatively you can put your hands together in front of your belly, which strengthens internal awareness and concentration.

Your chest is slightly lifted, your neck is straight, and your chin is barely tucked in, giving a small lift to the crown of your head. Your jaw is soft, your teeth are barely touching, and your tongue is lightly pressed against the hard palate just behind your teeth. Your mouth is relaxed.

What you do with your eyes will affect your mind. Work with the following three possibilities. Your eyes can be gazing forward, not grasping onto anything. They can be slightly open, gazing down at the floor. Or they can be closed. With your eyes gazing open, you can be with life as it unfolds, bringing forth a sense of luminosity to the phenomenal world. With your eyes slightly open, you are at the threshold between your mind and the outer world. Not entering either world, you bring both together in emptiness. With your eyes closed, you relax into an undistracted concentration.

Whatever sounds, sights, smells, tastes, or feelings arise, simply let them pass in and out of your awareness, as you keep your mind on your breath. Allow yourself simplicity. You are relaxing in such a way that you can begin to drop into a place that is deeper than your personality, deeper than your identity, deeper than your story.

Diaphragmatic Breathing

Now bring your attention to your breath and breathe into your belly. The diaphragm is a muscle that can hold fear. Let your deep and unrestricted inbreath move your diaphragm down. Let go of any hesitation, any fear that might be arising. This deep breath is an experience you will use to strengthen your awareness.

Awareness of the Breath

With your attention on your breath, silently count your outbreaths from one to ten. When thoughts, feelings, or sensations take your attention away from your breath, you will lose count. When you become aware that your concentration has faltered, simply label what has distracted you as 'thinking,' 'feeling,' or 'sensation.' Then return to counting your breaths beginning with 'one.' Keep your practice very simple and direct, gentle and precise.

You also may use words to help deepen your concentration. For example, you can say to yourself silently on the inhalation, 'Breathing in, I calm body and mind.' On the exhalation, 'Breathing out, I let go.' On the inhalation, 'Dwelling in the present moment.' On the exhalation, 'This is the only moment.'

One of the reasons we bring our awareness to the breath is to deepen our concentration. When the mind becomes very concentrated and stable, it is easier for us to see the world as it is. Not only can we have insight into reality, but we can also see directly, beyond language and concepts, into reality's very nature. Perceiving directly allows us to respond seamlessly – that is, with compassion and stability – to the world as it is.

When we have completed our meditation practice, we offer to others whatever good has arisen for us to others. We also remind ourselves to bring the spirit of practice into our everyday life in order to help others. Finally, we recall the elements of the practice that we are bringing into life – stability, strength, openness, flexibility, concentration, commitment, relaxation, confidence, courage, tenderness, compassion, and equanimity.

I suggest that a beginner to meditation receive instructions from a qualified teacher. There are many meditation teachers in America and Europe who have the skills to help one begin a stable practice. Mindfulness meditation can be used for stress reduction. It can also lead one to mental depths. A sensitive teacher can support you through the rough and placid waters of a developing practice.

I feel that a daily practice is very important. Sitting 20 minutes in the morning and 20 minutes in the evening can help us become acquainted with our mind. I also feel that doing at least one retreat a year can deepen and strengthen your practice. A Zen sesshin or a ten-day vipassana retreat at least once a year can be profoundly beneficial. These kinds of retreats always include private interviews with the teacher. This gives the practitioner the opportunity to have his or her practice evaluated.

Levels of Practice

Mindfulness practice has six interdependent levels – calming, accepting, harmonising, realising, engaging, and secret.

Calming

Most often we live in the conceptual mind, the mind of knowing. In mindfulness practice we begin to quiet ourselves, to calm ourselves. Through the experience of stilling and calming, we begin to see the nature of impermanence and perhaps discover the fresh mind of the beginner. In the beginning, we usually discover that we are neither calm nor clear. In stopping our usual external activity, we notice the relentless flow of the contents of the mind. As our practice develops, we become internally quieter when our capacity for self-observation and our experience of not-knowing deepens.

Accepting

The next realm of practice begins to open when we explore why, really, we are practicing. This is bearing witness. When we see the usefulness of non-doing and not-knowing, we may discover the spaciousness of patience. As our experience of practice deepens, we also begin to discover that reality is characterised by constant change. Being with the truth of impermanence can allow us more easily to surrender to pain, sickness, and yes, even death. Accepting practice as medicine to transform suffering and nurture awareness opens the way for us to experience spaciousness and the truth of change.

Harmonising

Our experience of alienation can result from poor synchronisation of mind, body, and the outside world, a lack of awareness of the interconnectedness of inside with outside. One of the most important effects of mindfulness practice is that it can produce a synchronisation of mind and body through the union of breath and awareness, and then a synchronisation of mind and body with reality.

Mindfulness practice can open the experience of harmonisation of mind and body with the world. The thread of the breath sews the mind, body, and world together. This is the basis for the tenet of healing.

Realising

When our body and mind are synchronised with the world, intuitive mind awakens. Since we are no longer caught in a web of concepts, it is possible to perceive directly, beyond language and concepts. We are able to realise our own suffering, as well as our wisdom and compassion. Again, we are touched by the tenet of not-knowing.

Engaging Practice

Once the meditator is in touch with her own suffering, she begins also to know the suffering of the world. Engaging practice of compassion in action is rooted in the tenet of healing. It takes us into the world, where our practice involves bearing witness to the suffering of others and engaging and serving them selflessly, with no attachment to outcomes. This is the realm of bodhisattvas, healers, shamans, teachers, and caregivers – those who have made a commitment to helping individuals and transforming social institutions, cultures, and environments.

Secret Practice

Finally, mature practice is invisible. In the best of circumstances, we realise ordinary mind, and experience the subtlety and richness of ordinary life. Mind, body, and reality have become one. Secret practice means that there is no separation between our practice and our everyday lives. We have no attachment to outcomes and play no special role as practitioners. Perhaps this is the deepest realisation of the tenet of healing.

This text is reprinted from *The Middle Way*, vol. 94 no. 4, February, 2020

ROBINA COURTIN

(1944–)

A Buddhist nun in the Tibetan Buddhist Gelugpa tradition and lineage of Lama Thubten Yeshe and Lama Zopa Rinpoche. Author, editor, feminist activist and international speaker.

Robina Courtin was born on 20 December 1944 in Melbourne, Australia. In 1996, she founded the Liberation Prison Project, which she ran until 2009. Courtin was raised Catholic, and in her youth was interested in becoming a Carmelite nun. She was a feminist activist and worked on behalf of prisoners' rights in the early 1970s. In 1976, she took a Buddhist course taught by Lama Yeshe and Lama Zopa in Queensland, Australia.

In 1978, Courtin ordained at Tushita Meditation Centre in Dharamsala. She was Editorial Director of Wisdom Publications until 1987 and Editor of Mandala until 2000. She created Chasing Buddha Pilgrimage, leading pilgrimages to Buddhist holy sites in India, Nepal and Tibet. Her life and work with prisoners have been featured in the documentary films *Chasing Buddha* and *Key to Freedom*.

She currently resides in the US where she continues to teach the Dharma online at her centre as well as looking after the welfare of prisoners.

Love or Attachment?

Robina Courtin, 2020

I would like to start with a little prayer, which expresses two things. The first part refers to anybody in the room who already identified with the Buddha, as it reiterates our reliance on the Buddha and his teachings, while the second two lines express our motivation. The Lamas would say: 'Set your motivation for what you are going to do.' In this little bit of time together, we will have the purpose to listen to the Buddha's viewpoints of the mind, which is the Buddha's expertise, together with the causes of suffering and the causes of happiness. The way of listening to it is to understand it as a tool, as an advice, and the advice is twofold: to develop wisdom, in order to be compassionate towards the beings around you. Wisdom and compassion, the two wings of the bird. That is our purpose today.

To say that the Buddha's expertise is the mind is very accurate, but it may sound a little bit odd, as we are used to thinking of the spiritual as opposed to the intellectual. But actually, as the Dalai Lama said, the Indians of 3,000 years ago are those who began this investigation of the nature of the self. The Buddha was born in that system, and then he diverged in his own direction, particularly in relation to his own experiential findings about the nature of self. These Indians created the technique we know today as mindfulness, which is actually called single-pointed concentration, a brilliant psychological skill which can be attained through hard practice. This single-pointed concentration represents a very subtle state of mind: in our modern views of the mind, we cannot even think that such a subtle level of being exists, and this is the great difference with the Buddha's approach and viewpoint. The Indians investigated internally, they unpacked and unravelled the contents of the mind. The map of the mind studied in Buddhist universities is coming directly from the Hindus: the Buddha learned and carried on the views on karma, the views on mind and what our potential is. He simply diverted and went in his own direction, providing a different interpretation, but still these amazing Indians are the source of all this.

We Christian Jewish Europeans are sometimes arrogant in thinking that it was Freud who began the investigation of the mind and of the nature of self, about 100 years ago. Now, the origins of this investigation, made by these amazing Indian thinkers, scholars and yogis, are finally becoming known and published. Indeed, their expertise was the mind, and the potential of the mind.

If we hold a Mahāyāna approach, we notice that the etymology of the word 'Buddha' tells us exactly what the goal is, which also implies the method. The root 'bud-' implies the utter eradication from one's mind or consciousness (which are broadly synonyms in Buddhist psychology) of all neurosis, all fears and all ego, all things that we, in our culture, instinctively feel as normal parts of one's own life. They seem so normal, that you think you are weird if you didn't have them. They are something that primordially we take as given. That also implies that we can develop to perfection everything else in our minds: love, compassion, kindness, the things that we know are nice. This is the result, and it implies the method: it is very clear. You'd better know your mind! The essence of being a Buddhist is knowing one's own mind, being one's own therapist. The reason why we should do that is clear, it is implied by the results. It is fundamental to give up attachment, anger, jealousy, pride: for the Buddha, these are the main sources of our suffering, and therefore of other people's suffering. Indeed, the Buddha tells us from his own direct experience that we must eradicate these things from our minds.

It is important to know that the Buddha is not a creator, but we also have to understand the implications of that. A few years ago, a scientist in New Zealand asked me a question, which would seem very usual if you take the classic approach of most religions. He asked: 'Who revealed the teachings to the Buddha?' He was kind of shocked when I replied: 'Would you ask Einstein who revealed the teachings about relativity to him?' Of course, Einstein used his own intelligence to absorb the world around him, and then he came up with his own findings and presented them to the world. That is the Buddha, no more and no less. We usually hold the view that religion equals a creator, assuming that he knows all the knowable. But that is not the Buddhist approach. The Buddha is a regular guy, he is not the creator. This is very important, because the implication of this is that these teachings are not revelations. Despite the word 'belief' having its own place in Buddhist psychology, I prefer not to use it, as it implies some kind of intellectual laziness. Indeed, Buddhism is not something you believe in, is something you do through practice and right effort.

Let us look at the Buddhist view of the mind, and at the difference between attachment and love. The Buddha would distinguish between mental consciousness and sensorial consciousness. That is why one needs mindfulness, single-pointed concentration, the skill that enables us to look internally in a rigorous and logical way, through unpacking and unravelling the contents. So, what should we unpack and unravel? The first thing to do in order to be able to choose between good and bad is to distinguish them. We could say that there are three kinds of states of mind. The first is the neurotic, deluded, negative, non-virtuous one, that causes us misery and causes us to harm others, and which is difficult to get rid of. Then, there are the virtuous states of mind, of love, compassion, intelligence, wisdom, which we can perfect and which are the sources of our happiness and of our ability to help others. The third kind is what I like to call the mechanics of mind. These are the things like concentration, good memory, discrimination, attention, intention. Whether you are a murderer or a meditator, you need these to function properly. These are developed in single-pointed concentration, the ones we need to distinguish between the neurosis and the good things. It seems pretty simple, but this is the hardest job we will ever do, as good and bad are completely mixed together like a big soup.

So, what is attachment and what is love? Love, kindness, generosity, forgiveness are valid states of mind, and they are valid because they are rooted in this dependent arising reality, where there is a sense of connectedness and interdependence. On the contrary, check when jealousy, pride, arrogance and attachment are prevailing: there is a vivid sense of being separate. These neurotic states of mind have got two functions: one is that they are disturbing, which is pretty evident. The other is a little bit tricky to spot, but if we recognise it then we really understand what Buddhism is, and we then are able to distinguish between the neurosis and the virtues. These states are delusions, and I believe that this English word really captures the meaning of it. These toxic emotions mainly cause us not to be in sync with reality. Understanding these functions is necessary if we want to practice Buddhism. Indeed, growing the virtues after having eradicated attachment is the actual job of a Buddhist.

I would say that in our culture we usually conflate attachment and love, and that the way we use the word attachment is as it has a good quality. So, we consider attachment to be a synonym for close and loving. Indeed, we all know that the same word, with the same spelling and pronunciation has also a different definition. It is crucial for us to really understand what attachment is, because for the Buddha it is indeed the source of all unhappiness and suffering. The Buddha's understanding of these states of mind is unbelievable: as we practice, we will reach the subtlest levels of this attachment, until we realise emptiness, which is so primordial. Only in that way we are then able to distinguish between love and attachment. On its primordial level, attachment means unsatisfaction, which is so important and present in our culture. Unsatisfaction is the profound feeling of not having enough, not being enough. Dissatisfaction means a bottomless pit of not enough. This feels so real that we never question it, of course: it is beyond pain.

Then, based on dissatisfaction, there is the attachment to the objects of the five senses, the grossest level of attachment. This means yearning, hungering for something that we feel we need: the more the hunger, the more the dissatisfaction, the more it manipulates and controls us in order to get the thing we desire. Attachment to an object of desire makes us forget the delusional nature of that object, and then makes us think that the object could bring us satisfaction and happiness.

Then, the next level of attachment consists in a massive expectation and anticipation of the happiness coming. Then we get emotional hunger, neediness, dissatisfaction, manipulation, control. All of these are the functions of attachment: we must recognise that. Attachment is limitless in finding things to attach to, and in making us think that once we find the things we want, then happiness will come. The first of the three toxic emotions is ignorance, unawareness, a very specific and primordial kind of ignorance. When it comes to the self, we call it ego-grasping, which consists in a concrete and solid posit of the concept of 'me'. Attachment continuously manipulates us in assuming that we will be happy once we obtain what we want.

Then, the third poison is anger, the most obvious and violent expression of aversion, which is indeed the reaction of not obtaining the object of our desire. Of course, this emotion manifests itself in a spectrum of manifestations, that could be milder or more intense. When we start to comprehend these poisons, then we comprehend what Buddhist psychology is, and we then understand ourselves and other people. Through mindfulness, we begin to acquire the skills to pay attention to what is going on. For the Buddha it is crystal clear that these emotions, these poisons, are the root of all suffering: what goes on in our mind is the source of our happiness and sadness, and not the world around us. If we prove that this is wrong, then all Buddhist thought would collapse in absurdity. It is interesting to notice that this approach is the opposite of our Western, scientific approach, focused on the idea that the biggest influence is given by the world around us. This is what we usually pay attention to in our daily life.

We should begin to investigate what is going on inside us, and then begin to identify it. Usually, it is only when it becomes physical, when our bodies are involved, that we feel something is going on. The vast majority of humans on this planet have absolutely no idea that what goes on in their mind plays any role in their life and therefore has an impact on their emotions. We usually think that the world outside is what influences us, that we are the products of the external world, a thought which is clearly reinforced in science and psychology. Of course, Buddhism does not argue with that, it does not argue with the fact that what happens around us influences us, as it would be absurd, being us products of interdependence. Despite that, its emphasis and expertise is what goes on in here, inside us and inside our minds. The reason why one should be mindful is to unpack and unravel the conceptual stories that inform our emotions.

So, what is the difference between attachment and love, then? Attachment is I-based, fear-based, its nature is the character of all neurosis. Attachment embellishes, it is hungry, frantic, needy, manipulating, possessive, it tries to convince us that once we get what we want, then happiness will come. Attachment is grotesquely over-exaggerating our sense of misery and indeed the function of the object of desire, until it causes disappointment. Attachment is emotional hunger, and it informs everything we think, do and say. So, what is love? Love is a virtue, is marvellous, is the delight in another person's happiness. 'May you be happy': that is love. Even more powerful, love is what pushes us to think: 'What can I do to make you happy?' We all recognise that this is altruistic, fantastic, and that the more the better.

The trouble is, we only have love for those we are attached to, and we are only usually attached to those whom we love. But the truth is that the more attachment, the less love. It is brutal, but it is the truth. What makes a relationship successful is the wish for the other person to be happy, which is compassion. That brings you to become a bit tolerant, patient, forgiving: it will allow all the positive qualities to flourish. That is the source of all happiness in a fruitful relationship. Attachment is so prevalent and pervasive that it is sometimes hard to see: it mixes with the positive and genuine feelings.

In the different meditations we do to develop compassion and love, in the compassion wing, the foundation practice is called 'developing equanimity'. There are different understandings of equanimity. In the first stage of the practice, it is what you develop to become more stable in your practice. On the other hand, in the compassion wing, equanimity is mostly in relation to the dynamics of friend, enemy and stranger. Equanimity, once you got it, would be the clear and heartful recognition that the person you call a friend, who is the object of your attachment, the person you call enemy, who is the object of your aversion and even irritation, and the object of your indifference, a stranger, are all equal to each other from one point of view. They all wish to be happy; they all wish not to suffer.

The Buddha said that there is one way of framing all the Buddhist teachings: be happy and stop suffering. Equanimity is what changes the reason for wanting somebody to be happy. Of course, also attachment is one reason for wanting somebody to be happy, but it is not the right reason of course. Attachment is also a symptom of a very unhappy person, a disconnected one, who has ego-grasping.

We have to recognise and begin distinguishing between those qualities which are rewarding and those which aren't, which are delusional instead. The Buddha gives us advices to first recognise attachment, and then to eradicate it. The difficult side of it is that it is extremely difficult to distinguish between love and attachment. It is only when the other person stops doing what your attachment wants that you recognise between the two. In fact, as soon as anger and aversion arise, you realise that this is a form of attachment. This is the moment to catch the mind and realise: 'This is attachment.'

The other thing, which is implied here, in this Buddhist view, is the intimate relationship between attachment and aversion. In the Buddhist map of the mind, there are 84,000 distinct mental problems, all connected to the three poisons of ignorance, ego-grasping and aversion, which in turn have a profound, intimate correlation with each other. Here there is an interesting mapping of the mind, made internally, which is indeed part of the unique approach of Buddhism.

Attachment is deeply rooted in all of us. Then, aversion, the response of not obtaining what attachment wants, has a spectrum, as I have said: the most brutal manifestation of it is anger, of course. And then of course there are mild manifestations of it: irritation, frustration, annoyance, anxiety; all manifestations which we often experience. The tragedy in our culture is that, because we don't pay attention to the mild things that are part of life, we just think they are normal, but then one day, when a really severe thing happens, then the serious problems come. But, the point here, is that at that moment it is already too late, and that is because you don't pay attention to our feelings until we don't arrive to the breakdown point, when it is too late and there is nothing to do anymore. To do mindfulness is to bring into your daily life the skills that help you recognise what is going on inside your mind. As you begin to develop awareness, you are then mindful to your thoughts, your feelings and emotions. In that way, you can really be your own therapist, and deal with everything inside you. In that way, you can be able to manage your life.

Originally printed in The Middle Way, vol. 95, no. 1. May, 2020

Robina Courtin

AJAHN SUNDARA

(1946–)

Buddhist sīladhāra *nun, author, teacher and leader of international meditation retreats.*

Ajahn Sundara was born in France in 1946 and has been a Buddhist nun for over 40 years.

In her early thirties she encountered the Dhamma through Ajahn Sumedho's teachings and a ten-day retreat that he led in England. Her interest in Buddhist teachings grew, and in 1979 she joined monastic community of Chithurst Monastery in West Sussex where she was ordained as one of the first four women novices. In 1983 she was given the Going Forth as a *sīladhāra* (ten precept nun) by Ajahn Sumedho. Since then, she has participated in the establishment of the nuns' community at Amaravati Buddhist Monastery in Hertfordshire, and has taught and led meditation retreats in Europe and North America for the last twenty years.

As of 2011, she lives at Amaravati Buddhist Monastery. She has published many books including *Seeds of Dhamma*, *Paccuppanna*, *The Present moment*, *The Body*, *Walking the World* and *Friends on the Path*.

She is a frequent lecturer and teacher at The Buddhist Society in London.

The Wisdom of Emotions

Ajahn Sundara, 2014

Our emotions can be triggered by something very small: a physical sensation, a passing thought, a sense contact, a feeling. In the context of Dhamma we begin to notice that emotions are constructs: amalgams of thought, feeling, perception, past conditioning, trauma, family stories; all these things come together to generate emotions. Sometimes for no apparent reason we start crying, or we become angry or confused. If we can't find a reason, we may think there is something wrong with us, that it's our fault. We make ourselves miserable because we don't understand that there is a bigger picture.

Emotions fluctuate constantly; they are indefinable. We may be sitting calmly in meditation and when somebody comes into the room our sense of calm changes. We are aware of a new feeling tone, perhaps an emotional charge in the body. Letting go of that emotional charge requires wisdom and understanding, so as to see deeply the characteristics of *anicca – dukkha – anattā* (impermanence, unsatisfactoriness and not-self).

The terms 'wisdom' and 'emotion' seem to be foreign to each other. We don't usually associate emotion with wisdom. Interestingly, emotions are closely connected to the water element. A well-known teacher in the Forest Tradition pointed out that we are concerned about ecology and the purity of the elements on the planet, but rarely consider how polluted our inner water element can be. When we are not mindful of emotions, they can become septic. Through that lack of awareness, they can also become extremely powerful and affect our whole inner environment, just as dirty water can pollute the natural environment.

It can be difficult to look clearly at some emotions because they are so painful. But the Buddha's path begins with the recognition of suffering. It is only when we are able to see suffering that we can know there is an end to suffering. *Dukkha*, suffering, is sometimes translated as 'stress.' This is a good translation. When we look at our emotions, we are looking at stress, at tension. But we may find that although we study our mind and our body, our inner stories and the way we relate to other people, we are not actually seeing the stress associated with them. We know there is something stressful but we can't see it clearly. Very often that's because it is too close to us. It's like a second skin; there's not enough space between us and that emotional resonance.

For many years I did not see that I was angry in certain situations. It took me a long time to see anger as an objective experience. The same with greed. In fact, it was the energy of greed that brought me to the Dhamma. I realised that desire is a bottomless pit; it's never satisfied. No matter how many delicious things you eat, how many wonderful holidays you have, how many wonderful relationships you enjoy, dissatisfaction is always around the corner. That's what the Buddha calls *dukkha*.

When you see desire clearly, you also see its characteristics of *anicca*, *dukkha* and *anattā*. Who is the 'I' who desires and is constantly dissatisfied? Who is seeking sensory gratification? Who is the 'I' who is righteously angry? Until you see through the illusion of 'I' you will be trapped in desire. Of course, even when there is some insight into the nature of desire and the emotional suffering which results, that doesn't mean the habit of desire doesn't continue, or that you won't be blinded again. But you have seen and known the patterns of desire and begin to realise the importance of developing wisdom with regard to your emotions.

Letting go of an emotion can take time. Even though it may have completely ended in your mind, your body can still be filled with residual feelings of rage, greed or sadness. The body and mind don't always talk to each other. You may need to be really patient and conscious of how the body absorbs and releases emotion much more slowly than the mind. You may think that these emotions are happening because of something you did, but actually they are reactions to what we find pleasant or unpleasant, what we like or dislike. We don't need to blame ourselves, but simply recognise that when mindfulness is not present, life happens on automatic pilot. This is an aspect of *anattā*.

Sometimes the mind can be so filled with emotion that the brain loses the capacity to think and we cannot express ourselves. At such times of heightened emotion, the mind seems to have a kind of protective mechanism, the capacity to disengage. When we have a strong emotional experience, we may overreact and lose clarity. Because we don't have the ability to respond to the situation, the mind simply shuts down.

When an emotion is present, we can see it as a priceless opportunity. Even though it may be painful, when we stay present and connected to the heat and energy coursing through us, we will see it change and lose its emotional charge. We will be able to let it go. But if we're not aware of it, it will revive a lot of old stories. If we believe our emotions, they drag countless stories along with them. Until we see through and understand those associations, they are a terrible burden.

A great master like Ajahn Chah would set up situations where his disciples would see their emotional nature. He would push their buttons to the point where they would become really angry, driving their minds into an intense emotional state. If this kind of teaching came your way, how would you respond? Would you start complaining and blaming? Would you criticise? Or would you use the situation as a teaching?

Life gives plenty of opportunities to challenge and test us. Somebody always seems to be 'stepping on our toes.' In that respect, life is our great teacher. You may think, 'No. I'm going to meditate so I can calm down. I'm going to stay away from all that.' But remember that the state of calm is just one aspect of the practice. A calm mind is compared to a clear lake, but if we overlook the rubbish at the bottom of the lake, we lose our chance to be free from delusion.

Walking the Path isn't hard in and of itself. But it is hard for the sense of self, that illusory entity called 'me' who is so resistant to liberation. This self is a collection of habits, it's not a fault. You don't have a 'me' because you wanted one. It just happened. You didn't want to have a deluded ego which you may hate right now. We are very good at self-denigration; indeed, it may even be a comfortable feeling.

So how can we start befriending our emotional nature? Perhaps at first the head leads. We may have read teachings on emotions and we are filled with good intentions. Then, as Dhamma practice becomes part of our life, we draw closer to the heart. This may be frightening because the heart has a soft, vulnerable, fluid quality, unlike the mental energy in our head, which can be hard and quite rigid. When we come into the heart area we begin to be in touch with a much more nebulous world. In the realm of emotions things are much less defined. There are no clear partitions and boundaries. Emotions can be treacherous because they can spread and affect other beings. For a mind which is attached to logic and intellectual clarity, practice can be difficult, because seeing clearly has nothing to do with having an idea about things; it is the ability to see things as they are, here and now, with presence of mind.

As we become very present with our emotions, this presence of mind can cool reactions in a very natural way. Just by staying fully present when emotions arise, we can witness how they change and fade away. Whereas if we are not aware of this straight away, our emotions can become a mountain of problems. But I'm sure none of us want to have a mountain of problems. We don't ask for them, they just happen. This is *anattā*. There is no self in control, just the results of habits. When we say, 'I wish I was not so angry. I wish I was not so jealous,' we still think we're in control of our emotions, but actually we are not. But we can start looking at emotions through the lens of mindfulness and clear understanding. In Dhamma practice, mindfulness and clear seeing are simply allowed to take charge. When we are able to look at ourselves in that calm, quiet light of mindfulness, without judgement, compassion naturally arises, and we can accept ourselves just as we are. That moment is a complete acceptance of what is.

Commissioned for a Buddhist Society workshop that took place in November 2018 and published in *The Middle Way*, August 2018, vol. 93, no. 2. This text appeared in the Forest Sangha Newsletter, Issue 93, 2014.

AJAHN CANDASIRI

(1947–)

Senior Buddhist Monastic sīladhārā nun at Amaravati Buddhist Monastery, teacher and leader of retreats.

Born in 1947 in Edinburgh, Scotland, Ajahn Candasiri encountered the Buddha's teachings in 1977 through Ajahn Sumedho, who was abbot of Amaravati Buddhist Monastery from 1984 to 2010, after exploring several meditation traditions.

Ajahn Candasiri became a renunciant in 1979, a white-robed, eight-precept *anagārikā*, at Chithurst Buddhist Monastery in West Sussex. She was one of four *anagārikā* women who carved out an existence in the early days of Chithurst Buddhist Monastery, along with a group of monks.

In 1983, Ajahn Candasiri took *sīladhārā* ordination (brown robes and ten precepts). It consisted of a unique set of 137 rules and a new version of the *Patimokkha* recitation created by Ajahn Sumedho so that the women monastics could be trained in Ajahn Chah's lineage.

Ajahn Candasiri was one of the pioneer *sīladhārā* monastics who were trained by bhikkhus (fully ordained monks), in parts of the *Suttavibhanga* and a version of the *Vinaya Patimokkha*.

Ajahn Candasiri stayed in the *sīladhārā* community and is one of the *sīladhārās* who have been allowed to teach and lead retreats. She lived at Chithurst until 1999 when she moved to Amaravati Buddhist Monastery in Hertfordshire, where she continues to teach.

As of 2015, she is one of the most senior monastics in the Amaravati Sangha. In 2015, she founded Milntuim Hermitage in Perthshire, Scotland as part of the siladhara community, where she often resides as Abbess. Her recent contribution is her work on the book by Amaravati Publications *Enlightened Nuns*.

My Life as a Nun

Ajahn Candasiri, 2018

When, in 1979, I had first received permission from Ajahn Sumedho to join the fledgling monastic community at Chithurst Monastery in West Sussex, my heart felt very happy. It felt settled. With the mind it was another matter; I'd find myself repeating in amazement: 'I'm going to be a Buddhist nun!' It was not what I had anticipated for my life. Now, almost 40 years on I still feel glad, settled – and I am still somewhat puzzled to find myself in these robes, living the Buddhist monastic life. While it's true that there are some things that I would enjoy doing that are prohibited by our monastic code (the Vinaya discipline), alongside this there is a tremendous sense of gladness, a certain lightness of heart.

When asked what is the most important thing I have learned in all these years, I sometimes reply: 'To enjoy life; doing what I want, and putting myself first.' This being rather different from the response that is expected, some explanation is usually needed to appreciate how this could possibly accord with the Buddha's teachings and their emphasis on the relinquishment of personal concerns and attachments.

For almost two decades I was a 'good' nun. I was dutiful, hardworking, dedicated to helping the community: my Sisters, Brothers and lay friends – and yet never deeply happy. Even though I had no interest in leaving my life as a nun, I recognised the lack of joy – but I was at a loss as to what to do about it, as I seemed to be doing all the 'right things.' It was a life-threatening illness that finally precipitated a shift in my understanding. The Buddha's teaching on the impermanence of things took on a whole new meaning: I now knew beyond any doubt that I was not going to continue for ever; one day my body would die.

As I began to recover from the illness, a process of reflection led me to consider what is important in life – with the surprising conclusion: to enjoy it. Of course I knew that it's simply not possible to enjoy everything. We are all subject to pain, loss, blame and countless other experiences that would not normally be considered 'enjoyable.' However, I found that there is a curious satisfaction that arises when I can stay inwardly steady in the midst of difficult circumstances. I found that when I could relinquish the struggle to avoid or to manipulate conditions according to my preferences, and simply, patiently, stay present, I would experience a deep sense of calm. I saw that just as pleasant conditions change, unpleasant conditions also change; and I could learn from all of them. As I began to relinquish that understandable desire for things to be different, I discovered a capacity to see things more clearly and to respond skilfully to the changing conditions of life, instead of constantly reacting to them.

I enjoy telling people that I put myself first, and sensing their surprise. Many of us have been brought up to be 'unselfish.' The Buddha's teaching is often interpreted as requiring that we get rid of the sense of self or that there is no self, so how can we think that putting ourself first is in any way suitable in one's life as a disciple of the Buddha?

As we contemplate the teachings of the Buddha, particularly the Noble Eightfold Path, we come to the understanding that our human life can be seen as a precious opportunity to do good. Furthermore, it is these bodies and minds that are the vehicles through which this opportunity can be fulfilled .... and it becomes obvious that if our bodies and minds are in poor shape, the capacity for doing good is significantly compromised. So we need to consider: what do this mind and body need? If we really want to help, to serve in the best possible way, it makes sense to make sure that we are in a state of inner balance and well-being. With this understanding, my priorities changed. Instead of compulsively putting others first, while nursing the subtle expectation (or demand) that if we help them they will help us, I began to acknowledge and to consider more carefully my own needs. That concern rose from the bottom to the top of the list.

What did that entail? I found that taking care of myself involves a careful watching over the state of mind. It involves checking any harmful thoughts and impulses before they take a hold and manifest in speech or action. It was no longer okay to do something 'good' with a mind of irritation, ill-will or resentment. I had done that for far too long, and the results were not gladdening ... So I began to attend more closely, and to make sure that I did only what I wanted to do.

I still do plenty of 'good' things – and there is joy. I do them because I want to do them, not out of a sense of duty, or to avoid disappointing someone, or even to win someone's affection or approval. I now see that my 'duty', as a daughter of the Buddha, is to liberate the heart from the subtle and not so subtle forms of greed, aversion and delusion. Of course it takes time. Our habits are deeply ingrained and, even after becoming aware of them and seeing clearly what is required, it can take a lot of kindly, persistent application to transform those harmful habits of thinking that undermine our sense of well-being. However, right now, I can't imagine a better way to be occupying myself for the remaining years of my life as a nun.

Originally printed in The Middle Way, vol. 93 No. 2, August 2018

Ajahn Candasiri

Both photographs of Ajahn Candasiri by Peter Kindersley

LAMA ZANGMO

(1952–)

Director of Kagyu Samye Dzong, Director of Rokpa Trust. Ordained Buddhist Getsulma nun

Lama Gelongma Zangmo was born in Denmark in 1952. She first became interested in the Dharma in 1974, and in 1977 she went to Kagyu Samye Ling Buddhist Monastery in Scotland where she met Akong Tulku Rinpoche. That year she took refuge, Bodhsattva vows and precepts with His Holiness The 16th Karmapa when he visited Samye Ling in December 1977. She lived at Samye Ling from 1977 till 1998, a total of 21 years, 11 of which were spent in strict retreat. Between 1977 and 1984 she received teachings from the following Lamas and Rinpoches; HH 16th Karmapa, Khenchen Thrangu Rinpoche, Tai Situpa, Gyaltsab Rinpoche, Jamgon Kongtrul Rinpoche, Akong Tulku Rinpoche, Lama Lhachog, Khenpo Tsultrim Gyamtso, Kalu Rinpoche, Lama Thubten and Lama Ganga.

She entered the first four year retreat at Purelands in March 1984 till March 1988. Ven. Lama Ganga was the retreat master. She received all the traditional retreat initiations from Venerable Thrangu Rinpoche as well as instructions in the practices. She was also instructed by Lama Ganga and Lama Thubten. During this first retreat she took life ordination as a Getsulma nun from Venerable Thrangu Rinpoche in August 1985. Ani Zangmo entered a second four year retreat in March 1989 till March 1993. During the retreat she received initiations and teachings from Venerable Situ Rinpoche and Venerable Thrangu Rinpoche and Lama Yeshe Losal Rinpoche.

Ani Zangmo entered the third retreat of 3 years and 3 months in November 1993 till February 1997 making her total number of years spent in retreat 11 1/2.

In the second retreat she started to instruct the new retreatants along with three other nuns. In the third retreat she was given full responsibility for instructing and helping the other retreatants.

She took full Gelongma ordination, as well as the Bodhisattva vow of the lineage in February 1998 in Bodh Gaya from the Taiwanese Master Hsing Yung, with the Venerable Lama Yeshe Rinpoche as preceptor. She has also received initiation and teachings from His Holiness 17th Karmapa. Gelongma Zangmo has been on pilgrimage to the Theravada countries of Sri Lanka, Burma and Thailand as well as to India and Nepal.

In 1998 Lama Zangmo was asked to run Kagyu Samye Dzong London and since then she has served others by teaching the Dharma as well as looking after the Buddhist centre.

Lama Zangmo's strong connection with the Kagyu lineage and in particular with Choje Akong Tulku Rinpoche and Lama Yeshe Losal Rinpoche has inspired her to work tirelessly and joyfully in service to the Dharma and helping others. In recognition of her long experience, selfless qualities and commitment, she became the first person in the UK to be honoured with the title of Lama at a heart warming ceremony in Kagyu Samye Dzong London in June 2001.

The Four Thoughts that Turn the Mind to the Dharma

Lama Zangmo, 2016

'The preciousness of our human life;
Impermanence and death;
The principle of cause and result and
The inherent dissatisfaction of samsara'

These four preliminaries in Tibetan Buddhism are sometimes called The Four Ordinary Thoughts and they are essential for turning the mind to the Dharma. We find that as Buddhists, even if we have been Buddhists for a long, long time, it is as if the mind is like a wild creature that wants to go off track here and there, and we have to gently push it along with these four thoughts to turn the mind to the Dharma.

This is the foundation of Tibetan Dharma practice and in that sense is not any different from any other Buddhist school, it just phrases or categorises in a slightly different way. These qualities are contained in the teachings of all Buddhist schools.

If we don't have that foundation, our mind strays. Our mind goes on side tracks. I see this very often; people come to see me, and for a period of time they come regularly to the Centre, and all goes very well, they are happy with their practice but then after some time, suddenly they are gone and I don't see them anymore. They disappear from circulation for a while, then after maybe three or six months, sometimes longer, one or two years sometimes, they come back and say, 'I just realised I couldn't do it on my own. I got distracted, my practise went downhill, I couldn't manage to continue on my own without the support of a Dharma centre.' So they come back to the source; in a way it's a bit like a wild animal that has gone off, and then they gently push themselves back on track. There are so many ways of distracting ourselves from the practice.

If these four thoughts haven't really been integrated and assimilated, making them part of our being, then we get lost. Imagine trying to build a house or a temple without the foundations, or if you have weak foundations and you try to build the walls and the roof, pretty soon the whole thing starts to crumble. It's like that with our Dharma path. Without a very firm foundation, progress on the Dharma path crumbles and begins to disintegrate.

In Tibetan Buddhism we say, 'Renunciation is the feet of meditation, devotion is the head of meditation and non-distraction is the body of meditation.' This is describing the Dharma path, saying that renunciation is what gets us onto the path; it's what makes us move on the path. And in a sense these four thoughts are mainly the renunciation aspect; renunciation is the foundation.

Without renunciation we get distracted into all sorts of worldly activities, not that all worldly activities are bad in themselves, but they pull us away from Dharma practice. So renunciation is the necessary aspect. It's the thing on the ground that makes us move; it makes us turn towards the Dharma.

And then devotion is the head. The head is where we have all the sense impressions; we see, we hear. Without the head we can't do anything. So devotion is a very important aspect as well. It gives us inspiration, gives us direction, gives us perspective. We carry the guru above the head, or the lineage holders or the teachers; we develop appreciation and inspiration to keep us going.

The main body, the torso, is non-distraction, which is what we are trying to develop. By developing non-distraction the whole thing is built up. That's what our path is mostly about, sitting meditation. So renunciation is the four thoughts.

When the Buddha was still Prince Siddhartha, the king tried to protect his son because he didn't want the prophecy that his son would become a great spiritual guide and teacher to be fulfilled. He wanted his son to become the next king. So he tried to protect him from anything that could possibly plant the seed of renunciation in him. It is said that everything was beautiful in the palace, and even the flowers got whisked away when a tiny leaf started to whither. There was not a sign of decay in his world. The king was a very powerful, wealthy person and at the snap of a finger all the servants were there, keeping it all pristine and perfect; we would think of it as a god realm, perfection. There was no hint of suffering surrounding the Buddha. Sick people would be whisked away, old people would be whisked away.

Everything was kept completely perfect. But the prince, being young and inquisitive, one day left the palace and saw a sick person for the first time in his life, showing very visible signs of illness. He was very shocked and he asked his attendant, 'What is this?' and his attendant replied, 'This is sickness;

anybody who has been born is going to become sick at some point in their life.' The prince went back to the palace, but his curiosity had been awoken and again he went out and came across an old person. Again, Siddhartha was shocked and asked, 'What has happened to this person? What is wrong with him?' And he was told, 'This is old age; this is what happens to everybody. With birth, there is sickness and there is old age.' And again this gave him food for thought; and another day he left the palace once more, and this time he came across a funeral procession. Again he was struck by this sight because he'd never seen a dead body. He was not aware of death or imperma- nence. Again he was told by his very honest attendant, 'This is what happens to everybody; we are born, we get old, we get sick and we die. Everybody who is born has to die.' And so the last time the Buddha goes out he comes across a holy man, someone who had renounced the ordinary world and was looking for spiritual revelation. Again the prince is struck by this, and when he goes home he sits in the palace gardens for the first time in meditation under a wood apple tree. The Buddha needed to explore and investigate, and his path was clear. He chose the spiritual path. After sitting under this tree and contemplating he thought, 'There must be some way, there must be some solution to this problem, there must be something I can do for all those beings out there who are suffering.' So it was the seed of compassion and the seed of renunciation. But for the Buddha, this was not the seed really because it was said he had had 500 lives of virtuous activity before that, where he did amazing things. And through all the merit gathered throughout those 500 lives he had come now to the last life, and in that life he was ripe and ready to achieve Buddhahood. The story then describes how eventually he left the palace in the dark of night and goes in search of a remedy for the human condition of birth, old age, sickness and death.

We may or may not feel that our life is so bad that it needs a remedy. We are very fortunate here in the West. We have hospitals and health services. But, of course, what the Buddha's teachings tell us is about the inherent suffering of samsara, the inherent suffering of existence. And that's what happened to the Buddha at that time. He woke up. It was his final moment of turning his back on samsara. Due to all the past merit and purification of his past lives he was now at the point of Buddhahood. This also shows us that it's a long path of purification and accumulation.

But this moment – where Siddhartha sits under that tree and starts to contemplate and think, 'What can be done?' – you could say was the moment of renunciation. The feet that took him on the path and moved him along in a spiritual direction, as opposed to his direction of becoming a king and having a world of splendour and power and influence, but only in a purely worldly way, had not with the power to give ultimate freedom from suffering. This was the choice that the Buddha made. And when we talk about these Four Thoughts and the foundations with the Dharma, that's what it means; it's about recognising that however much we search externally, it's not going to really solve our problems, it's not going to really give us all the answers, it's not going to give us true freedom. It doesn't mean turning one's back completely on wealth and money, or necessarily becoming a monk like the Buddha, but it means having a certain perspective.

The way these four thoughts can be summarised is:

1) Appreciation of our present condition: appreciation of our own potential, we have to really recognise how much potential we have.
2) Impermanence: that fact that what we've got now we could lose tomorrow, in an hour, any time. We don't know how long we've got it for.
3) Cause and effect: meaning that whatever we have we try to use for good purpose, for the utmost purpose. We try to make the most of our life.
4) Recognition of dissatisfaction in life: the fact that all this running around in circles is really tiring.

So these are, in summary, the Four Thoughts, the foundations for our Dharma practice. These four thoughts are what we need to really integrate in order to stay on the path. We need to continually come back to these four thoughts to remind ourselves about them, contemplate them, study them. If we don't, it's very likely that negative emotions, and attachment and aversion will take over. Attachment and aversion will rule our life. If we don't really assimilate the four thoughts and forget about them, it's very likely that we will be side-tracked or will have a weak foundation, like those people who disappear and eventually find that their Dharma practice has become stale and died on them like an old motor whose battery needs to be recharged. That's what happens when we forget. We need to think about those things, to keep them alive and keep them very relevant for ourselves, not just theory, as something the Buddha said, but very much to the heart of our own daily experience. If we can do that, then we will find that it keeps us on track.

So, thinking about precious human birth – the first of the four thoughts – the Buddha taught the Six Realms of Existence. That's relevant whether you talk about Theravada or any of the schools of Buddhism, they all talk about the Six Realms of Existence. We say that we are very fortunate to be born in a human realm. But if you find it difficult to relate to the Six Realms, then simply just think about our life, or the world as we know it. It's very easy now with modern communications, with the internet and news and anything you have available to you, to see how fortunate we all are. Here in the West, in many ways we have all the freedoms and assets of human life. We have wealth, we're not poor, we don't have to struggle to feed ourselves. We have a roof over our head, we have services to look after us if we are ill, we have all sorts of material wealth and comfort. Wealth can give us a lot of freedom, and we have freedom to make choices, which is a wonderful thing if we make the right choices. But if we become prisoners of wealth, and our whole life is spent going to work, making money, paying bills, paying mortgages, getting more things … our whole life is caught up in this wealth cycle of trying to keep up with it all. We're going at a speed where it's very difficult to stop and then we become prisoners of that.

At the same time, in the West we are very fortunate because we have freedom, freedom to practice, freedom to study, we have so many freedoms. At a personal level, if you think of your own life, it's about looking at how fortunate you are rather than seeing all the things you think we are lacking. It's also about recognising Buddha Nature, seeing that we have potential, realising that we all can change. If we work on ourselves, we can change. We have everything it takes to change, and we have every- thing it takes to make changes as well. We can all make a change in our own life, in our society, in our family – we have these freedoms and choices and possibilities. So we are extremely fortunate. It's about appreciating everything we've got, because if we don't appreciate it, we don't make use of it – we don't benefit from it. So this first thought is like summing up all your wealth, putting it all in a big basket and saying, 'Wow, this is amazing, look at this, I thought I was poor, but I've got all of this.' There's no end to the wonderful things that we could say that we have. You should make a list as an exercise, literally write down all of the amazing, wonderful things you have going for you.

They'd be all different lists, but they'd all be very long and very positive if you really think about it. So that's one thing we can recognise – our wealth.

The next thing is impermanence. It's about saying to ourselves, 'I have all of this, but it's all impermanent, so I'd better make use of it now, because it could all evaporate; it could all be lost.' The reason we think about impermanence, and the reason it's so important, is so that we don't miss the opportunity, so that at the end of our life we don't think, 'It's too late now, I had all these opportunities, and now they're gone.' Take someone who has put all their wealth in the bank, and then when they die, it's just sitting there, it's been completely and utterly useless. They could have used it to accumulate some merit, to give to the poor, to build temples, to help our children's education, or do something good with it. But if it's sitting in the bank, unused, it's been totally useless. It's like that with our life, but not in a material sense, we're talking about our spiritual path. The Buddha only talked about the spiritual path, about our mind, about finding freedom from suffering, about finding ultimate liberation. What he was saying is that we have all of these opportunities, and this is what he discovered in his own life. He thought because there is sickness, old age and death, I'd better do something. He got the message of impermanence, and he did something about it with his wealth, his mind, his Buddha potential – and he went and worked on it.

He didn't just sit back and say, 'I'll practice tomorrow, I've got plenty of time, I'm only 35.' Of course, we don't know how long we'll live. There is this whole contradiction of how we live our life, we know so well that everything is impermanent, we know that we can't guarantee that we'll get old, but we still live our lives as if that's going to happen.

We are encouraged to think about death and dying as a way of waking ourselves up to the fact that we don't have all the time in the world, and so we should get on with it. Recognise that everything in our life is impermanent. Recognise that your relationships are impermanent, so make the most of them. Recognise that your own body is impermanent, so make the most of it and use it for good purposes. Check whether we have our values right. Are we using our time well? If you went to the doctor and you were told that you only had a few months to live, how would you feel? How would you react? This is how you can tell if you've got your values right. At that time, we don't want to feel regret, we don't want to feel too terrified. Ideally we want to be at a place where we can die joyfully; if we can do that, that's a very wonderful place to be.

The teaching says that, 'An ordinary practitioner dies without regret.' It means that we have used our life to a point where, although we may not have attained great powers or wealth, but we have spent enough time on practice in our life where we can feel that we've done our best to live our life as a good person, we can die without regret. So if we are a practitioner, hopefully we can face our end like that.

Check whether we have no regrets, that we have no fear. And that means we have practised to an extent where we have maybe faced our demons. Maybe we have managed to tame our inner demons to a point where we have some mastery of our mind. It's not just basic practice, but we have achieved a level of mastery and acceptance of death and impermanence. We have no great grasping, we have managed to dissolve our attachments and our aversions to some degree. We can let go. One of the biggest things to face is our own death, and fear at that time is a big thing; leaving our most treasured possession – our body.

Then it says that a superior practitioner is someone who has no regrets, no fear, and great joy. Someone who has seen that there's nobody there to die, nobody there to be afraid, nothing to hold on to, has really seen through the illusion of the self, of 'I'. I'm sure there are many examples of this when we look through all the different lineages at the lineage masters. And one that we know in our generation is the Sixteenth Karmapa, who died of cancer in 1981 in a hospital in Chicago. There is a film where the doctor who worked in the hospital at the time speaks about how amazed they all were with him, how his joy never diminished and how his compassion and care for others never diminished. There were no signs of pain, even though he died from cancer. This story is quite amazing when you hear it. His state of mind had no sadness for himself, no concern for himself. His only concern was for all the people around him. This is a story that we can clearly see was true, it happened in the present day, in an environment that was not a Buddhist environment, not hundreds of years ago where we might think that the story had been exaggerated a bit over time. Because they were all so inspired, they allowed his body to be left untouched for four days in the hospital. They saw he was a unique, exceptional human being and they all developed this great respect for him. So the Karmapa showed us how to die. It's a great inspiration for everybody. But of course, for us, that's a whole other level; we need to prepare ourselves for death, and we need to do that by thinking about impermanence. And thinking about impermanence is like the plug that we put into the generator to charge our batteries, because then we wake up and think, 'I can't waste my time, because sooner or later I will be in a situation of having to separate from everything that is near and dear to me.'

The third thought is Cause and Effect. How are we going to use all this wealth that we have? What are we going to do with this life that we have? It's about getting our priorities right. It's about looking at our lives and deciding how we best make use of them. In simple ways, it's about doing good and using our lives for positive things, trying to have good speech, good action, positive thinking, good motivation. And trying to give up, of course, negative actions. You may be familiar with that verse from the *Dhammapada* that says to give up negative acts, to practise positive acts, to tame our minds. Those are the teachings of all the Buddhas – all contained in these few lines. So Cause and Effect is in there. Look at the Noble Eightfold Path – Right Speech, Right Action, Right Intention, Right Livelihood. If we live our life according to those principles, that is part of the foundations. We need to recognise that everything we do has an effect. We're not beyond Karma, Cause and Effect, until we are enlightened. We are Karma carriers until that point. Everything we do has an effect, so we'd better invest it in doing good things.

There's a story about a father whose son had a terrible temper. He was always angry. His father was at his wit's end. So finally he came up with a task for him to do. He said, 'Every time you lose your temper or do something bad, go down to the bottom of the garden and hammer a nail into the fence.' So every time he lost his temper, he went down there and put a nail in the fence. Eventually the fence was full of nails, but then there was one day when he managed not to have to go down to the fence and put a nail in. He was very proud of himself and told his father. His father said, 'Very good, son, so now, each day you manage to not lose your temper, go down to the fence and pull out one of those nails.' As time went on, he took the nails out of the fence one by one, and eventually the son went to see his father and told him that all the nails were gone. So the father said, 'Well done, son, but let me show you something.' He took his son down to the bottom of the garden and said, 'Look, all those nails you put in and pulled out have left a hole, every nail you left there left a scar. Every time you lose your temper, it creates a scar.' This was showing him cause and effect; even if we try to repair damage when we get things wrong or we make mistakes, it leaves a scar. It's very difficult to completely purify these things, we tend to leave scars wherever we go. So Cause and Effect is about recognising that, and to help us to ensure that our efforts are going in the right direction, to be aware of our actions of body, speech and mind.

The fourth of these thoughts is Recognition of this general dissatisfaction in life, samsara. There is the underlying dissatisfaction and suffering, even when we have a good life with all the freedoms and assets. It's there as long as there is an underlying sense of self, as long as everything is ruled by 'me' and 'mine' – what I like and I don't like. We are constantly chasing after things that we want, and we are constantly trying to avoid the things that we don't like and have an aversion towards. This constant chasing is samsara. We are constantly running around in the circle of samsara. Attachment and aversion is what makes up our samsaric life. Even if we have a good life, there is underlying suffering, if nothing else; that is due to impermanence because we can't hold on to the things we like, and we can't always avoid the things we don't like or don't want. So the fourth thought is about the general irritations, the ups and downs in life – we have to contemplate them and recognise that as long as we are striving to perfect our externals, it's not really going to get us very far, as we're still running in circles. So as long as we're looking outside, we're looking the wrong way. The Buddha's message was to look inside. If we want to free ourselves, it's about looking inside and taming our mind. It's through taming our mind that we can really and truly give up the negative and can practise the positive; it gives us the power to do that. If we don't work on training our mind, we don't have the power – we are ruled by attachment and aversion.

So these four thoughts are what tell us that we have to meditate. If we don't meditate to tame our minds, it means we are caught up in the circle of chasing after externals that we are attached to, or trying to avoid the externals that we have aversion towards. The wheel of samsara is continuously turning. By our running, we are keeping the samsaric wheel spinning. Instead of looking outside for solutions, we should start to look inside; this was really the Buddha's message.

So this is why we say that the body is the meditation, the body is non-distraction. The feet are renunciation – where we begin to say that we can't really fix anything out there. We can deal with life with good motivation and try to do the right things, positive things; all of that we have to do. But we can't really fix it unless we turn inside. And that's through developing this non-distraction – working on the body of meditation.

So we need to have these two 'wings' in order to fly – the view and the meditation. We need to have enough understanding of the Dharma teachings, the theory, but we also have to practise. One of them is not enough. We have to understand the Dharma teachings and where they take us, but it has to be applied in actual, personal experience, and that is the meditation. Without that, it just remains concepts and ideas to fill our busy minds. But what we need to do is learn how to deal with all these thoughts, to see the nature of thoughts, try and see how the thoughts themselves are like clouds in the sky, so that when there is attachment and aversion we don't get pulled in, because they're just thoughts. We get pulled in because we allow the thoughts to overpower us, because our meditation, our mind training, is not strong enough. The training of the mind is the remedy: it is the Path.

This text was adapted from a talk given at The Buddhist Society and first published in *The Middle Way*, vol. 94, no. 2 August 2019.

Lama Zangmo

MAURA SOSHIN O'HALLORAN

(1955–1982)
Darcy Biddulph, 2018

Ordained in Japan as a Zen Buddhist nun, completed Koan training, determined and extraordinary at a young age, of Irish decent, with rare insight into the nature of Buddhist practice. Diarist and author.

Outside a Zen Buddhist monastery in Japan is a statue dedicated to Maura Soshin O'Halloran, an Irish American Zen practitioner who trained at Toshoji Temple in Tokyo and Kannonji Temple in Iwate prefecture between 1979 and 1982. She received Inka in 1982. Her monastic name was Soshin meaning 'open heart' or 'great enlightenment.'

Maura was born in 1955 in Boston, the eldest of six children. Her father Fionan was from County Kerry and mother Ruth was from Maine. Maura moved to Ireland aged four and returned to Boston in 1966. Her father did graduate work at MIT and was killed in a road accident in 1969 aged 43. Maura was killed in a road accident in 1982 aged 27. She was 14 when her father died and helped her mother raise her five younger siblings.

Maura studied at Sacred Heart in Ireland and Boston, then at Trinity College Dublin and received a combined degree in mathematics and sociology. She worked at the Rudolf Steiner school in Northern Ireland with autistic students. She also studied photography and travelled widely before her Zen training. She started meditating in college and was known to fast for nine days. She had a tomboy look and was not much concerned with her clothes. She travelled to Tierra del Fuego on her own. She said while very young that if she turned 26 and had not done all she wanted she would commit suicide. She had this burn-through attitude.

She kept a diary of her training which her mother subsequently published in 1994 as *Pure Heart Enlightened Mind: The Zen Journal and Letters of an Irish Woman in Japan*. A second extended version was later published. The diary is an intimate portrayal of Zen training for the priesthood and a rare glimpse of koan practice which that involves. Koan study is only a part of the training and consists of questions called koans which the Zen Master asks during a series of interviews. The questions go back centuries and there are many interpretations in Zen texts. Maura described her interviews with Go Roshi, a peaceful and vibrant Zen priest who gave Maura her first koan, Mu. The description is a welcome insight for anyone in koan study struggling with their very first koan. Answering Mu and the daily practice of cooking, gardening, cleaning and meditating gave her the insight into what Buddhism was really all about. Through the daily practice she realised the question could not be solved intellectually and had to be answered in the body. She knew that Zen was the school of realisation.

For those of other Buddhist traditions that are not familiar with Koan study, the question called 'Mu' is translated as, 'Does a dog have Buddha nature?' The student answers, Mu (nothingness). It is essential to answer the question through realisation in order to be given another koan. The student begins to understand that only through the daily practice of living the routine of the monastery and zazen, or meditation practice, can 'Mu' be realised. Once there is the discovery that there is no other, there is no self, there is no me and no you, no birth, and no death, a joyous release and freedom is experienced which is the backbone and foundation of practice. A good Roshi will push relentlessly until he sees that the realisation is in the body. This is when it all starts to connect and things begin to change. Most students take many, many years of training before they can answer their first koan. The practice was mainly limited to Japanese monasteries for those wishing to enter the priesthood, before Zen became popularised and travelled to the West. It was an ancient and strict training process under institutional monastic control in Japan, not open for the general public to declare themselves as Zen Masters. The koan process had to be completed before entering the priesthood or becoming an incumbent of a training monastery.

In 1979 Maura was indeed a rarity and was often interviewed on Japanese TV. She was female, foreign and very young, in one of the toughest and coldest training monasteries in the country. The Daikan or 'great cold' without central heating in the Zendo during meditation was notorious. The Japanese were fascinated by her and could not understand why she chose this kind of life, especially the begging part of Zen practice as she went around in robes in the freezing snow. They began to revere her as some sort of Irish Zen saint and an incarnation of the Goddess of Mercy.

Her diary describes trips to Kamakura and Korea and gives an account of the local Buddhist sites and inhabitants. It also describes her teaching English to local families and her daily tasks in the monastery which were mostly domestic. It was the endless daily tasks of weeding in the garden, cleaning and cooking which taught her the essence of Zen, how to just do the task at hand without prejudice, without a sense of self, without the I, me, mine, interference in just getting on with it. She describes while working incredibly physically hard, exhausted from sleeplessness on a freezing cold winter's day, the complete joy she had and the beauty of the frozen morning.

The sesshins or zenkai were with Go Roshi, who gave Maura her second, third and subsequent koans, along with the warning that they would become progressively more difficult. One of her fellow monks told her, 'When you are your mother, when you are Roshi, then you are Enlightened.' Maura answered the koans after putting herself through the most intense daily training. She was not alone and there were many comings and goings and relationships with the different practitioners that are humorous and often dramatic. Some ran away from the monastery but Maura stayed on through sheer will power, often weakened from poor nutrition, infection, sleeplessness and cold. She always chose the ancient or hard way when begging, which is a big part of the practice. For instance, she often wore no socks in the snow, as they might have slowed down her burn-through-it attitude.

There were a few westerners who participated in the practice during the period Maura was training but not many lasted. She did not speak much Japanese or know much Buddhism when she arrived in Japan but had a friend in Ireland who studied Buddhism and that may have inspired her. However to endure such a profound and rigorous study is hard to understand. Perhaps what led her to Buddhism was the death of her father and the suffering that caused just at the time of her puberty. Many of the greatest Buddhists experienced trauma with the early death of one of their parents. For the Buddha it was just seeing a dead person, becoming aware of such a thing as death which led him on his path.

UNESCO asked her to a conference to give talks about her life and she was filmed again by Japanese TV and managed to remain modest despite her celebrity in Japan. The letters she wrote to her family and friends revealed her insight into Buddhism; in one letter she observed that where Christianity preaches original sin, Buddhism preaches original enlightenment. She had been raised in Catholic schools, winning a scholarship to Trinity College. Her mother wanted her to continue her studies and complete a PhD but Maura wanted to go further into Zen practice. She was given the Zen koan 'Kyogen' which presented such difficulty that she embarked on a new resolve and answered multiple koans within six months. She then enjoyed a real sense of finally belonging to the Sangha.

A senior monk asked her to marry him but she refused, thinking the proposal was merely a set up to continue the lineage of the monastery with any children she might have, and he also needed a good cook. She did not believe love had much to do with it and showed no interest in breeding as giving further purpose to her life. There was a daily difficult relationship with him and she finally complained of his treatment towards her. Once she stood up to his male bullying and dominance in the monastery her life improved and she began to progress rapidly, set free.

Maura was convinced people in Japan did not want to study zazen, but they did in Ireland. She wanted to go back home and start a dojo. Over three years she wrote heart-breaking letters to her mother to visit her in Japan and finally she did in October 1981, but Maura did not go back home with her. Go Roshi had cancer and his health started to fail after the age of 70. He explained that a Roshi is like your mother, who comes halfway round the world to make sure her grownup daughter is all right, so no matter how good a student is, a Roshi will worry and push and push.

Go Roshi gave a lecture and revealed that Maura was the only successor to the Zen heart in Japan today. Maura had a loving relationship with the venerated teacher and this helped her greatly in making Zen her life study. He wished her to succeed him and stay in Japan but she may have had ideas of her own to start a dojo in Ireland.

As she wrote in a letter to home: 'We are allowed to wear socks with straw sandals, so we usually wear several pairs plus plastic bags to keep out the wet. In the old days, though, the monks used to go barefoot on crushed ice, but as Go Roshi says, if you just take one step at a time, you can do anything and you can.' Maura helped to run two temples for Go Roshi and was asked to translate two of his books. A certificate to teach Zen takes ten years in Japan and Go Roshi was afraid that he might die before the date of Maura's *Hishinsai* or koan graduation ceremony, so he moved the date forward. The last entry of a koan mondo in her diary has Maura asking, 'Go Roshi, the stone that is now preaching the Dharma, is it living or dead?' Go Roshi answered, 'Stone, what stone, this stone? Ask the stone.' Maura answered, 'I am asking the stone,' and they both laughed.' She completed the koan process and graduated at the ceremony.

Another ceremony is the Denpo-shiki or the transmission ceremony which takes place over one week and involves 3,000 bows, breathing deep from the hara, repeating the words of homage to all the buddhas of the Three Worlds. Maura completed this as well.

Her brother Scott visited her at the monastery and they did zazen together. He seemed to take to it instantly. They travelled together to Thailand where she boarded a bus to see Chiang Mai before the scheduled flight home with Scott to Ireland. The bus driver fell asleep and the bus overturned. Maura was killed along with the driver and two others. She was 27 years old.

The inscription on her statue at Kannonji Temple reads:

Maura Kannon (A Brief History)

Miss Maura O'Halloran from Ireland
On the tenth of October in the 54th year of Showa 1979, at
Toshoji Temple she became a Nun and completed 1,000 days
of continuous Zen practice at Toshoji and Kannonji Temples.
Her daily practice included three hours of sleeping in the zazen
position and 20 hours of devotion to her studies in order to attain
salvation not only for herself but also for all people.

On the seventh of August in the 57th year of Showa 1982, she was
conferred an authorised certificate of Enlightenment achieved on
the 22nd of October, on her way back to Ireland, at Chiang Mai,
Thailand, by some traffic accident her life ended at the age of 27.
She was given the posthumous name of Great Enlightened Lady,
of the same heart and mind as the Great Teacher Buddha. Miss
Maura has been a real incarnation of Kannon Bosatsu to be loved
and respected forever. We dedicate the Maura Kannon Statue
here to her extraordinary memory.

Nirvana Day February 15th in the 58th year of Showa 1983 by

Tetsu-gyu So-in, founder of Kannonji Temple.

Maura's memory provides inspiration, encouragement and hope to everyone in Buddhist practice.

Maura wrote:

Creaking to the post office
on my nasty bike
I saw one purple iris
wild in the wet green
of the rice field.
I wanted to send it to you,
I can only tell you
it was there.

Originally published in *The Middle Way*, vol. 93, no. 2, August 2018.

Darcy Biddulph also writes under the name of Flynn. She is Editor of *The Middle Way* and a co-author of *The Teachings of the Buddha, The Wisdom of the Dharma from the Pali Canon to the Sutras*. Co author of *365 Ways to Live a Buddhist Life, Insights on Truth, Peace and Enlightenment* and *1001 Pearls of Buddhist Wisdom, Insights on truth, peace and enlightenment.*

Moira Soshin O'Halloran in Japan

The Buddhist Perspective on Evil

Darcy Flynn, 2022

Does evil as a self-existent principle come into Buddhism? Does evil exist? Do we act in an unskilful way because of this principle? Are there forces at loose in the world that could be considered an evil principle, the source of agency outside ourselves?

Buddhism does not engage with these philosophical questions, nor does it believe in these ideas. Salvation comes from developing the innate but underdeveloped capacity for wisdom and compassion, more commonly known as love. Love and hate exist in the heart of man.

Buddhism, being non-dualistic, does not see the world as a drama where forces oppose each other: good opposed to evil, right opposed to wrong, man opposed to nature, the body and its irrational and disruptive impulses opposed to the mind and rationalism etc., nor even inside opposed to outside.

In Buddhism there is no concept of an enduring principle of evil as in dualistic or Manichaean religions engaged in perpetual warfare, of good against bad. The Jungian approach could suggest that consciousness stands in opposition, the 'shadow'. Jung however was at pains to point out that evil was an absentia bonum, and the 'shadow' was not evil but the part of ourselves we never see, being the potential for creative individuation.

In ordinary language things are of course good and bad, they cause pain and suffering. If a Buddhist monk is tortured by a Chinese member of the CCP, he (CCP) is not evil; it is the ignorance that has led him to commit an intentional unskilful and degrading act.

Questions such as 'Is there a God?' or 'Where do we come from?', or 'What exists before God?' were usually met with the 'Noble Silence' by the Buddha. In the southern, the oldest tradition of Buddhism, philosophical questioning is avoided; the teaching and practice confines itself to the immediately known and experienced, and speculation of any kind is not encouraged as it delays the urgent action needed to escape the wheel of repeated rebirth by creating attachment to ideas and encouraging pointless speculation.

There are Buddhist answers to these questions however, particularly in the developed Mahayana, where questions relating to consciousness are directly addressed. Here the trikaya (three bodies) doctrine describes reality as we know it. Nevertheless these are accorded both a metaphorical and descriptive role of what is experienced in the higher levels of meditation (jhanas Sanskrit). Although Buddhism is not dualistic, it is not monistic, as everything is interdependent, and ultimately empty and void.

The first is of the three bodies (kaya sanskrit) the dharmakaya, the dharma body, represents the unity of all things existent and non-existent, the origin of everything in the manifest universe, that which is unknowable yet informs all that can be known. That which contains all the apparent opposites, co-mingled with the known, but timeless and limitless. The universe and reality are indivisible but the discursive mind bound to instinct (Karma) separates, judges, compares, looks for a primogeniture, seeks more, and then less, creates ascending and descending values, creates a hierarchy of needs and then wants but cannot see the whole, and thus experiences and declares life to be an alienated state.

Buddhism as a religious teaching and praxis is concerned with the problem of suffering; the eschatology is profoundly practical, based on the human condition. Suffering comes in all forms and these varieties of suffering have been reduced to a fairly simple formula, to the simplest teaching, and most obvious observations of the nature of life experience by anyone in a body.

Firstly, The Buddha's teaching: 'Suffering I teach, and the way out of suffering'. This encapsulates the entire teaching life of the Buddha. (The Four Noble Truths and the Noble Eight-fold Path)

The Buddha goes on to define the suffering of which he speaks in its two forms, again in a simplified language where suffering is seen as twofold: physical and mental. 'Birth is suffering, sickness is suffering, old age is suffering, dying and death are suffering'. As for mental suffering: 'Being separated from what one likes is suffering. Being conjoined with what one dislikes is suffering. Not getting what one wants is suffering'.

'Birth is suffering' means the process of coming into life (including the birth process itself) and the process of growing up and learning through one's mistakes, and the entire process of maturation with all its pitfalls, risks and dangers, that includes ecstasy and joy as well as disappointments and defeats and is laced with suffering and uncertainty.

'Sickness' 'old age' and 'death' are to be understood as the biological life process itself. The Buddha is often described as a Doctor who not only diagnoses the illness, because he understands the aetiology, but also prescribes the treatment.

The 'cause of removeable suffering' is said to be 'thirst', (tanha sanskrit) 'craving', 'longing', (for things to be different from how they are now), for pleasure and the pleasurable as well as sensual objects, longing to avoid the unpleasant, to be a 'someone', an 'I', a 'Person', a 'being', and a 'life', and finally the longing for personal 'annihilation'.

These desires are dependent on first being born and having a human body, with the inherited characteristics that the human body brings with it. That is, the whole inherited instinctual capacity that orders the world into a hierarchy of desirable and essential objects, beginning with the first cry, the scream of the newborn baby. The longing for pleasure is associated with the idea of 'contact', either physically or through the mind.

The law of cause and effect in Buddhism teaches: because 'this' arises, as a consequence so does 'this'. If 'this' does not arise then 'this' will not arise. If desire arises, then 'grasping' arises, and if 'grasping arises', 'attachment' arises, if 'attachment' arises, so do 'old age' 'sickness' and 'death'. Because there is 'contact' with a pleasurable or unpleasurable object, there is desire, and desire is suffering and anxiety if ungratified.

If we are not born, we do not suffer. Hence this accent on cause and effect in the southern traditions leads to the idea to reach a state where one will no longer be reborn. This can only occur when desire for life has been extinguished, Nibbana.

We are born as a result of Karma - intentional action, accumulated past actions that can be seen as the evolutionary and Darwinian processes. It could be looked at as the human genome, but specifically our own genome, instinct (accumulated past Karma).

Ignorance is a blind force and is responsible for setting in motion the sequence of causes and effects that give rise to desire and to birth, and the whole of suffering. Instinctual action (that is action that is carried out without awareness) as it is blind gives rise to results; this is the process of karma unmediated by awareness, wisdom or compassion.

Karma (kamma in pali) means action; intentional action is karma-producing. It also has the connotation of the consequences of our actions which are either wholesome or unwholesome, hence the expression 'that's good karma', or 'that's bad karma' meaning there will be a good outcome or a bad outcome to certain actions, dependent upon our intentional actions.

The question arises, why do we do things that have negative consequences, i.e. create more suffering for ourselves and others? What is happening when we do things that create beneficial effects. The Buddhist answer is that we are acting intentionally, sometimes out of the force of ignorance. In this sense ignorance and the habit patterns of Karma can be aligned with the Jungian 'Shadow'.

Generally, in most Buddhist schools and traditions there is not much said of the 'unconscious' as it is conceived in modern psychology; things, dhammas, psychic objects, are either known or seen in the light of awareness or they are not. For something to be connoted it needs to have an object, an organ of sense and consciousness. In this system consciousness only exists in the presence of a body. The object of practice and all praxis is to increase awareness of the arising of impulses, desires, reactions and wholesome practice, and to avoid blind, unskilful action and unwholesome action that produces negative karma.

In the northern Schools of Buddhism the human composite is essentially good. Due to ignorance the human being can be unskilful and cause much suffering for himself and others. Underlying all human behaviour is the idea that, if ignorance can be removed, human beings will behave in a harmonious way with each other and with nature, and the mental turbulence that comes with the sense of conflict is stilled.

The concept of the collective unconscious has a Buddhist counterpart in the idea of the alaya vijnana the store consciousness, and the dharmasantana or stream of dharma objects (objects of consciousness).

In practice, once it has been accepted that life brings with it inevitable suffering, it becomes possible to move forward in an attempt to reduce human suffering through the mental sphere, and here we are at one with all the modern schools of western psychology in the recognition that it is the emotions that cause us to suffer. As the emotions always give rise to some sort of re-action, we are inescapably bound to behave or refrain from behaving, in a way dictated by emotion. The refusal to feel or denial of emotions (repression, disassociated states) gives rise to unskilful, painful action as it is devoid of feeling, wisdom and compassion and arises as a way of refusing to live the emotions. If the emotions can be 'seen', brought into awareness, they will cause us less suffering and their consequences in unskilful action can be eradicated through the process of practice.

In some ways it could be said that this is the case because emotions and feelings are not truly 'mine', they have an impersonal quality; this is why they are often depicted as deities, but they too are impermanent. And this is why it sometimes seems that people are possessed by an 'evil' entity, but the truth from the Buddhist point of view is that these powerful emotions have not been truly owned, in the sense that a dynamic conscious relational connection with them has not been established.

Once that connection has been made, then these seemingly opposed entities merge into the new being that functions with all the power of the emotions, but transformed in the alchemy of relational love into a new being that sees nothing as outside, yet functions independently guided by an innate, un-nameable intellect that never errs, (is sinless) in which the two dynamic factors of wisdom and compassion are fused into the single eye of the whole man or woman.

The image of Amitabha from the Mahayana (Great Way of the Northern Tradition) is the Buddha of infinite light and life. This Buddha dispels the darkness of ignorance, and the illuminating rays of love and discernment streaming forth cleanse all defilements. It produces the shadowless light of Amidha (Amitabha) Buddha. Our own light (photon, electromagnetic wavelengths) is a mere reflection of this inner Buddha light.

The Buddha light has no shadow; the Buddha nature is Nirvana.

This was reprinted from *The Middle Way*, vol 97 No 4, Winter 2022-2023

Darcy Flynn

The compassionate work of Ama-la

Jetsun Pema

Interview with Dr. Desmond Biddulph CBE
President of The Buddhist Society

27th October 2023

Dr. Desmond Biddulph

Welcome Ama-la to the Buddhist Society. The Buddhist Society is an old institution, one of the oldest Buddhist institutions in the West. It was started in 1924, and our patron, your brother, is His Holiness the Dalai Lama. It is a great joy for us to have you here with us today. Many of the people watching us will probably know who you are, but I think I should say just a few things to introduce you.

You were born in Tibet in 1940, and then later, left Tibet and had your education at St. Joseph's Convent, in Kalimpong. Then you went to Darjeeling with the Irish Loretta nuns, before eventually going to Switzerland and to London, and returning to India at the end of 1963. At that time, you then took over the management of the Tibetan Children's Village (TCV).

Jetsun Pema

Yes, the Tibetan Children's Village was started in 1960. His Holiness sent his officials to collect the children from the road construction camps, because that was the only kind of work that the government of India could give at that time to the refugees pouring in, following His Holiness into exile, was the construction of roads in the high regions of India. For the children it was very difficult, and so they were brought to Dharamshala. There were 51 children at the beginning, and then His Holiness entrusted these children to our elder sister, who started the Children's Village in 1960.

Dr. Desmond Biddulph

I want to give people a rough idea of the things that have happened, because you remained, doing that job for 42 years, and during that time, you established five Tibetan Children's Villages with associated schools: seven residential schools, seven day-schools, ten day-care centres, four vocational training centres, four youth hostels, four homes for the elderly, and an outreach programme for over 2000 children. And in all, there have been 15,000 children and youths in the Tibetan Children's Villages.

Jetsun Pema

Yes. Now the number has dwindled down: we are getting less and less children coming from Tibet, whereas before we used to receive each year over 1000 children from Tibet, because the border was open. Sometimes, in one year, as many as 1000 children would come across the border. And once you have the children in the village, you have to keep them until they finish their schooling. So, they remained with us, depending on their age, for eight, ten, or twelve years. So, the number was always increasing in the Children's Villages. But today, because of the Chinese policy, there are no more Tibetan refugees: hardly anyone is coming across the border. The unfortunate thing is that Tibetan children today are sent to Chinese boarding schools, as the Chinese are trying their very best to make the Tibetans as Chinese as possible. So even little children as old as six years are sent to boarding schools against the wishes of the parents. That is a very distressing news for us to learn. And this is what's happening at the moment in Tibet.

Dr. Desmond Biddulph

I think we did the same in Canada, by taking Inuit children away from their parents and putting them into residential boarding schools. And in Australia, we did the same thing with disastrous consequences.

Jetsun Pema

Yes, unfortunately. The Chinese should learn from these episodes, because now the governments of the United States, and Canada, are apologising to the communities for the mistakes they made. But the Chinese, still today, are doing the very thing which in the West we think was a mistake. It is terrible that one does not learn anything from the history of human experience.

Dr. Desmond Biddulph

I would like to ask you some questions, but before that I should say that you were you were given the honour of being called the Mother of Tibet, for your work with all these children's homes. You came here to London on this visit as a guest of the alumni of the school. Have you enjoyed your stay?

Jetsun Pema

We arrived here just two days ago, and I have been meeting with some of the ex-students: it has been a very enjoyable two days. It is wonderful to see how well they are flourishing: when you look back and think of why they are doing so well today, it is because of the education that they have received. It was always His Holiness's dream or wish, ever since we came into exile, to give our children a good education, a modern education but at the same time, an education which is deeply rooted in our own culture and religion, so that the Tibetan children growing up in exile could retain their identity as Tibetans, and this is what we have been doing. We just celebrated 63 years of TCV existence, and during those 63 years, over 52,000 children have left from the Tibetan Children's Villages, and they are scattered all over the world. Here in England there are around a hundred of them, and they are the ones who invited me here this time.

Dr. Desmond Biddulph

Yes, it is really a remarkable achievement.

Jetsun Pema

We are very proud that one of our ex-students is working for the Buddhist Society: we are very proud that he is able to serve you here.

Dr. Desmond Biddulph

We are very delighted that he is here too, I have to say. I will start with the first question. You have seen some of the drawings here. When you look at them, you realise that many of the children have endured a great deal of pain and suffering in the course of their early life. What do you think we can learn about the possibilities of transforming those difficulties into something really positive through education?

Jetsun Pema

Many of these children were either orphans or semi orphans, in the beginning of the Tibetan Children's Village. Then later on, the children coming from Tibet had to leave their parents in Tibet, and come to India to stay in the Children's Village. And I think the most important thing for the children, even though they might have had a very difficult life, is that they got an education, and even more than the education it was important to provide them with a home. We had this idea of having homes established as they have in the Pestalozzi Children's Village here in England and also in Switzerland. When I was a young student in the West, I visited these children's villages, and I realised that, more than anything else, what the children need is a home to grow up in with a with parents who will give them the love and affection that they need. And if that is given to traumatised children, a loving, caring mother and home, that they can grow up and call their own, then I think that is something which transforms their life, because that is the security which the children need. This is something that we provided for them, and that made a lot of difference. Indeed, no matter how much the children have suffered in their early years: once they are in school, they have a home to go to, with foster parents, where all the children are like brothers and sisters. This big family heals their soul, and whatever kind of problems they might have, somehow, they realise they are not the only one, all the other children also coming from Tibet, they have gone through the same thing, and that sharing and caring heals a lot of things.

Dr. Desmond Biddulph

And how important do you think it is maintaining the Tibetan language in that?

Jetsun Pema

Well, the spoken and the written language, for anybody, is the foundation and the pillar of their identity. So, I think the spoken language is so important, because we do not have our country, we are in exile and Tibet has been occupied by the Chinese, where the Chinese think that Tibetan culture is nothing and Tibetan people are treated as second class citizens. This is the reason why His Holiness always tells the young people "you must retain your identity as Tibetans". Of course, there are many things which are not necessary to retain in this 21st century, but whatever is good and makes you a good human being, those are the things of our culture which you must retain, and retain your identity as a Tibetan, because this is what is being destroyed in Tibet. So, we feel that we have to keep this up. And we owe this to the Tibetans in Tibet. And so, this is what we're trying to do. And I think, to a certain extent, we have not failed, because wherever we see Tibetan people today, of third and fourth generation living in exile, they are all making an effort: the children speak the language, and they are brought up in a Tibetan atmosphere, where they learn to retain what is Tibetan. And that I think is very important.

Dr. Desmond Biddulph

I think there is a good reason why they call it the mother tongue, because it also communicates all the important values that children require, through the warmth and affection which is carried in the language.

Jetsun Pema

In 1963, there was a resolution passed in the United Nations, saying that children up to the primary school level should be educated through their mother tongue, because if you are educated through your mother tongue, you retain your identity. I think that is an important thing, because children learn best through their mother tongue. So, in our schools, up to the age of twelve or thirteen, we teach them in Tibetan language for the lessons, be it geography, history, whatever. Then, from the sixth grade, which is like the middle school, English is taught, because we have to give young kids a recognised education. So, English comes to be their first language and Tibetan becomes their second language, but at that point they have a good foundation in Tibetan.

Dr. Desmond Biddulph

Well, the important thing is that for children, the basis of morality and strength, comes from the bonds of affection. You can be disciplined if you are loved. If you discipline someone who is not loved or does not feel it, then it seems like a punishment.

Jetsun Pema

Discipline should not be from outside: discipline should be from within. That is the lasting discipline.

Dr. Desmond Biddulph

Indeed, and that gives not only a sense of identity, but also a sense of morality, which is natural for the person, and not simply a lot of rules they are following. And then when you come to English, as cognitive as it is, it is just something that goes on in the head, but not in the heart, so that then becomes a second language.

Jetsun Pema

It is important that they have an education which is recognised. Now we have Tibetan language courses in our own college, but in most of the secondary schools and high schools where they have to sit for Board Examination, they have to do it in English. According to the regulation of this Board of Secondary Education in India, it is either in Hindi, or in one of the regional languages that are recognised, and at the moment, in the high school, Tibetan is recognised only as a second language for the Board Examination.

Dr. Desmond Biddulph

It is a wonderful thing to have that opportunity to be brought up with your own language and culture. You have experienced educating children who have suffered a great deal. What advice would you give for teachers and charities that are now looking after orphans? At the moment there is a terrible war going on, that is generating huge numbers of orphans, who are going to leave their own country. In fact, all over the world, we see families being broken up and children losing their parents.

Jetsun Pema

Well, that is a very sad situation. And that is where the world is today. Then, at the same time, I think, whether they are Muslim, Israeli, Tibetan, or British, or whatever nationality they might be, what children need most is the security of a home: they need to feel secure, to feel that they are loved and protected. I think that is important, and that is something we can offer in our schools. In our Children's Village, we have the house parents, and we always emphasise that those people who are looking after the children must have a feeling for the children. I always used to tell our teachers and our house mothers "if you decide something, you have to think that you are deciding this for your own child: if you just make that decision as if that child was your own, then you do not make any mistake". So, this personal feeling of warmth and kindness is really important because that gives the child the security and the self-confidence. If you believe in the child, and you let the child know that you are there for them, then you have won their trust. And once you have won that trust, they will do anything that you ask them, because they will know that what the person is saying is always for their good. They realise that. And that's the important thing.

Dr. Desmond Biddulph

That is probably the most difficult thing to do, isn't it?

Jetsun Pema

Yes, it is, but most of the things that are difficult are something that we aspire to do, and I think we have to keep on trying, until we reach that goal. The human spirit is always there, and you can always remind yourself, "I must do this". And if you keep reminding yourself, I think, then somehow, you are always going in the right direction.

Dr. Desmond Biddulph

It must be very difficult in the children's homes, as you have shortages of all kinds, and quite a lot of children.

Jetsun Pema

The homes were actually built for 25 to 30 children. But then, when we had influx of children coming from Tibet, we had as many as 45 to 50 children. And it was really overtaxing the work for the mothers. But we realised that we had to do this because there was no alternative. And then if everybody tries to do their best, somehow, some results will come out, and there are always people all over the world who are very generous and give their support. That support is so important. And it is also so encouraging that the work gets going.

Dr. Desmond Biddulph

I see that you still have a programme where people can actually support a child.

Jetsun Pema

Yes. The work of the Tibetan Children's Villages, in the homes and in the schools, it is all through sponsorship. At the moment, a sponsor pays like $60 a month for the upkeep of that child. That takes care of the education, the food, the clothing, everything.

Dr. Desmond Biddulph

And do the people who donate have some sort of connection with the children?

Jetsun Pema

Oh, yes. It is like a foster parent. We call them sponsor parents, and there is contact between the child and the sponsor. And when the children are young, there is always the sponsorship secretaries who keeps in touch, and the child makes a few drawings and maybe write a few words, then later on, when they go to the higher classes, they get to know the sponsors through letter writing.

Dr. Desmond Biddulph

That must be very pleasing for both parties.

Jetsun Pema

Also, the sponsors feel that they know exactly where their money is going, for the education of that particular child. They are also informed of the various programmes we have for the children. And I think that gives them a lot of satisfaction. We have sponsors who have been sponsoring children for the first 12 years of their life, and then they are still in touch when the child has gone to college. Then, they sponsor another child from the age of eight or nine: there are some sponsors who are sponsoring now their fourth children in the Children's Village. I was just talking to a sponsor this morning, who said that his sponsored child has been educated through TCV, has finished college and has gone to the United States, and now she is going to visit his family. So, that contact has been going on for twenty or thirty years.

Dr. Desmond Biddulph

I remember when I went to visit Dharamshala in the 1960s, many children were coming from Tibet, and there was a lot of malnutrition, which was creating a lot of quite serious difficulties.

Jetsun Pema

In the 60s it was really difficult. We did not have enough of clothing, food, or shelter.

Dr. Desmond Biddulph

Indeed everything was a real problem. But it is amazing to see what you have actually achieved over that period.

Jetsun Pema

Well, that was actually due to the far-sightedness of His Holiness, who was saying that we have to give a good education to the children. Then, secondly, it is because of the kind people all over the world who helped us to educate the children. We would not have been able to do this without the help that we have received, both from the individuals who sponsored the children, and from the organisations that put up the buildings and gave money for different projects, such as hospitals, hostels and so on.

Dr. Desmond Biddulph

Many of the children are sort of damaged or they have a lot of trauma from their childhoods. Do they have any particular special education to meet their needs?

Jetsun Pema

Many young people have been trained as counsellors, and they help the children. The home mothers or the teachers will identify certain children that need some sort of counselling, or special treatment. In reality, there are very few, because they live in the Children's Village, and everybody has the same kind of problem, then they heal each other's pains. They say, "I'm not alone, my eldest sister went through the same thing". When you feel this, then your own problems become less. That is another way of sharing, learning and accepting something that has happened to you, and to realise that this is something that is in the past. Us Tibetans have a saying: "yesterday is something which is already finished, tomorrow will take care of itself, let's make the best of the present". You must live in the present and try to make the best of that. That is the important thing. And I think that as soon as you realise that, then you are a happier person.

Dr. Desmond Biddulph

Of course, for children who desperately miss their mothers it is so difficult to live in the present.

Jetsun Pema

That is true, but there is always somebody there, being the house mother, or a teacher. We say that our Children's Village is one big family, and that sense of family and of unity, that sense of saying that we all are together and that the house mothers and the teachers are there for the children, I think it builds something. Today the ex-students, who are now working and who have been educated, still feel that they have to do something for TCV. Around 25% of the revenue for running the Children's Village It's coming from the Tibetan community, and most of the Tibetan community it is made of the ex -TCV students who have been going to live in the USA, In England and all over the world. That already gives us a lot of hope, for the future.

Dr. Desmond Biddulph

I think so, because I think if people are prepared to give money for something they have been through themselves, it is obviously a vote of confidence, isn't it? They think: "this was good for me, and I want it to be good for somebody else too." It is a real sign of success.

Jetsun Pema

The motto of TCV is "others before self". And that is a very Buddhist teaching. One day, His Holiness came to TCV, and he was speaking to the children. He was accompanied by one of our donors, Dr. Hermann Gmeiner, who started the SOS Children's Villages in Austria. His Holiness said: "Well, children, you are here getting an education, and you are able to gain all this, and enjoy life, because of the help of all these donors, then one day, when you are able to stand up on your own feet, you must be able to repay back what others have done for you, and you must also think of helping others". So then, after His Holiness left, we were discussing among the staff members, and we thought why not make our motto "Others before self"? I think that has left an imprint on the children's minds, and that makes a lot of difference. Because wherever they are, they want to help the children who are there now, and many of them are sponsoring children and sending donations.

Dr. Desmond Biddulph

Very often Western people do not see it in that way, but "others before self" it is actually more natural than "self before others", even if we tend to think of it the other way around. But in fact, that is the right thing to do, that is the way to be happy. So, if one has limited amounts of money, what do you think is the best goal to actually target that money towards?

Jetsun Pema

Well, it depends. At the moment, the old hospital that we had In TCV, that was built by the Swiss Red Cross in the early 60s, is now falling apart. So, we are building a new hospital, and we got a lot of help from a German organisation. But then, once a hospital is built, you have to furnish it, you have to buy medical supplies, instruments, everything. So, in that respect, there are always projects where it would be most useful if somebody was to donate 10 pounds or 100 pounds. The president of TCV, was formerly one of the children, educated in TCV. He was admitted at the age of five, when I was working there. Today he is 67 years old, he has become the president of the Tibetan Children's Village, and he is doing a wonderful job. He has a team of young people working with him, and they always have very good ideas where the money will be best utilised. Then the project manager keeps in touch with all the other schools, to understand what their needs are, and what are the ones that are most urgent. It is always the most needed project that is put on top of the list. So, you can rest assured that whatever is sent to TCV, is never wasted.

Dr. Desmond Biddulph

Yes. Because in these gigantic organisations, which are kind of impersonal, like the NHS, so much is wasted with all sorts of ideas and schemes. But it sounds as if everything that you do is very personal, very direct and immediate.

Jetsun Pema

Yes. And this means that very little spent on administration. Before retiring around 18 years ago, I calculated that administrative expenses were only around the 3% of what we received. And I do not think now it is much higher, as since the number of children has gone down, the staff number has also gone down. So, it will still going to be around 3% or 4%, not more than 5%, that is being spent on administrative expenses.

Dr. Desmond Biddulph

I think that is very important for donors, and for anyone watching this programme, to know that any money they are giving will not be going up the sort of administrative chimney, and that they will actually be spent directly on what is needed. And I am sure that the work that you have done has been extremely inspirational to other people. Would you have a sort of message from all these years?

Jetsun Pema

I have always been trying to do what His Holiness envisioned for the children. He always calls the children "the future seeds of Tibet". And then, I have always felt that it is so important to nurture these future seeds properly. When you have this feeling in your heart, then I think, whatever you do, there will be good results. For example, when you are doing gardening, in order to have these tulips coming out well, you have to water them. Similarly, to have the children blooming into wonderful human beings, us that look after them need to have this kind of feeling. And if you feel this dedication and this conviction, then you do not make a mistake. That is the most important thing. His Holiness is always an inspiration for us. His guiding force is always there, and that makes us go a long way.

Dr. Desmond Biddulph

I think you have made a very good point. And also, what makes the tulip beautiful its already there in its seedling, and that is the same with human beings: its all actually already there, we just have to give them the right things. It must have been deeply satisfying for you over the years to see so many alumni coming out as happy people, who obviously started with great difficulties.

Jetsun Pema

His Holiness always says that once you are born as a human being, the most important thing is that you lead a good life, a life that helps others. And I think that doing the work for the children was my way of doing something good with my life. And I am satisfied, I am grateful that I was given that opportunity to do the work that I did. That is the greatest satisfaction.

Dr. Desmond Biddulph

I think that the people you meet will be inspired to follow in your footsteps, to make a contribution.

Jetsun Pema

I hope that the ex-students are all doing a wonderful job, and contributing in the way that they can.

Dr. Desmond Biddulph

We tend to think, "I cannot do anything, it is all too difficult, I cannot help other people". But of course, one can.

Jetsun Pema

One should never give up. His Holiness says, "never give up".

Dr. Desmond Biddulph

I would like to ask you, what do you think about the present situation in Tibet, and about the possible future for the Tibetan people.

Jetsun Pema

The present situation in Tibet it is very sad. I was telling you about the children being sent to be brought up as Chinese. That is a terrible thing, and there is nothing we can do about that. Those of us who are living outside of

Tibet, under the guidance of His Holiness, we are all doing well. And we never give up our hope that we will return back to Tibet. And I think, as long as that hope is there, we Tibetans, we will flourish well. We all have to keep that in our mind and do our best, as parents as teachers, whatever we are doing in our life.

Dr. Desmond Biddulph

We have been mostly concerned for the climate changes that are taking place in Tibet, because of the drying-out, of the Tibetan Plateau.

Jetsun Pema

Tibet is known as the third pole. But the glaciers in Tibet are all melting down much faster than what it used to be before. With the global warming, Tibet plays a very important role, because all the rivers in India, in Southeast Asia, are all flowing from Tibet. So, when the glaciers all melt, there will be flooding everywhere. And then, if the rivers dry up, that would be a terrible disaster for more than one third of the world's population. So, I think that is something that people, especially those working with climate change, have to be made aware of. I think that is a very important issue to address, because it is not just for the Tibetans, it is for the whole of Asia, and I think not many people are aware of this.

Dr. Desmond Biddulph

We attended a conference on climate change, and we were very surprised and shocked, that the Tibetan plateau was hardly mentioned, as the consequences for the drying of the Tibetan Plateau is the fact that, as you say, one third of the world's population will be without water or very little water. That is catastrophic, really. And I suppose that as a Tibetan you are able to make people aware of this issue.

Jetsun Pema

As you have mentioned, nobody seemed to be aware of this when you attended the conference. It is those leaders who should be aware of these things, but I do not think this issue reaches up to the leadership of the countries.

The Tibetans can cry about this, but then, if it does not reach the people who are making the decisions, it is a hopeless situation.

Dr. Desmond Biddulph

Do you think that over time the autocratic regime of China will soften towards the Tibetan people? Or do you think it will continue to try and Sinicise the whole of the Plateau?

Jetsun Pema

Well, we are all hoping that things will improve. But at the moment, when you look at the situation in China, there does not seem to be much change. Their policy towards Tibet is now harsher than ever. The borders are guarded by the military. And then this is also true for the neighbouring countries like Nepal: the Nepalese police do not allow Tibetans to cross over easily, and if Tibetans do come, they hand them back to the Chinese. That's the reality, which is very sad. We hope things will slowly change, but I do not know how soon. Anyway, we keep hoping that things will change for the better.

Dr. Desmond Biddulph

One of the things is that Tibetan people are not allowed to travel, they have no travel documents. So, they are unable to leave their own country.

Jetsun Pema

Seven or eight years ago, there were Tibetans who were given a passport to travel to India or to Nepal. But now they are not giving any more passports.

Dr. Desmond Biddulph

It does look very dark, doesn't it, the future? Well, tomorrow, you are going to have another celebration with the alumni. How long will you be staying in the UK?

Jetsun Pema

We are leaving on the 31st. We will be back in Delhi, and then back in Dharamshala soon.

Dr. Desmond Biddulph

Well, it has been a wonderful opportunity. And I am very grateful to you for being able to talk to us.

Jetsun Pema

Thank you to the Buddhist Society. Thank you for having us.

Dr. Desmond Biddulph

It is a great joy, a great pleasure and a privilege. I hope anyone watching this short interview will take inspiration from this, and see what can be done through the power of warmth and human contact, not through huge amounts of money, but through just ordinary human, natural communication between grown-ups and children, which can then create a community and give people a proper future as human beings.

Originally printed in The Middle Way vol. 98 no. 4, Winter 2023-24, The Hundredth Anniversary Year of The Buddhist Society 2024

Jetsun Pema as a young woman

Jetsun Pema, photo by Lei Lei Qu

BIBLIOGRAPHY AND BOOKS WRITTEN BY CONTRIBUTORS

Contributors in order of inclusion:

Darcy Biddulph (Darcy Flynn)

1001 Pearls of Buddhist Wisdom, Insights on truth, peace, and enlightenment (co-author, London, DBP, 2006)
Teachings of the Buddha, The Wisdom of the Dharma from the Pali Canon to the Sutras (co-author, London, DBP, 2009)
365 Ways to Live a Buddhist Life, Insights on Truth, Peace & Enlightenment (co-author, London, Watkins, 2020)
Guest Editor of The Middle Way, Quarterly Journal of the Buddhist Society (2011-19)
Editor of The Middle Way (2019-)

Otagaki Rengetsu

Otagaki Rengetsu: Springs of Times Past, by Ray Hughes (2011) The Gallery, Sidney
Rengetsu: Life and Poetry of Lotus Moon by John Stevens (2015)

Caroline Augusta Foley Rhys Davids

Publications:
Buddhism: A Study of the Buddhist Norm (London, Butterworth, 1912. Reprinted London, Williams, 1947)
Buddhist Psychology: An Inquiry into the Analysis and Theory of Mind in Pāli Literature (London, G. Bell and Sons, 1914. Reprinted Charleston, Nabu Press, 2010)
Old Creeds and New Needs (London, T. Fisher Unwin, 1923)
The Will to Peace (London, T. Fisher Unwin, 1923)
Will & Willer (London, Williams, 1926)
Gotama the Man (London, Luzac & Co., 1928)
Sakya: or, Buddhist Origins (London, Kegan Paul, Trench, Trubner, 1928. Reprinted Delhi, Gyan, 2021)
Stories of the Buddha: Being Selections from the

Jataka (London, Chapman and Hall, 1929. Reprinted Delhi, Low Price Publications, 2010)
Kindred Sayings on Buddhism (Calcutta, University of Calcutta, 1930)
The Milinda-questions : An Inquiry into its Place in the History of Buddhism with a Theory as to its Author (London, Routledge, 1930. Reprinted London, Routledge, 2014)
A Manual of Buddhism for Advanced Students (London, Sheldon Press, 1932. Reprinted Delhi, Asia Educational Services, 2004)
Outlines of Buddhism: A Historical Sketch (London, Methuen, 1934. Reprinted London, Routledge, 2018)
Buddhism: Its Birth and Dispersal (London, Butterworth, 1934) - A completely rewritten work to replace *Buddhism: A Study of the Buddhist Norm* (1912)
Indian Religion and Survival: A Study (London, George Allen & Unwin, 1934)
The Birth of Indian Psychology and its Development in Buddhism (London, Luzac & Co., 1936. Reprinted Delhi, Gyan, 2021)
To Become or not to Become (That is the Question!): Episodes in the History of an Indian Word (London, Luzac & Co., 1937. Reprinted Luzac & Co., 1965)
What is your Will (London, Rider and Co., 1937) - A rewritten edition of *Will & Willer* (1926)
What was the original gospel in 'Buddhism'? (London, The Epworth Press, 1938)
Wayfarer's Words, Vols. I-III (London, Luzac & Co., 1940-42. A compilation of most of C. A. F. Rhys Davids' articles and lectures, mostly from the latter part of her career. *Vol. I* (1940), *Vol. II* (1941), *Vol. III* (1942 - posthumously))

Translations:
A Buddhist manual of psychological ethics or Buddhist Psychology, of the Fourth Century B.C., being a translation, now made for the first time, from the Original Pāli of the First Book in the Abhidhamma-Piṭaka, entitled *Dhamma-Saṅgaṇi (Compendium of States or Phenomena)* (1900,

reprinted Kessinger Publishing, 2010)
Psalms of the Early Buddhists: Volume I. Psalms of the Sisters (London, Pāli Text Society, 1909)
Points of controversy; or, Subjects of discourse; being a translation of the *Kathā-vatthu* from the *Abhidhamma-piṭaka*, (C. A. F. Rhys Davids and Shwe Zan Aung, 1915)

Articles:
'On the Will in Buddhism' (The Journal of the Royal Asiatic Society of Great Britain and Ireland, pp. 47–59, 1898)
'Notes on Early Economic Conditions in Northern India' (The Journal of the Royal Asiatic Society of Great Britain and Ireland, pp. 859–888, 1901)
'The Soul-Theory in Buddhism' (The Journal of the Royal Asiatic Society of Great Britain and Ireland, pp. 587–591, 1903)
'Buddhism and Ethics' (The Buddhist Review Vol. 1 No. 1, pp. 13–23, 1909)
'Intellect and the Khandha Doctrine' (The Buddhist Review. Vol. 2 No. 1, pp. 99–115, 1910)
'Pāli Text Society' (C. A. F. Rhys Davids and Shwe Zan Aung, The Journal of the Royal Asiatic Society, pp. 403-406, 1917)
'The Patna Congress and the "Man"' (The Journal of the Royal Asiatic Society of Great Britain and Ireland, pp. 27-36, 1929)
'Original Buddhism and Amṛta' (Melanges chinois et bouddhiques, pp. 371–382, 1939)

Alexandra David-Néel

Publications:
Pour la vie (written under the pseudonym Alexandra Myrial. *In Praise of Life: A Libertarian Essay*, Brussels, Bibliothèque des Temps Nouveaux, 1898)
Le modernisme bouddhiste et le bouddhisme du Bouddha (Paris, F. Alcon, 1911)
Voyage d'une Parisienne à Lhassa (Paris, Plon, 1927. *My Journey to Lhasa*, Boston, Beacon Press, 1955)
Mystiques et Magiciens du Tibet (Paris, Plon, 1929. *Magic and Mystery in Tibet*, New York, University Books, 1958)
Initiations Lamaïques (Paris, Adyar, 1930. *Initiations and Initiates in Tibet*, London, Rider, 1938)
La vie Surhumaine de Guésar de Ling le Héros Thibétain (Paris, Adyar, 1931. *The Superhuman Life of Gesar of Ling*, New York, Kendall, 1959)

Grand Tibet; Au pays des brigands-gentilshommes (Paris, Plon, 1933)
Le lama au cinq sagesses (with Lama Yongden. Paris, Plon, 1935)
Le Bouddhisme, ses doctrines at ses méthodes (Paris, Plon, 1936. *Buddhism: Its Doctrines and Its Methods*, translated by H.H. Hardy and Bernard Miall. London, Bodley Head, 1939)
Magie d'amour et magic noire; Scènes du Tibet inconnu (Paris, Plon, 1938. *Tibetan Tale of Love and Magic*, Jersey, Neville Spearman, 1938)
Sous des nuées d'orage; Récit de voyage (Paris, Plon, 1940)
Au Coeur des Himalayas: Le Népal (Paris, C. Dessart, 1949)
Ashtavakra Gita; Discours sur le Vedana Advaita (Paris, Adyar, 1951)
Les Enseignements Secrets des Bouddhistes Tibétains (Paris, Adyar, 1951. *The Secret Oral Teachings in Tibetan Buddhist Sects*, Calcutta, Maha Bodhi Publications, 1951)
L'Inde où j'ai vecu; Avant et après l'indépendance (Paris, Plon, 1951)
l'Inde: Hier, aujourd'hui, demain (Paris, Plon, 1951)
Textes Tibétains inédits (Paris, La Colombe,1952)
Le Vieux Tibet face à la Chine nouvelle (Paris, Plon, 1953)
La Puissance de Néant, by Lama Yongden (Paris, Plon, 1954. *The Power of Nothingness*, London, Thorndike, 1954)
Grammaire de la langue tibétaine parlée (Publisher unknown, 1954)
Avadhuta Gita (Paris, Adyar, 1958)
La connaissance transcendente (with Lama Yongden. Paris, Adyar, 1958)
Immortalité et réincarnation: Doctrines et pratiques en Chine, au Tibet, dans l'Inde (Paris, Plon, 1961)
Quarante siècles d'expansion chinoise (Paris, La Palatine, 1964)
En Chine; L'amour universel et l'individualisme intégral: les maitres Mo Tsé et Yang Tchou (Paris, Plon, 1970)
Le sortilège du mystère; Faits étranges et gens bizarres rencontrés au long de mes routes d'orient et d'occident (Paris, Plon, 1972)
Vivre au Tibet; Cuisine, traditions et images (Paris, Morel, 1975)
Journal de Voyage; Lettres à son Mari, 11 août 1904 – 27 décembre 1917 (Vol. 1, Ed. Marie-Madeleine Peyronnet. Paris, Plon, 1975)
Journal de Voyage; Lettres à son Mari, 14 janvier 1918 – 31 décembre 1940 (Vol. 2, Ed. Marie-Madeleine Peyronnet. Paris, Plon, 1976)

Le Tibet d'Alexandra David-Néel (Paris, Plon, 1979)
La Lampe de sagesse (Monaco, Rocher, 1986)

Carmen Blacker

Publications:
The Japanese Enlightenment: a study of the writings of Fukuzawa Yukichi (Cambridge, Cambridge University Press, 1964)
The Catalpa Bow: A Study of Shamanistic Practices in Japan (London, Allen & Unwin, 1975)
Collected Writings of Carmen Blacker (London, Routledge, 2000)

Other editions:
Zen (Abbot Sogen Asahina, translated by Carmen Blacker, a brief introduction to Zen for Westerners. Tokyo, The Kawata Press, 1976)
Women and Tradition: a neglected group of folklorists (edited by Carmen Blacker and Hilda Ellis Davidson. Durham, Carolina Academic Press, 2001)
Carmen Blacker: Scholar of Japanese Religion, Myth and Folklore – Writings and Reflections (edited by Hugh Cortazzi, with James McMullen and Mary-Grace Browning. Amsterdam, Amsterdam University Press, 2017)

Mihoko Okamura

Okamura was the translator for two of the potter Bernard Leach's books, *The Unknown Craftsman* (1972) and *Hamada, Potter* (1990) subject of various TV features including a recent documentary.

The Buddhist Society has a special relationship with both the D.T. Suzuki Museum in Kanazawa and the former home of D.T. Suzuki, the Matsugaoka Bunko, of which Okamura was a Trustee.

From 2014, The Buddhist Society Trust in association with the University of California Press has begun to publish the *Selected Works of D.T. Suzuki, vols 1–5*. The fourth volume, *Buddhist Studies* by Mark Blum, was published in 2020.

Other editions :
The Faces and Infinite Presence of D. T. Suzuki – An Album of Photographs from His Final Years (Photography by Shizuteru Ueda and words

by Mihoko Okamura, Kyōto, Institute for Zen Studies, 2005)

Sōetsu Yanagi and Bernard Leach: Letters from 1912 -1959 (translated by Mihoko Okamura, Tokyo, Japan Folk Crafts Museum, 2014)

Beatrice Erskine Lane Suzuki

Beatrice Lane Suzuki (by Kachiko Yokogawa and Elaine Blakc Stanley. Published in Japan after her death in 1939. Reprinted California, 2009)

Although Beatrice Lane Suzuki published relatively few titles, they have sold in very large numbers and continue to so long after her death.

Kōya San: The Home of Kobō Daishi and his Shingon Doctrine (three editions written by D.T. Suzuki and edited by Beatrice Lane Suzuki, published in English between 1931 and 1936)
Nogaku : Japanese Nō Plays (London, John Murray, 1932. Fourteen editions published between 1932 and 1980 in English and other languages)
Buddhism and Practical Life (Nagoya, Shindo Kaikan, 1933. Three editions published between 1933 and 2006 in English)
Buddhist Readings (four editions, parts 1 and 2 covering all aspects of Buddhist life, published between 1934 and 1937 in English. Kyōto, Hirano Shoten)
Impressions of Mahayana Buddhism (written by D.T. Suzuki for The Eastern Buddhist and edited by Beatrice Lane Suzuki. Kyōto, The Eastern Buddhist, 1940. Five editions published since 1940)

Most widely-held works by Beatrice Lane Suzuki:

Mahayana Buddhism (with a foreword by Christmas Humphreys. London, The Buddhist Lodge, 1938. Fifty-five editions published between 1938 and 2009 in four languages
Mahayana Buddhism: A Brief Outline (London, George Allen and Unwin, 1959. Twenty editions published between 1959 and 2004 in English)

"In this outline, the author confines herself to the teachings of Mahayana Buddhism, which accepts many of the doctrines found in all

*forms of Buddhism. Mahayana accepts many
of these doctrines but holds some of them less
important. What is most important in Mahayana
is Enlightenment, freedom from illusion, and the
aspiration after Buddhahood, and this not only for
a few wise monks but for all beings. Mahayana is
the religion of the Buddhists of the North and East
of Asia and, as such, deserves to be studied and
appreciated.*" (Publisher's description)

Buddhist Temples of Kyōto and Kamakura (two
editions drawn from The Eastern Buddhist,
of which Beatrice Lane Suzuki was a founder
member with her husband D.T. Suzuki. Edited
and updated by Michael Pye, editor of The
Eastern Buddhist. Kyōto, The Eastern Buddhist,
reissued Sheffield, Equinox Publishing, 2103)

Translations

Il buddismo mahayana (Florence, Sansoni, 1960)
and *Budismo Mahayana*. (Four editions published
between 1961 and 2014 in Italian and Spanish)

Miriam Salanave
Publications

A Tryst With The Gods (pp. 1-39 from the series
An Eastern Rosary, 1932. Reprinted Delhi, Gyan
Books, 2020)
*India, An Impression; Prolusion to A Tryst With The
Gods* (Oceano, Harbison and Harbison, 1932)
An Oriental Tale Spin (Oceano, Harbison and
Harbison, 1932)
Buddhist Roll Call (1935, reprinted Delhi, Gyan
Books, 2020)
Tributes to Dwight Goddard (Miriam Salanave and
Chas. R. Cumming, *American Theosophist Vol. 27
No.9*, 1939)

POEMS SECTION:

Wayne Yokoyama

Editor, translator and editorial assistance to
works including:
John Maraldo's essays on modern Japanese
philosophy (2017–),
Cultivating Spirituality with Mark L. Blum (2011)
The Nirvana Sutra with Mark L. Blum (2013)
The Suzuki English diary 1920–1955 edited by
Kirita Kiyohide for the Matsugaoka Bunko
Foundation

His translations include:

Coffinman: The Journal of a Buddhist Mortician by
Shinmon Aoki (1993)
Nishida Kitarō's essay 'Coincidentia
oppositorum and love' (1997)
'Zen and Shin' the dialogue between DT Suzuki
and Soga Ryōjin (1994)
The Suzuki English diary 1920–1955 edited by
Kirita Kiyohide, for the Matsugaoka Bunko
Foundation
Leaves of My Heart by Kujo Takeko (2019)

POETS:

Kaga no Chiyo-jo

Featured in *The Penguin Book of Women Poets*
(London, Penguin Books, 1978

Yamada Fusako

Rokoko No yakata: Yamada Fusako Kyushū
(Tokyo, 2000)

Kujo Takeko

Life of Baroness Takeko Kujo by Kenji Hamada
(Honolulu, Honpa Hongwanji Mission of
Hawaii, 1962)

Okamoto Kanoko

Okamoto Kanoko Shu by Katsuichiro Kamei
(Tokyo, 1979)

Selected bibliography of works in English

Three tanka (translated by Asatoro Miyamori
in *Masterpieces of Japanese Literature, Ancient and
Modern* (London, Greenwood Press, 1936)
'Scarlet Flower' (translated by Edward
Seidensticker, Japan Quarterly 10-3, 1963)
A Mother's Love (translated by Phyllis Birnbaum
in *Rabbits, Crabs, etc: Stories by Japanese Women*,
Honolulu, University of Hawaii Press, 1982)
Modern Japanese Tanka: An Anthology (translated
by Makoto Ueda, 1996)
This contains a biography and a number of
poems by her, as well as a bibliography of
related works including dissertations.

Portrait of an Old Geisha (translated by Cody Poulton in *The Oxford Book of Japanese Short Stories*, Oxford, Oxford University Press, 2010)

Ruth Fuller Everett Sasaki

Publications:
Far East for 90 Days (narrative of a trip to Japan and China in 1930. Ruth and Edward Everett)
The Zen Koan: Its History and Use in Rinzai Zen (with reproductions of ten drawings by First Zen Institute of America, Kyoto. Ruth Fuller Everett Sasaki and Isshu Miura, New York, Harcourt, Brace, 1965)
The Recorded Sayings of Layman P'Ang: a Ninth-Century Zen Classic (translated by Ruth Fuller Everett Sasaki, New York, Weatherhill,1971)
The Record of Linji (translation and commentary by Ruth Fuller Everett Sasaki, Kyōto, Institute for Zen Studies, 1975. Revised version Honolulu, University of Hawaii Press, 2008)

Her literary works included *The Record of Linji*, a collection of sayings of Linji, the founder of the Rinzai sect of Zen Buddhism, who died in 861, which she translated with a commentary. The publication was edited by a prominent team of scholars and translators around her in Kyōto, including Iriya Yoshitaka, Kanaseki Hisao, Yokoi Seizan and four Europeans, Philip Yampolsky, Burton Watson, Gary Snyder and later Walter Nowick, who were all distinguished in their own way. The work remained unfinished for many years after her death until the Zen scholar, Thomas Kirchner, took up the incomplete 1975 manuscript. The completed and fully annotated version was published as *The Record of Linji* by the University of Hawaii Press in 2008.

Louise Janin

Bibliography:
Louise Janin by Jean-Jacques Lévêque (Paris, Ishtar, 1959)
Louise Janin (by Edan Milton Hughes)
Janin by Elie-Charles Flamand (Paris, Galerie Hexagramme, 1974)
Erotique de l'Alchimie by Elie-Charles Flamand (Paris, Payot, 1989)

Isaline Blew Horner / IB Horner

I.B. Horner began her writing career in 1930 with *Women Under Primitive Buddhism: Laywomen and Almswomen*. Numerous books followed as author, co-author, translator or editor. These included translations of the sutta pitaka as well as translations of commentaries on *The Jatakas*, *The Milindapanha*, *The Vinaya-Pitaka*, *The Bhikkhuni Khandhaka and the Bhikkhuni-Vibhanga*, *The Therigatha*, *Early Buddhist Theory of Man Perfected*. *Papanchasudani*. *The Book of Discipline (Vinaya-Pitaka)*, translation. She worked with others, for example David Snellgrove, Edward Conze, Arthur Waley and Ananda K. Coomaraswamy. Many of her books were published by the Pāli Text Society. Below is a list of her works in chronological order:
Women Under Primitive Buddhism: Laywomen and Almswomen (London, Routledge, 1930. Reprinted Erie, Gutenberg Publishers, 2011)
Papanchasudani Vol.3, Commentary on the Majjhima Nikaya (London, Pāli Text Society, 1933)
The Early Buddhist Theory of Man Perfected (1936, reprinted Delhi, Munshiram Manoharial, 2017)
The Book of the Discipline (Vinaya-Pitaka) (translated by I.B. Horner, 1938, reprinted Oxford, Legare Street Press, 2022)
Alice M Cooke: A Memoir (memoir of an historian who taught at Owens College, Manchester, University of Leeds and Newnham College, Cambridge. Manchester, Manchester University Press, 1940)
Early Buddhism and the Taking of Life (Kandy, Wheel Publications, 1945, reprinted 1967)
Madhuratthavilāsinī nāma Buddhavaṃsaṭṭhakathā of Bhadantácariya (A.P. Buddhadatta Mahathera, edited by I.B. Horner. London, Pali Text Society, 1946, reprinted London, Routledge and Kegan Paul, 1978)
The Living Thoughts of Gotama The Buddha (with Ananda K. Coomaraswamy, 1948. Reprinted Delhi, Raj Publications, 2015)
The Collection of the Middle Length Sayings (translated by I.B. Horner, Oxford, Pāli Text Society, 1954. Reprinted Delhi, Motilal Banarsidass, 2003)
Ten Jataka Stories (with Pāli text, London, Luzac, 1957)
'Women in Early Buddhist Literature' (talk to the All-Ceylon Buddhist Women's Association. Kandy, Buddhist Publication Society, 1961)
Early Buddhist Poetry (Colombo, Ananda

Semage, 1963)
Milinda's Questions (translated by I.B. Horner, Oxford, Pāli Text Society, 1963)
Buddhist Texts through the Ages (translated and edited by Edward Conze in collaboration with I.B. Horner, Arthur Waley and David Snellgrove, New York, Harper & Row, 1964. Reprinted London, Oneworld, 2014)
Noble Quest: Ariyapariyesana Sutta (Kandy, Buddhist Publication Society, 1974)
Minor Anthologies of the Pali Canon Vol. 3: Vimanavatthu and Petavatthu (translated by I.B. Horner, Oxford, Pāli Text Society, 1974)
Minor Anthologies of the Pali Canon Vol. 4: Buddhavamsa and Cariyapitaka (translated by I.B. Horner, Oxford, Pāli Text Society, 1975)
Apocryphal Birth-stories: Paññāsa Jātaka (translated by I.B. Horner with Padmanabh S. Jaini, Oxford, Pāli Text Society, 1985)

Princess Poon Pismal Diskul

Thai Traditions and Customs (English text, Thai translation by Prayudh Payutto)
Buddhism and the Young (Bangkok, Bangkok Times Press, 1931)
The Relevance of Buddhism in the Modern World (Kandy, The Buddhist Publication Society, 1969)
Buddhism for the Young, Thai Traditions and Customs (Bangkok, Prachandra Press, 1975)

Li Gotami Govinda

Tibet In Pictures, Expedition To Central Tibet (Dharma Publishing, 1979)
Tibet In Pictures, Expedition To Western Tibet (Dharma Publishing, 1979)

Norma Levine

The Spiritual Odyssey of Freda Bedi (Shang Shung Publications, 2018)
The Miraculous 16th Karmapa (Shang Shung Publications, 2018)
Blessing Power of the Buddhas: Sacred Objects, Secret Lands (1993)
Chronicles of Love and Death, My Years with the Last Spiritual King of Bhutan (2011)
A Yearbook of Buddhist Wisdom (Godsfield Press, 1996)
Stepping Stones; Crossing the River of Samsara 2023

Joan Watts

The Collected Letters of Alan Watts, co-editor (New World Library, 2019)
Anne Watts

The Collected Letters of Alan Watts, co-editor, (New World Library, 2019)

Freda Newth Wint

'The Luminous Mind', parts 1, 2 and 3 (The Middle Way, Quarterly Journal of The Buddhist Society)
'Three Buddhists Talk About Meditation' (Freda Newth Wint, Derek Wright and Damaris Parker-Rhodes, Theoria To Theory, Vol 6 No. 2, April 1972)

Venerable Myokyo-ni

Publications:
Wisdom of the Zen Masters (under her preordination name Irmgard Schlögl – New York, New Directions Publishing Corp., 1976)
The Zen Way (London, Sheldon Press, 1977, reissued London, The Buddhist Society Trust in association with The Zen Centre, 2021)
Introducing Buddhism (London, The Zen Centre, 1978)
Gentling the Bull: The Ten Bull Pictures, a Spiritual Journey (London, The Zen Centre, 1980, reissued London, The Buddhist Society in association with The Zen Centre, 1996)
Living Buddhism (London, The Zen Centre, 2000)
The Daily Devotional Chants of the Zen Centre (2008, reissued as The Great Wisdom Gone Beyond, London, The Buddhist Society Trust in association with The Zen Centre, 2021)

Translation and editing:
The Record of Rinzai (under her preordination name Irmgard Schlögl – Boston, Shambhala, 1976)
The Ceasing of Notions (with Sōkō Morinaga Rōshi and Michelle Bromley – London, The Zen Centre, 1988)
The Bull and his Herdsman by Daizokutsu R. Otsu (London, The Zen Centre, 1989) from the German *Der Ochs und sein Hirte* by Tsujumura and Buchner
The Discourse on The Inexhaustible Lamp of the Zen School by Torei Enji Zenji (also translated by Yoko

Okuda, London, The Buddhist Society, 1989)
Other writings:
Introduction, *On Zen* by Thomas Merton
(London, Sheldon Press, 1976)
*Look and See: Buddhist Teaching Stories with
Commentaries* (London, The Buddhist Society
Trust, 2017)
Towards Wholeness: Essays on Zen Buddhism
(London, The Buddhist Society Trust, 2017)
Yoko Daishi's Realizing The Way (translation and
commentary – London, The Buddhist Society
Trust, 2017)

Ayya Khema

Being Nobody, Going Nowhere (Boston, Wisdom
Publications, 1987), winner of the Christmas
Humphreys Memorial Award
Be An Island, The Buddhist Practice of Inner Peace
(Boston, Wisdom Publications, 1999)
When The Iron Eagle Flies, Buddhism for The West
(London, Penguin Arkana, 2000)
*Visible Here and Now: The Buddha's Teachings
on the Rewards of Spiritual Practice* (Boston,
Shambhala, 2001)
Who Is My Self? A Guide To Buddhist Meditation
(Boston, Wisdom Publications, 2002)
*Come and See for Yourself: The Buddhist Path to
Happiness* (Birmingham, Windhorse, 2002)
Know Where You're Going (Boston, Wisdom
Publications, 2014)
*The Path to Peace: A Buddhist Guide to Cultivating
Loving-Kindness* (Boston, Shambhala, 2022)

Nina Coltart

Publications:
Slouching Towards Bethlehem (London, Free
Association Books, 1992)
How To Survive as a Psychotherapist (London,
Sheldon Press, 1993)
The Baby and The Bathwater (Madison,
International Universities Press, 1996)

Gelongma Tsultrim Zangmo

Where The Bees Are There The Honey Is, a memoir
(Eskdalemuir, Dzalendra Publishing, 2014)

Francesca Fremantle

Tibetan Book of the Dead (Shambhala, 1975)
Luminous Emptiness (Shambhala, 2001)

Roshi Joan Halifax

Standing at the Edge, (Flatiron Books, 2019)
*The Fruitful Darkness: A Journey Through Buddhist
Practice and Tribal Wisdom* (Grove Press, 2004)

Robina Courtin

Working With People In Prison (Springer, 2018)
How To Meditate, co-author (Wisdom, 2015)
Transforming Problems Into Happiness, co-author
(Wisdom, 1993)

Ajahn Sundara

Walking the World (Hemel Hempstead,
Amaravati Publications, 2011)
Friends on the Path (with Ajahn Candasiri –
Hemel Hempstead, Amaravati Publications,
2011)
The Body (with Ajahn Candasiri and Ajahn
Metta – Hemel Hempstead, Amaravati
Publications, 2013)
Seeds of Dhamma (Hemel Hempstead, Amaravati
Publications, 2016)
Paccuppanna: The Present Moment (Hemel
Hempstead, Amaravati Publications, 2017)

All available from Dhamma Books at Amaravati
Buddhist Centre.

Ajahn Candasiri

Simple Kindness, Dhamma Books, Amaravati
Buddhist Centre

Lama Zangmo

Only The Impossible Is Worth Doing (2020)
contribution to chapter on three year retreats,
Dzalendra and Rokpa Trust, 2020

Maura Soshin O'Halloran

*Pure Heart Enlightened Mind: The Life and Letters of
An Irish Saint* (Wisdom, 2007)

*Pure Heart Enlightened Mind : The Zen Journals
and Letters of Maura Soshin O' Halloran* by Sann
Bruno (audio literature by Audible Books, 2004)

ACKNOWLEDGMENTS

It is a privilege to have edited this collection of articles written by women from *The Middle Way*, The journal of The Buddhist Society. *The Middle Way* started in the 1920's and was the first periodical in the United Kingdom to introduce Buddhism and give a voice to those interested in it. It's an honour to have this collection published in the Centenary Anniversary Year of The Buddhist Society 1924-2024. This collection presents an opportunity to map the historic context of when these women practiced Buddhism and my sincere thanks firstly goes to the contributors. Many are well known authors while others are not known at all. The chance to share their valuable contributions has been a great honour and education. I hope it will give inspiration to women to write about their practice and contribute to progress the chart of the growth of Buddhist thought in the West.

I would like to thank all of the past editors of *The Middle Way* for their vocational work over nearly one hundred years providing an outstanding quarterly journal held in high esteem by Buddhists, libraries and universities. It continues to stand out based on Buddhist Practice, not just academic content. In that way *The Middle Way* paved an individual identity different from the Buddhist periodicals that followed. Today there are many magazines and journals on Buddhism but *The Middle Way* was the first and only to provide this type of content which inspired so many to practice and gave comfort to those who were already practicing. It also served to join together the Buddhist communities in the East and West and continues to do so today.

I also wish to thank the charity, The Buddhist Society and it's staff for their effort. The head of the publishing team at the Buddhist Society Trust deserves a special thanks for his unceasing contribution and support, Desmond Biddulph CBE.
The consultant Jonathan Earl deserves much gratitude for staying with the development of the book. I thank Peter Armstrong for his long standing legal expertise.

I am grateful to Buddhists I was fortunate to meet, in particular Soko Morinaga Roshi and His Holiness The Dalai Lama and Ven. Chimyo Takehara and Junichi Miyamae, who each changed my life in the most profound way. There are no words to describe my gratitude and good fortune.

I am grateful to every woman in this collection for her contribution to *The Middle Way* and its editors who commissioned their work which has given a huge amount to Buddhism. Women in this book demonstrated bravery and courage exploring Buddhist countries during times when women barely left home. They explored Buddhist thought and practice during periods of female oppression and discrimination. We can all be grateful for their fearlessness, creativity and devotion to The Dharma.

Finally I thank the Buddha for his teachings. Buddhism has no gender, there is no male or female duality, it is and always has been an open door to an open heart. I hope this collection celebrates The Dharma and inspires us all to strive on heedfully in our Practice.

Darcy Flynn

GLOSSARY

Abhidharma *Abhidharma/abidhamma*, Higher Dharma. The last of the three baskets of teachings that goes to make up the *tripitaka/tripitaka*. Categorization of all experienced phenomena arising into consciousness through the sense bases, of eyes, ears, nose, taste, and sensation, that includes the mind itself, into moral categories. Neutral, wholesome, unwholesome, and shows that they are all conditioned, interdependent, a source of suffering, without substantiality, and impermanent. They are all conditioned except the last: *nirvana/nibbana*. These elements or dharmas/ dhammas, go to make up the world we falsely experience as permanent, substantial, and real, and to which we are attached. The only nondependent *dharma/dhamma* (element) is *nirvana/nibbana*.

Bhikkhu A monk or nun. In Theravada (the Pali based traditions) countries the ordination of nuns ceased to occur many centuries ago. The ordination of women in the northern tradition however continued without a break. More recently western women monastics have sought ordination through the Mahayana transmission line that is still flourishing. The first ordained women were by the Buddha, his foster mother and his aunt. It seems that the Bhikkhuni ordination died out as a result of social pressure rather than doctrine indicating a women's inadequacy for the role.

Bodhicitta Mind of enlightenment. *Bodhi* awakening, *citta* mind heart. A (psychological) force that opposes the passions, or the three fires of desire anger and delusion, and drives and moves towards enlightenment.

Bodhisattva *Bodhisattva/bodhisatta*. *Bodhi* Awakening. *Sattva/satta* being, thus 'enlightenment being', or one who strives for enlightenment.

Brahma Viharas The 'divine abodes' 'immeasurables' *apramāṇa* or 'infinite minds', in Chinese of *Maitri/ Metta*, loving kindness or good will, *Karuna*, compassion *Mudita* sympathetic joy and *Upeksha/ Upekha* serenity, or equanimity associated with the fourth *Jhana*. These characterize the four responses that arise following contact with the objects of the five senses. These arise spontaneously, but can also be practiced to encourage the cultivation of the opposite of arrogant schadenfreude and spiteful indifference.

Buddha The awakened one. From the vedic root *Budh;* awake, to open as a flower. Usually applies to the historic Buddha, Gautama Siddhartha, Shakyamuni Gautama (Sage of the Shakyas), 563-483 BC. Siddhartha was the last of a line of former Buddhas, and will be followed by other Buddhas. The historical Shakyamuni Buddha merely 'rediscovered an ancient path to an ancient city.'

Chan The Sanskrit word for absorption, meditation is *dhyana/jhana* Pali. The transliteration of this word *jhana*, into Chinese sounds like Chan, this word when used in spoken Japanese became Zen, thus the Zen Schools of Buddhism in Japan are derived from the *Chan* schools from China and the meditation absorption schools of early Buddhism. *Chan*, in China is a separate school, within the Mahayana tradition, traces its origins to Bodhidharma the first Chinese patriarch, an Indian monk who it is claimed haled from the south Indian aristocracy, it is also said he was an Indo-Iranian monk from Central Asia, said to have had blue eyes who arrived in China during the reign of the Buddhist emperor Wu 464- 569 with whom he had a fabled meeting and exchange.

Huineng was the sixth Chinese patriarch. The first Indian patriarch was said to be Mahakasyapa a close disciple of the Buddha to whom the transmission was passed. All schools abide by the principal that Chan is a special transmission outside the scriptures, a non reliance on the written word, and direct seeing in to the (Buddha) nature, and becoming Buddha.

Citta Mind/heart. Pronounced chitta. It is said that the great Indian translator Kumarajiva first translated the Sanskrit word *citta* into Chinese using the character heart, *shin*, to make it understandable to the Chinese readers. *Citta* is the world of mentality in all its forms, and is a sign of sentience, to include the different 'states of mind' and emotion. The third collection of the sutras known as the *abhidharma* admits of only 4 divisions of all that can be perceived; *citta* mind, mental concomitants (content of consciousness, wholesome, unwholesome, or neutral) *cetasika. Rupa* or matter, and finally *nirvana* Sanskrit, *nibbana* Pali.

The Eightfold Noble Path i. Right View, ii. Right Resolve, iii. Right Speech, iv. Right Conduct, v. Right Livelihood, vi. Right Effort, vii. Right Mmindfulness, viii. Right Concentration

The Four Noble Truths The First Noble Truth; Suffering exists. The second Noble truth; there is a cause for suffering. The Third Noble Truth; There is cessation of suffering; The Fourth Noble Truth; The path or way to the cessation of suffering; the Noble Eightfold path.

The Great Vehicle Mahayana; (*maha*; great, and *yana*, vehicle) The Buddhism of Tibet, Bhutan, China, Taiwan, Nepal Japan and Vietnam are mainly Mahayana, as are those of Mongolia Buratia Kalmykia and the Siberian republics in the Russian Federation. Hong Kong, Malaysia, Singapore and Taiwan, Korea, and Japan the texts are Sanskrit based, translated into local languages from Sanskrit, the original texts often having been lost. Literally the great vehicle, the form of Buddhism that is practiced following the separation of the Buddhist Community after the second Council, that took place in India into what are now called the southern and northern traditions. Because the greater number left remaining at the Council following the disagreement on the discipline, the larger body numerically was called the *maha* greater *yana* vehicle (to enlightenment) or Great way. It is a numerical reference not a moral one.

Haiku A poetic form that developed from earlier poetic forms in Japan. The syllables usually arranged as 5, 7, 5. the Most famous Haiku collection are by Basho, Buson and Issa. The form is derived from earlier forms, and contains a cutting word that adds 'spine' and 'centres' the verse.

The Jatakas The Birth Stories of the Buddha, collected from contemporary and pre-Buddhist times, assimilating folk stories, fables, and legends. They are in essence moral tales that show that all living creatures take part in the moral drama in which Gautama Shakyamuni, the Buddha to be, and all beings find themselves moving either upwards towards the heavenly realms or enlightenment, and less suffering, or downwards, towards the hell realms or a less favorable incarnation, and unhappiness

and more suffering, as a consequence of their moral actions. The Buddha is the central figure in these stories as in his previous lives, he moves towards enlightenment through selfless acts of virtue. He is also able to see the previous lives of others, and thus often recounts episodes from his previous lives, in which he and his disciples were present.

Kensho A Japanese Zen term often used to mean seeing into the Buddha Nature, one's own nature, reality.

Koan Literally a *case*. Their origin lies in the way in which a student would approach the teacher and ask a question for example 'What is Buddha?'

The teacher would give a public reply. Now questions are put to students, and they need to answer to satisfy the teacher that they have insight. Zen students are given a koan on which to work in order to aid them in their understanding of the teachings. There are various layers of Koan from beginners koans to advanced koans. Koans are recorded in various collections the most well known being the *mumonkan*, The Gateless Gate, and the *hekiganroku*, The Blue Cliff Record, and there are others.

Students need to pass their Koans in order to progress in their practice. To be fully fledged Zen teacher must pass these koans in order to be able to use the Koan sytems an aid to transmission to their own students, Rinzai sect uses Koans more than Soto sect and the Obaku.

Language The Buddha taught in the language of the people. His sermons were later memorized by monks following his death and as a result of the first Council.

There are as many languages used in Buddhism as there are countries where it is practiced. However the historical texts in which they were preserved and written down (as opposed to memorised) some four centuries after the Buddha's death and later, are Sanskrit, Pali, Tibetan, Chinese (Khotanese) as well as the vernacular European languages. The Buddha spoke in a middle indic dialect of Maghadi, *prakrit*, of the middle Ganges valley, and his words preserved in the *sutras/suttas* were committed to memory before being written down. The most complete record was committed to writing about 500 years later in Pali language, in Aluvihara by Buddhaghosa of the Theravada tradition. following a famine and the fear that the *sutras/suttas* might get lost. The scripts used are varied, such as Brahmi, Devanagari, Kharoshti, etc., and recently of course Roman.

The language of the Brahmans the Vedic priests was old Vedic (from which sanskrit is derived), a language most ordinary people would not have understood. The Buddha spoke in the vernacular language of the people to whom he came into contact. This distinguished him from the Vedic priestly cast. Sanskrit, the language that succeeded Vedic, the old language of the Rig Veda and the sacred language of the northern Indo-Aryan invaders of India in the bronze age in which the memorized, prayers, rituals, and sacred matter, were remembered and chanted, and the mantras and prayers were recited. The poems and Gathas bear a close language resemblance, to old Persian and Homeric Greek which has pointed to the possibility of the reconstruction of Proto Indo-European language that is the origin of all Indo-European languages of which Sanskrit is an example. Succeeded by Sanskrit a language written in Devanagari one of many scripts extant at the time and formalized by the great grammarian Panini. Classical Sanskrit became the court language to many Indian kingdoms, both in and beyond India in south east Asia, and aided the spread of the Mahayana along the Silk Road. The sacred texts of the Northern tradition known as the Mahayana were first committed to writing in Sanskrit. All of the Mahayana sutras were originally written in Sanskrit although they were later translated into Chinese, Khotanese, Tibetan, and other languages and are now written in vernacular languages.

Lama The Tibetan word for teacher, usually an ordained member of the clergy.

The Lesser Vehicle Often called the *Hinayana*, *(hin)*small *(yana)*vehicle, to be distinguished from the *Mahayana*; the greater vehicle. The term is still used but has a slightly pejorative tone, and the word 'lesser' should not in any way suggest that as a means to enlightenment it is an any way deficient in comparison with the Greater vehicle of the Mahayana. (See Mahayana) The Theravada tradition of southern Buddhism (the way of the elders) is the only continuous unbroken tradition that goes backto the time of the Buddha.

Madhyamika A central school within Mahayana Buddhism derived from the teachings of Nagarjuna. These teachings are laid out in the *prajna paramita*

sutras. Nagajuna is said by some to be a second Buddha.

Mahayana see the great Vehicle.

Mantra A word or phrase repeated for its enlightening function. There are various mantra traditions within Mahyana Buddhism.

Meditation Strictly speaking the formal practice of absorption. Composed of two elements calming, and insight. Insight arises from stillness of the mind.

The Middle Way The first teaching of the Buddha that encapsulates the entire teachings, the avoidance of self indulgence and hedonism and the other extreme of self privation. To be distinguished from the middle way tmadhyamika.

Nirvana Nibbana The enlightened state of being.

Maha-nirvana The final extinguishment of desire in the body, in corporeal death.

Pali Pali the middle Indic dialect of Maghadi, known as *prakrit*, closely approximating to the language the Buddha used when teaching. The language of the *sthaviravada*, an early sect out of which the Theravada arose. The language in which the fullest record of the three baskets of the teachings is preserved.

Paramitas the virtues that arise from selflessness. Only a Buddha's actions are naturally completely selfless but to behave selflessly and to practice the vitues is meritorious and leads to a gentling of the passions.

Rinzai one of the Zen sects of the three sects of Japanese Zen Buddhism of which Obaku and Soto are the other two. Founded by the Chinese Chan master Linji, said to have died in 866, the school came into being after his death based on his very direct teachings which were written down as the *Rinzai Roku*. The Soto sect also derived from Chinese Chan Buddhism was founded by Dogen Zenji in the thirteenth century. Obaku Zen was founded in the 17th Century. (1661)

Rohatsu An annual retreat held in the Zen Schools of Japanese Buddhism that begins on 1st day of December and culminates at the rising of the morning (Venus) star on the eighth day of December to celebrate the enlightenment of the Buddha. The Buddha's birth enlightenment, and death is celebrated in different days in the far east.

Samkhya A school of Indian philosophy that is essentially dualistic, spirit matter and witnessing consciousness.

Samanera A novice in the Theravada tradition.

Samsara The world of delusion and suffering.

Samadhi Blissful absorption.

Sangha Community, this refers to the Buddhist community both lay and monastic, but more generally the monastic community of ordained mendicants. The Sangha is considered one the three jewels of Buddha Dharma and Sangha Taking refuge in the three jewels is a universal practice throughout all schools of Buddhism.

Sanskrit The language that succeeded old Vedic, the language of the Rig Veda and the sacred language of the northern Indo-Aryan invaders of India in the bronze age in which the memorized, prayers, rituals, and sacred matter, were remembered and chanted, and the mantras and prayers were recited. The poems and Gathas bear a close language resemblance, to old Persian and Homeric Greek which has pointed to the possibility of the reconstruction of Proto-Indo-European language that is the origin of all Indo-European languages of which Sanskrit is an example. Sanskrit is a language written in Devanagari one of many scripts extant at the time and formalized by the great grammarian Panini. Classical Sanskrit became the court language to many Indian kingdoms, both in and beyond India in south east Asia, and aided the spread of the Mahayana along the Silk Road. The sacred texts of the Northern tradition known as the Mahayana were first committed to writing in Sanskrit. All of the Mahayana sutras were originally written in Sanskrit although they were later translated into Chinese Khotanese Tibetan and other languages and are now written in vernacular languages as well as languages that are no longer used.

Sati *Smrti/sati*; Alert and awake. Awareness and presence of mind, watchfulness of mind, as well as being collected in the present. This requires remembering what one is about, recalling, and remembering to pay attention. Equivalent to the Greek *nepsis*. Both a practice and a state of mind. In the vedic tradition smrti referred to texts that had to be memorized. The Buddha's use of *smrti* to refer to remembering the present moment, the here and now, be aware now, rather than remembering the texts of the Vedic religion, pointed away from language, towards direct living experience.

Satori Seeing into 'one's true nature'. A Japanese term derived from the verb Saturu. The act itself is described as *Kensho*. Also means enlightenment, as to who one is, seeing into ones own nature.

Shin Shin Buddhism, the most popular form of of Buddhism in East Asia and Japan. Based on achieving rebirth in the pure land or Buddha field of Amida Buddha. The origins go back to the earliest sutras and teachings including the Mahavyuha sutra and others founded by Shinran.

Soto One of the traditional Schools of Zen Buddhism found in Japan, Rinzai, and Obaku, are the other two. Dogen (1200-1253) was the founder of the Soto sect of Japanese Buddhism.

Shakyamuni The Sage of the Shakya's. The name used to describe the historical Buddha. Gautama Shakyamuni. Shakya was the clan to which the historical Buddha belonged

Skandhas The five heaps, or necessary constituents for experienced reality.

Body *rupa*, feeling *vedana*, cognitive perception, naming, *Samjna* formulations *samskharas*, consciousness *Vijnnana*

Sutra/sutta the sayings of the historical Buddha. Sutta literally means a thread. In the Theravada Buddhism suttas are the remembered sayings of Gautama Shakyamuni, in the Mahayana there are many sutras that are attributed to the Buddha and are literary compositions containing profound teachings but also attributed to the Buddha..

Temple In the early days of Buddhism the monks were homeless, wandering from place to place, begging for alms, rather like the friars of Christianity. They first began to stay in one place during the rains or monsoon. This eventually gave rise to places where monks lived all year round, although the tradition of begging for alms continued. A temple is now a generic term for a place of residence for ordained members of the Buddhist clergy, either male or female. Also called *Vihara,* in the southern tradition. In the northern tradition the term monastery is used. Large monasteries may house many hundreds if not thousands of monks, at various stages of their development. Himalayan Buddhism has developed a form of architecture called the *Dzong* a fortifies monastic and administrative centre. The eremitic tradition gives rise to hermitages.

Theosophy A movement that begun in New York in 1875 by Henry Olcott, Helena Blavatsky, and William Quan Judge that went on to become a worldwide movement exploring the roots of religion, that drew to it writers philosophers artists.

Theravada Theravada; 'The Way of the Elders'. The Buddhist tradition that is practiced in most of the countries of south, and south east Asia where Buddhism is practiced; Sri Lanka, Myanmar, Thailand, Cambodia, Laos, and Vietnam practice Theravada Buddhism,. The Theravada tradition arose in the years following the death of the Buddha, when the 'sects' arose, and after the second Council, following a disagreement regarding the *vinaya.* Theravada Buddhism is still represented in Japan as a Buddhist tradition.

The Three Signs of Being The Three Signs of Being; Suffering, Impermanence, and No I.

Tripitaka The Three baskets or divisions of the teaching, comprising the words of the Buddha , hiis sermons and other utterances as recorded by his disciples, Sutras/*suttas,* the Discipline, the moral rules / *Vinaya,* and the *abhidarma/abidhamma.* The higher (*abhi*) teachings. Initially, confined to memory, remembered, recited , and then committed to writing around the first century CE.

The Twelve Linked Change of Dependenc 1 *Avidya* (ignorance) 2 *Samskara* (formations) 3 *Vijnana* (consciousness) 4 *Nama-rupa* (name and form) 5 Six *ayatanas* (six sense bases) 6 *Sparsa* (contact) 7 *Vedana* (sensation) 8 *Trishna* (thirst) 9 *Upadana* (grasping) 10 *Bhava* (becoming) 11 *Jati* (birth) 12 *Jara-marana* (old age and death).

Upanishads The Late and most recent part of the *vedas* that form the basis of the Hindu philosophy, the Vedanta.

Vedas The oldest teachings in vedic Sanskrit language the latter part have gone on to form the foundation of

modern Hinduism. The oldest is the *Rig veda* followed by the *Samaveda* followed by the *Atharvaveda.* Each Veda is presented in four sections; the *samhitas* the *aranyakas* the *Brahmana* and finaly the *upanishads.*

Vesak, Wesak The celebration that occurs in Theravada countries, at the full moon in May, and commemorates the birth enlightenment and death (*parinirvana*) of Shakyamuni Buddha the historical founder of the Buddhist religion. It is the biggest religious festival of the year, a time of celebration.

Vijnana *Vijnana/Vijnnana*; consciousness. In Buddhism Consciousness is not seen as something that exists outside a human body because it is seen as a function only present when there are at least two other factors involved its existence outside of human life is not considered particularly relevant to practice but somewhat speculative.

Vinaya Discipline, usually referring to the rules of the monastic order, that all Buddhistic monastics and lay people adhere to, in different levels. Women have by tradition had the largest number of rules to live by. Throughout Buddhism regardless of country or whether of southern or northern tradition, the *vinaya* is remarkably consistent throughout the Buddhist world, whatever the doctrinal differences maybe. The Vinaya forms the first collection (basket) of the (Tripitaka), the teachings sermons of the Buddha (*Sutra/sutta*) being the second, and the third the higher dharma. (*abhidharma/abhidhamma*) The Vinaya grew with the monastic order as and when a rule seemed necessary to maintain the harmony and smooth running of the community to facilitate the practice towards arahatship.

Waka A short poetic form (*Tanka*) made up of thirty-one syllables 5-7, 5-7, 7 typical of Japanese court poetry of the 6th-14th century.

The Wheel of Life A dharmic 'psycho-cosmogram', or diagram depicting the not only the teachings, in pictorial form but also states of mind, indeed it depicts all we need to know to lead a Buddhist life. For this reason the depiction is often placed near the entrance of the monasteries so the monk can point out to anyone the wheel of life with a central hub in which a cockerel snake and pig chase each other, these represnting the 'three fires' of the teachings, Desire (cockerel), Anger (snake) Delusion (pig), the central part of the wheel is divided into 6 realms representing

states of mind or states into which we could be reborn.
The rim of the wheel depicts the twelve *nidana* or links
on the twelve linked chain of causation.

Yogacara A school of Buddhist philosophy developed
and practised in Buddhism and developed within
India by Vasubandhu and Asanga. Also known as the
'mind only school' of Buddhism.

Zazen The word used in the Zen tradition for formal
meditation.

Zen The Japanese forms of the Chan schools of China,
Japanese Zen, in Korea, Son Rinzai Soto and Obaku.